For Fred

December 2001

Ian

OUNDLE

A CELEBRATION IN COLOUR

by
Ian Bishop

Photographs by the Author

JEMA PUBLICATIONS

Published 2001 by Jema Publications

Printed in Great Britain by
Woolnough Bookbinding Ltd
Irthlingborough, Northants

ISBN: 1-871468-19-1

Publisher's Note
Every care has been taken in the preparation of this book. The publishers cannot accept responsibility for any inaccuracies or for any loss, damage or inconvenience resulting from the use of this book.

JEMA PUBLICATIONS
40 Ashley Lane
Moulton
Northampton NN3 7TJ

Contents

Bibliography

A History of the Oundle Schools	William Walker	Grocers' Company 1956
Estate Publications Town Plan of Oundle	Northamptonshire Red Book	Estate Publications 1999
Exploring Oundle and Surrounding Villages	Ian Bishop	Jema Publications 1995
Oundle and the English Public School	Raymond Flower	Stacey International 1989
Oundle in the 18th Century	Alice Osborn & David Parker	Spiegl 1994
Oundle Pub and Brewery Trail (leaflet)	Oundle Museum Trust	OMT 1997
Oundle Town Guide and Trail	Oundle Town Council	OTC 1987
Oundle's War	Michael Downes	Nene Press 1995
1:25,000 224, Corby	Explorer Maps	Ordnance Survey 1999
1:25,000 227, Peterborough and Oundle	Explorer Maps	Ordnance Survey 1999

Introduction

In compiling this collection of photographs, I have been impelled by the realisation that nothing stays static for very long and there is a need to place on record how the town looked at the start of this new millennium. In the twelve years I have lived and photographed the town there have been many changes; some minor and others quite dramatic, and in some cases the changes themselves have been changed again. Those of us who see this taking place every day notice them but may not grasp how much of our history is vanishing before our eyes. Footpaths have been created, hundreds of houses built and buildings have changed their use.

Perhaps one of the biggest social changes, which is intimately tied up with how we purchase both essential and leisure products, are the number of business premises in the town centre which have changed hands several times in the last decade. And in the past few months we have acquired a spate of new pedestrian crossings and have lost, inevitably, as it was dead, one of the delightful walnut trees which dominated St Peter's churchyard. The by-product of this loss, however, is that the tower and spire of the Church can now be seen to far greater effect from the south side of the churchyard.

Indeed it has become apparent that this book is a mere snapshot in time. A record of Oundle around the turn of the new century. In ten years time much will be different, and, if the world continues, in another hundred years, those who come after me will be amazed at the differences even if, as I suspect, they will be looking at my images on some sort of portable viewer linked to a central library located somewhere in the world – if not on one of the satellites which orbit the planet.

The layout of this book roughly follows the Town Trail in my previous book, "Exploring Oundle and Surrounding Villages" (Jema 1995), though of necessity this has had to be expanded as many of the pictures are outside the scope of the orginal trail. I have included a map of the main thoroughfares of Oundle; it should be reasonably easy to locate the locations of the various sections from this.

The "trail" starts from the East Road car park, moves through St Osyth's Lane to the Market Place, then northwards to St Peter's churchyard and up New Street and the Glapthorn and Cotterstock Roads. Returning to the town centre we go out along Milton Road and Benefield Road and then across to Stoke Doyle Road, Warren Bridge and the Catholic Church area. Then the south of the town is covered from the South Road artery and its "tributaries", returning to the start of Benefield Road and along West Street to the Market Place. The penultimate section winds its way towards the North Bridge and the bypass that largely follows the line of the old LNWR. and which was completed in the late 1980's. The final section has a collection of photographs taken around the town during the severe floods at Easter 1998.

Most of the photographs were taken from 2000 to 2001; also included are a small selection of aerial photographs of the town. I am indebted to John and Janet Lister of Winwick for these. John flew me over Oundle in his delightfully restored 1941 Piper Cub in August 2001 – the photographs you see here are the best of those. I am also grateful to Estate Publications of Tenterden, Kent, for allowing me to include a modified map of Oundle within the text. Their Red Books are well drawn and have often assisted me on my travels.

I would like to dedicate the book to all who love Oundle. Both at work and in my recreation I have met them around the country; they speak favourably of the town as a nice place to live and work. May they go on enjoying its delights as the century progresses.

Ian Bishop
October 2001

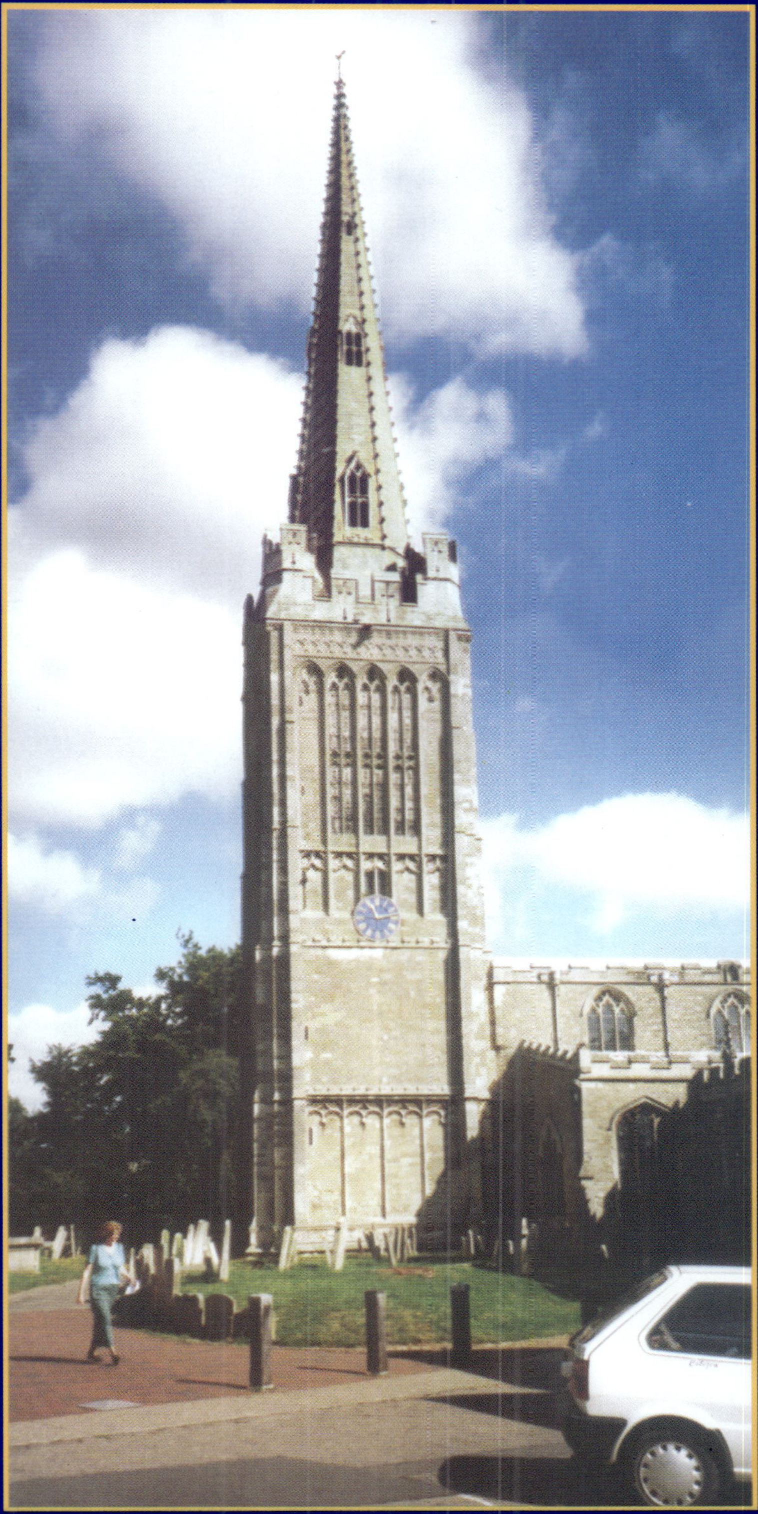

Oundle

Oundle

The growing town of Oundle, currently with a population of around 4,500, nestling in the north-east corner of ancient Northamptonshire, has a long and distinguished history. Known thirteen hundred years ago as "Undolum" it was at one time the highest navigable point on the River Nen (now corrupted to Nene). Historical records suggest that it had a greater importance then than now, being centre of a province which included other, now independent, towns. After the 9th Century Danish occupation and influence of the whole area, in the following century the eight English "hundreds" at the northern end of the shire were organised into a judicial unit administered from Oundle. Its influence extended from Wellingborough in the south almost to Crowland in the north, maybe 35 by 15 miles at its greatest points, but largely following the course of the River Nen.

Such was importance of that waterway that it remained a vital part of the town's trade for centuries until the mid nineteenth century. The backwater Oundle Wharf and some fittings are still visible alongside one of the two northern-most bridges that span the entire flood plain from the town to the relatively recent bypass. The river was a vital route to bring needed supplies into the town as the roads were deeply rutted muddy tracks in winter and baked ruts in summer. Even today the river is used for pleasure both fishing and boating and there are many footpaths following its banks and into the surrounding villages.

Oundle Market, still held each Thursday, dates back before the Domesday Book, firmly establishing the town as a centre of commerce from at least Roman times. The creation of an ever better road system after the demise of local railways has allowed the town to become part of the commuter zone, with easy access to both London, the Midlands and the North. Much of Oundle's present-day reputation comes from its association with the public school founded in 1556, on a bequest from Sir William Laxton, a "local boy" and former Lord Mayor of London. The present-day Laxton Long Room is a replica of the original in which the School was established. Just recently the three parts of the public school, junior, day and boarding, have amalgamated under the one name, Oundle School, and work has started on Laxton Junior's new enlarged premises off East Road.

Set in a largely agricultural setting with sheep, cattle and arable crops predominating, Oundle also has a number of other industries, of which boat-building is probably the largest with the successful Fairline Boats and its subsidiaries having sites around the town.

The main thoroughfares of

OUNDLE

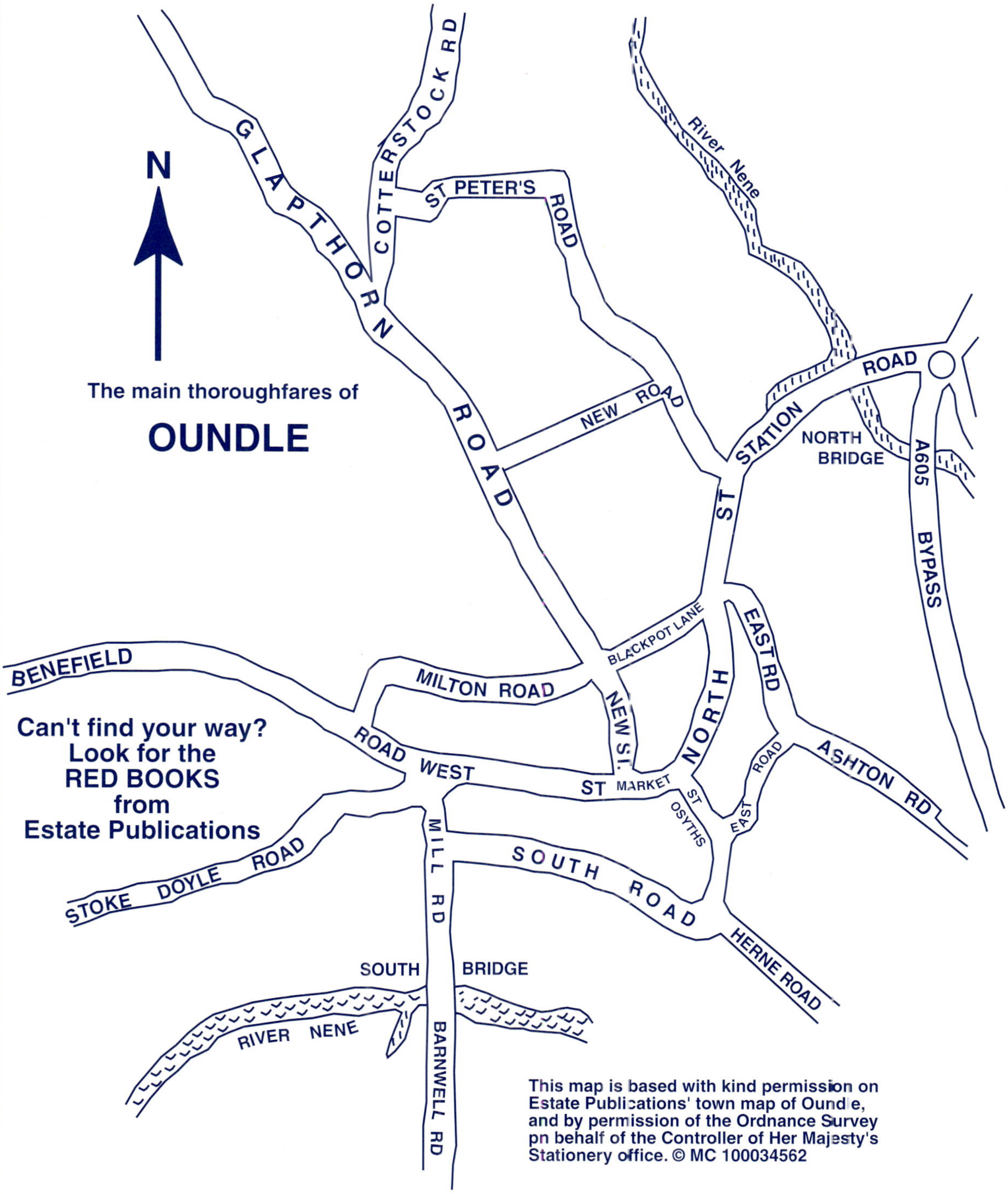

Can't find your way?
Look for the
RED BOOKS
from
Estate Publications

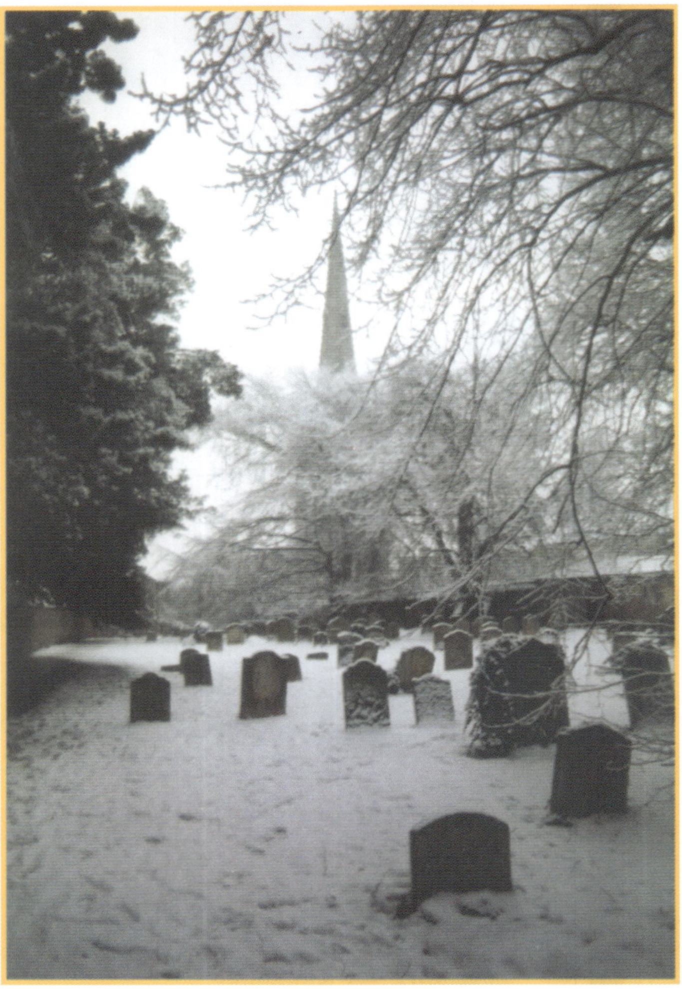

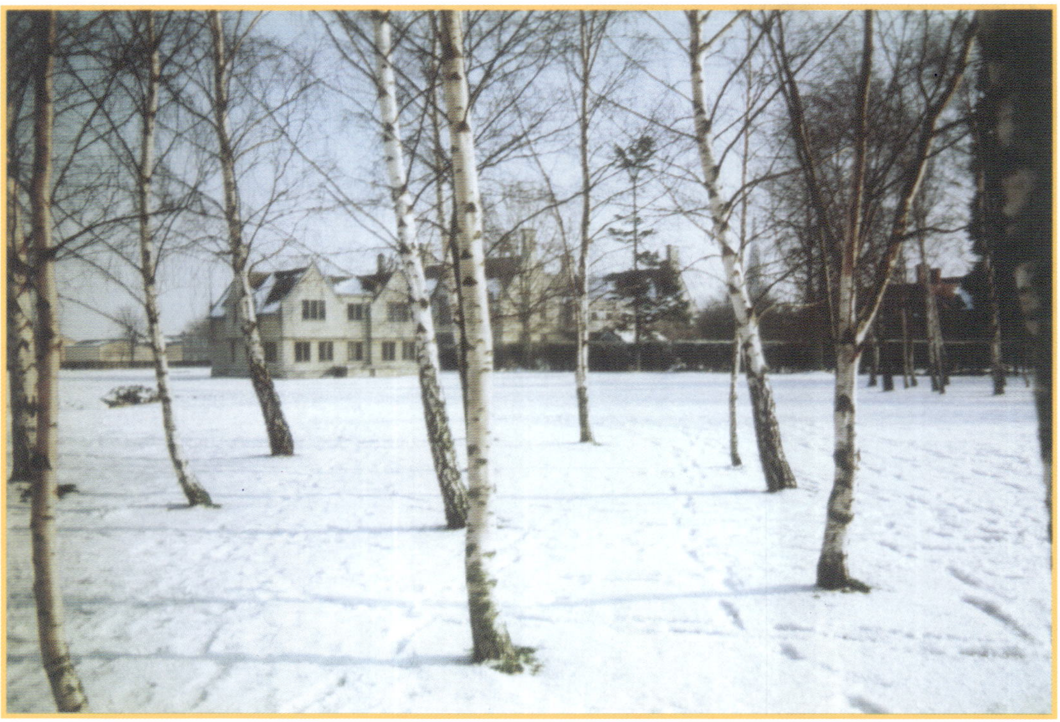

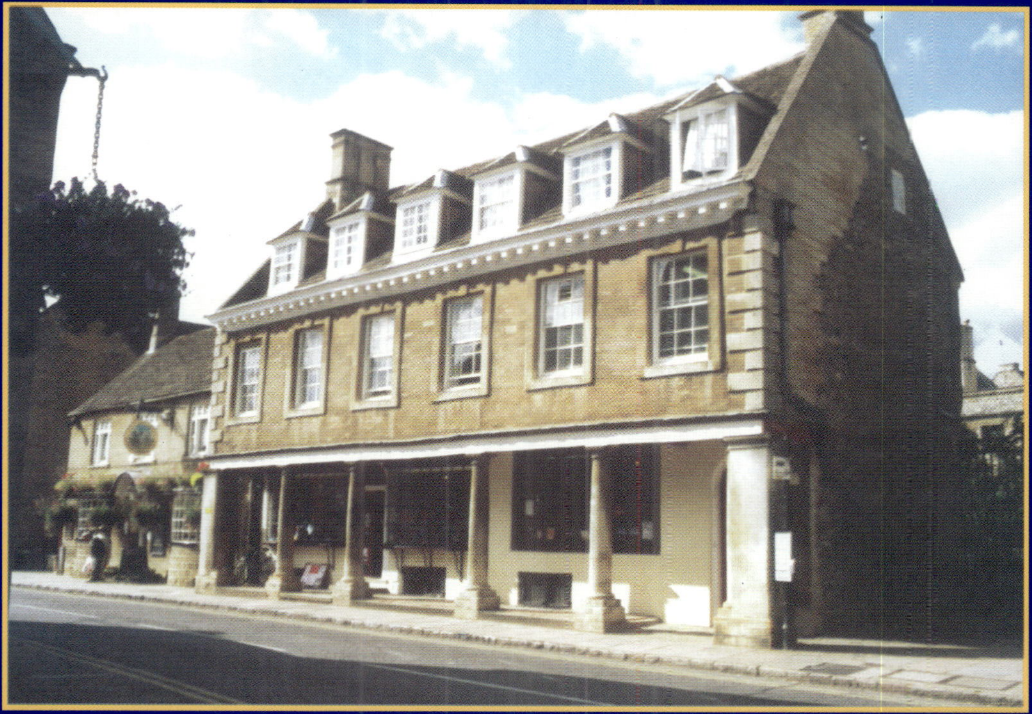

Market Place and Eastern Oundle

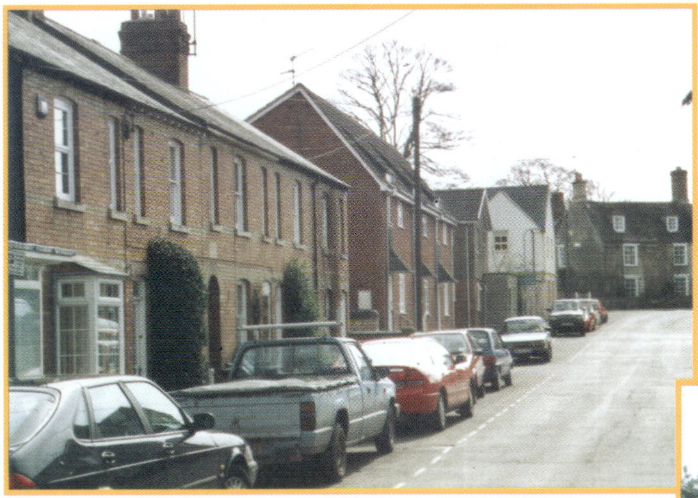

East Road (left) is an important thoroughfare linking North Street, Ashton Road and South Road. Off it are a long stay car park and the vital district recycling area, plus a small trading estate.

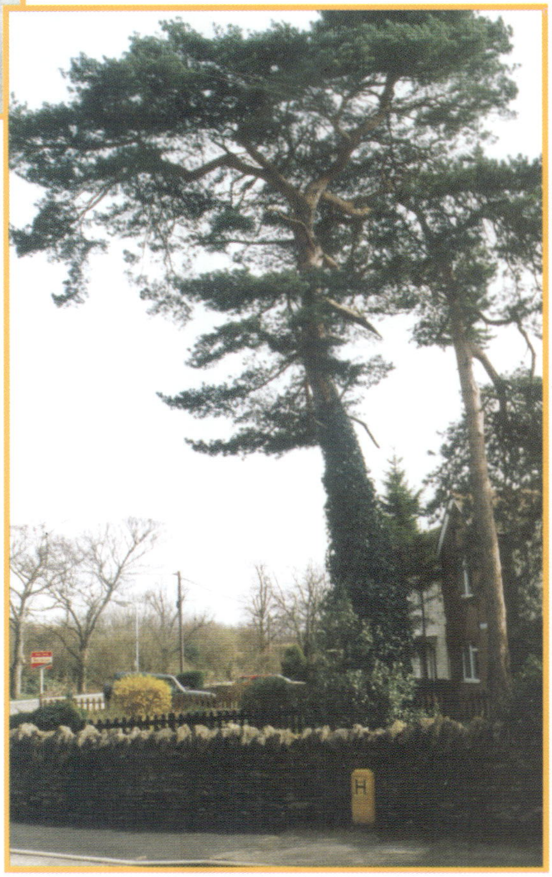

The magnificent tree (right), standing proud at the corner of Ashton Road and East Road. How many changes has this old tree seen? A trading estate, a new housing complex, a supermarket?

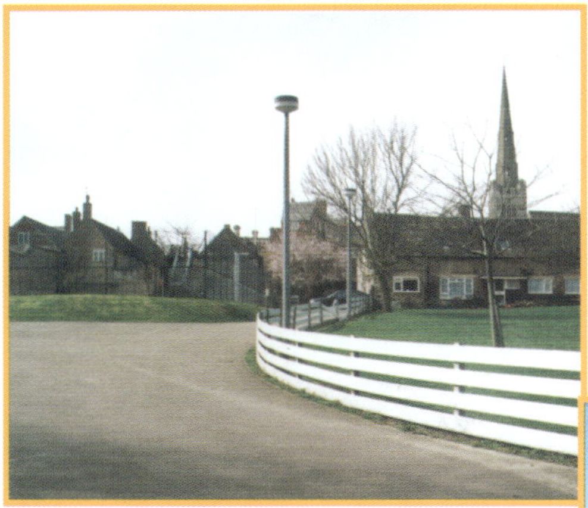

Above, and in the distance on the left is Laxton Junior, the right photograph is the site of the new school buildings.

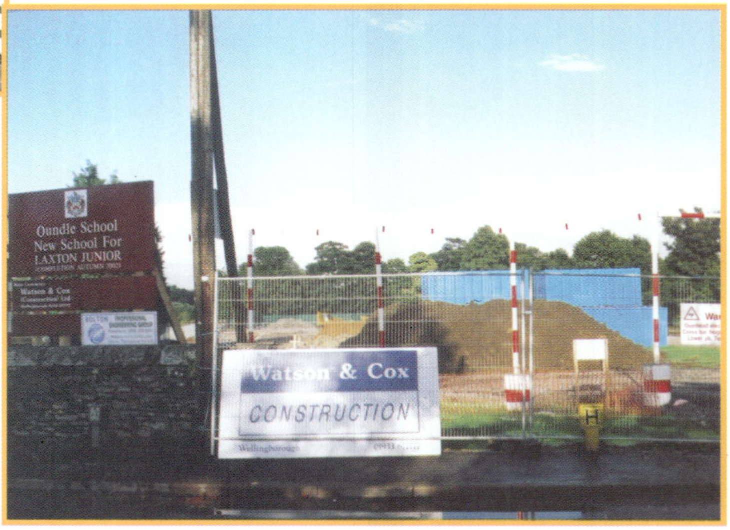

Ashton Road Estate, developed during the late twentieth century, has provided much needed housing on the edge of the town without imposing on the unique character of Oundle.

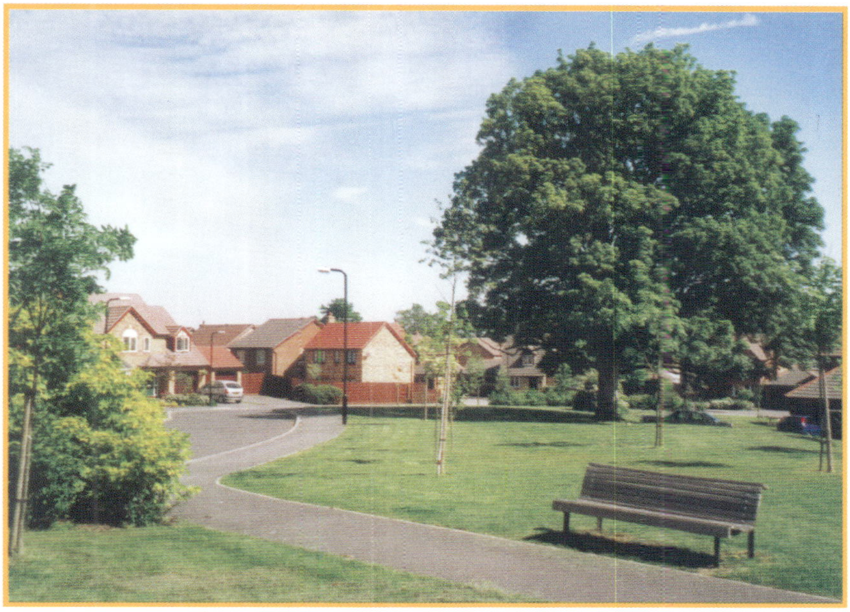

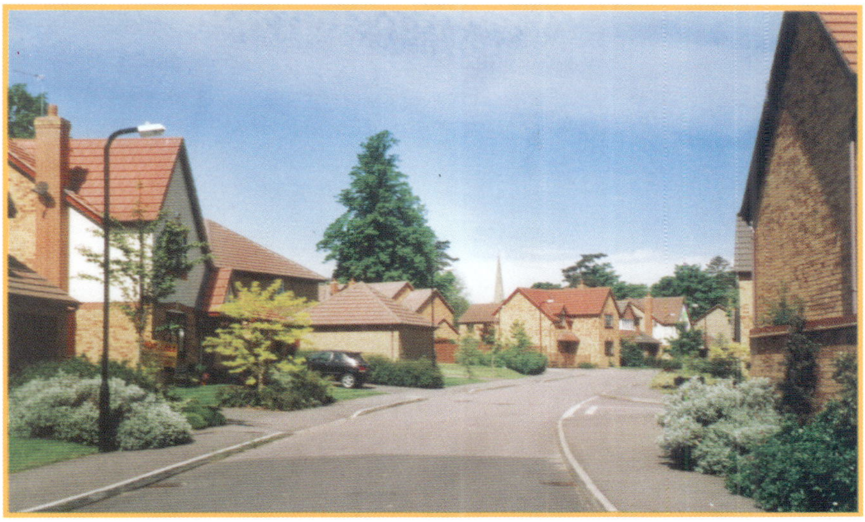

Part of the East Northants Plan has been to develop new housing in towns such as Oundle. The 2001 census will show a significant population increase over that of 1991.

One of the few remaining "wild areas" of Oundle is situated between the Ashton Estate and the bypass. This known locally as "the tip" - what are buried here?

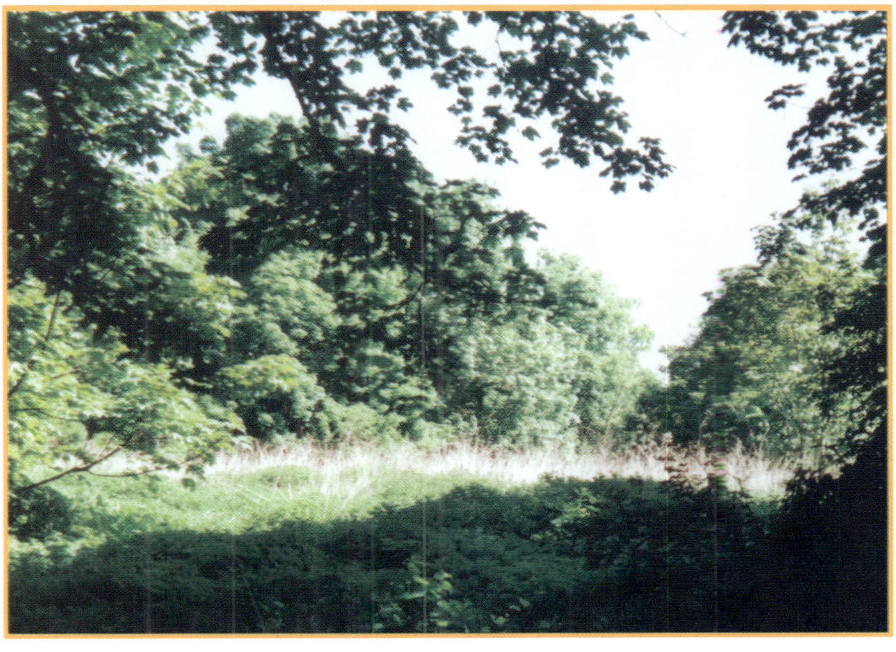

An unexpected joy.

A delightful grazing paddock between houses in the south of the town and below St Peter's Church dominating the area around West Street and the Market Place. Also see the sight of the new Laxton Junior visible at the top of the photograph with the Oundle School Cloisters to the left of the church.

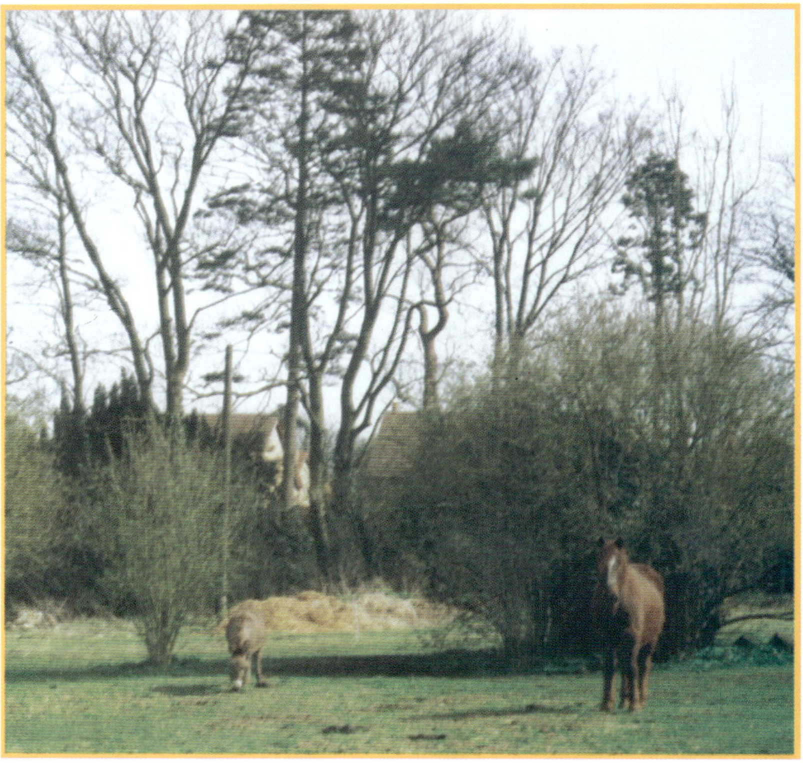

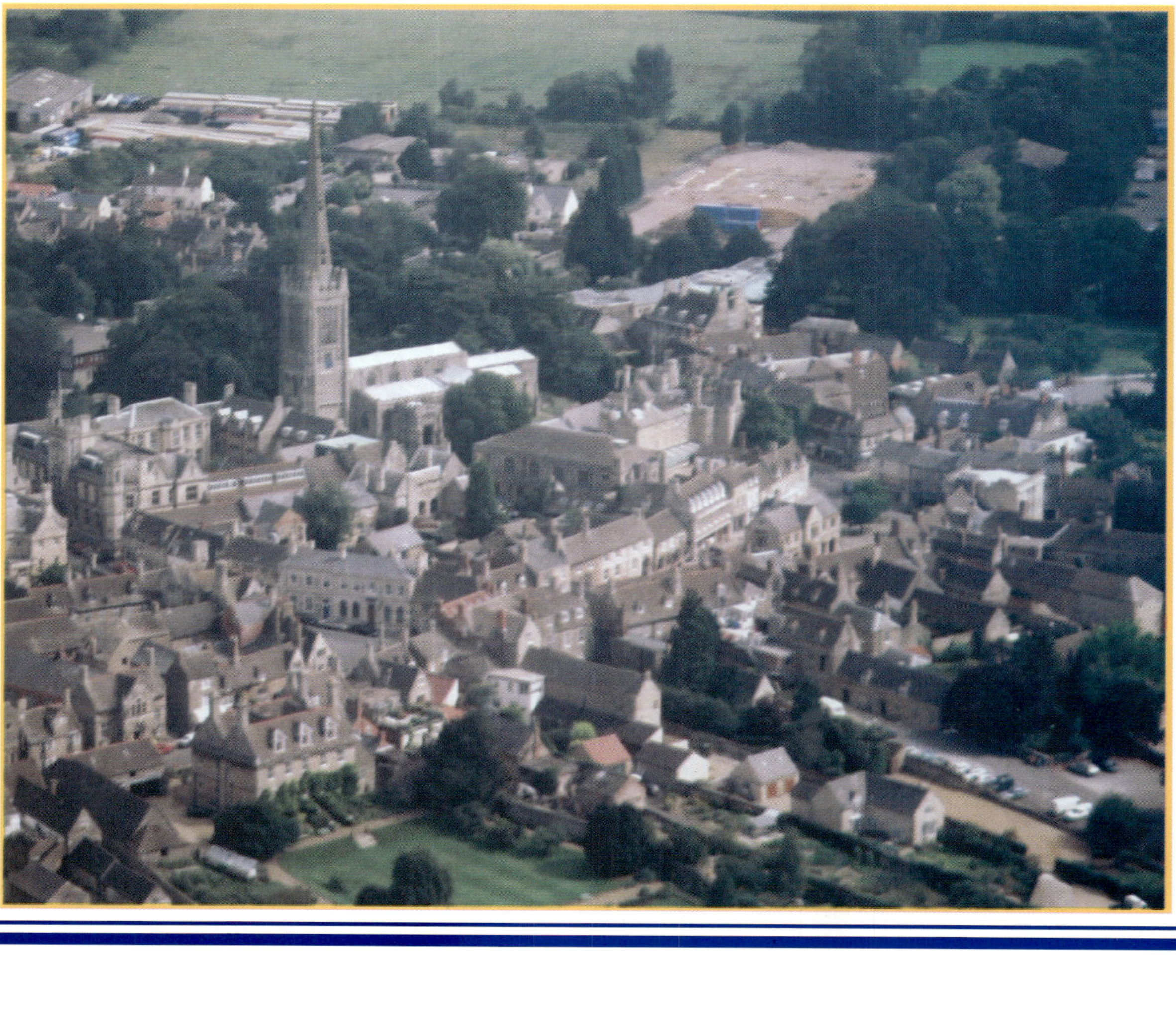

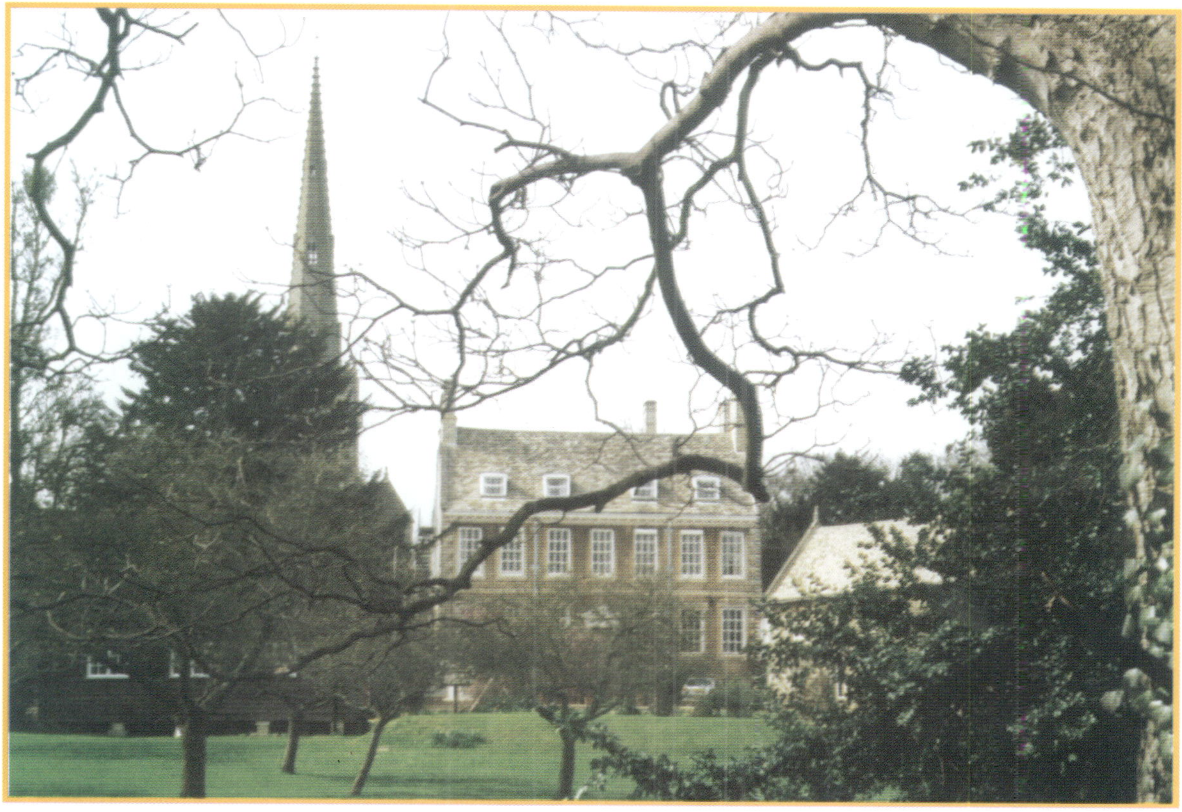

Above, the original frontage of the large town-house known as the Berrystead. One of Oundle's finest seventeenth century buildings and bought by the school in 1911. It is now the boarding house for Oundle School's youngest pupils.

Below, at the corner of East Road and South Road is the cottage which served as Oundle's Air Raid Precautions (ARP) command post during the Second World War.

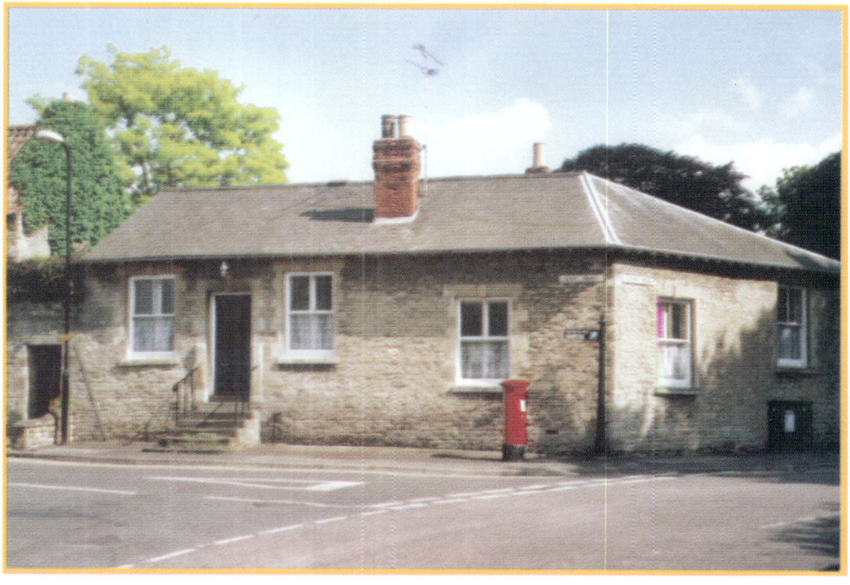

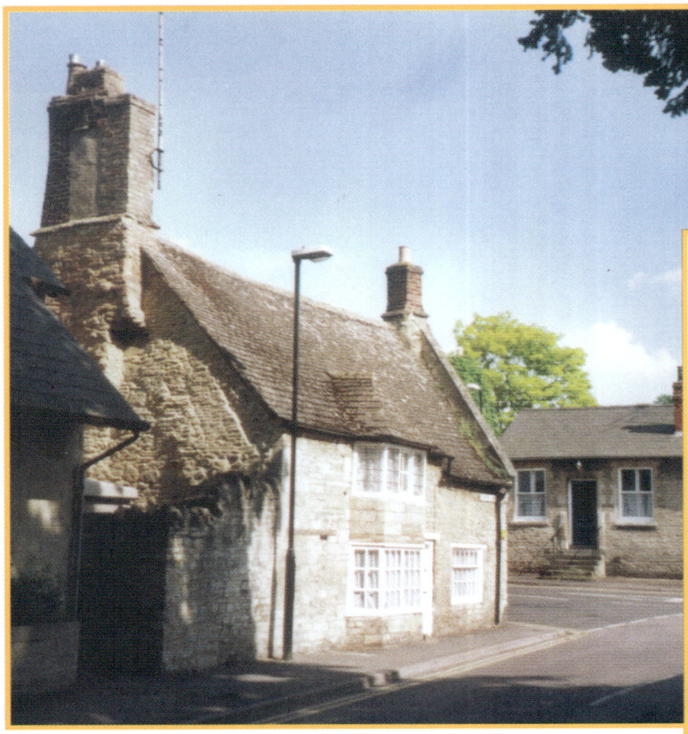

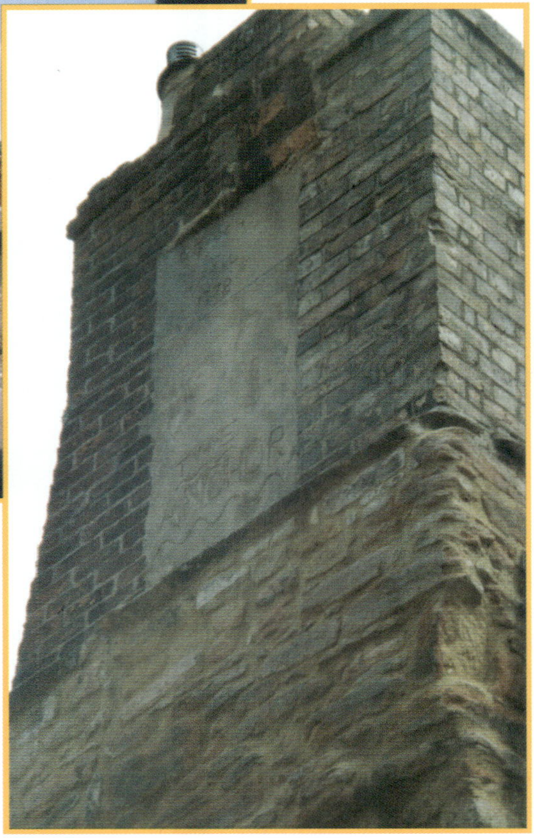

On the opposite side of the road to the ARP command post is the old Anchor Inn which closed in 1956. Now a private residence the building was also known as 'The Duck's Nest' and on the south gable (below) are the initials JM and the date 1637, but it is thought that the building is probably of an earlier date. The Lamb pub was once next door but now is situated the ultra-modern Co-op building which serves as Oundle's main grocery store.

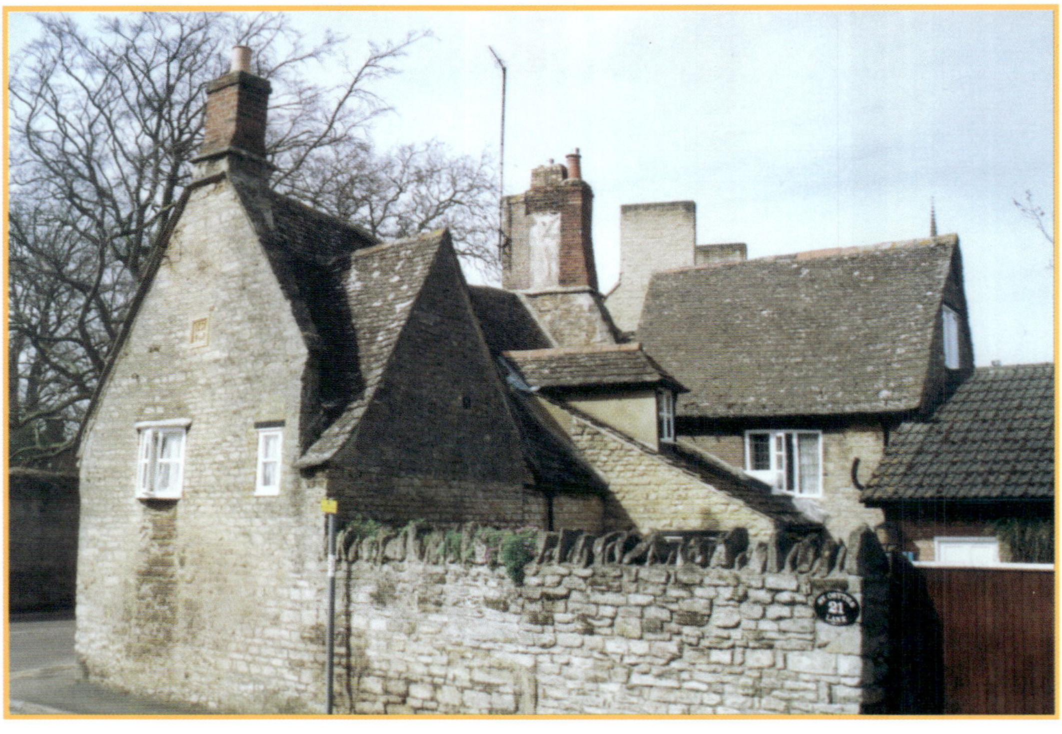

St Osyth's Lane, looking towards the Market Place with "The Angel" on the east side opposite Bramston House and the paddock. The Angel public house has occupied this spot for some time being mentioned in the records of the 1780's. Just visible in the right photograph is the Co-op developed in the early 1990's.

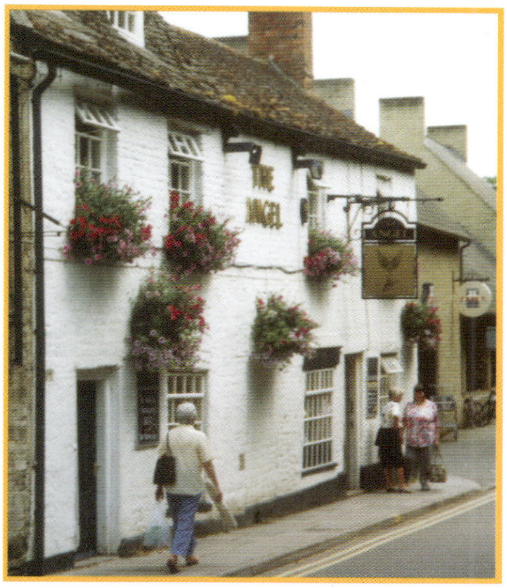

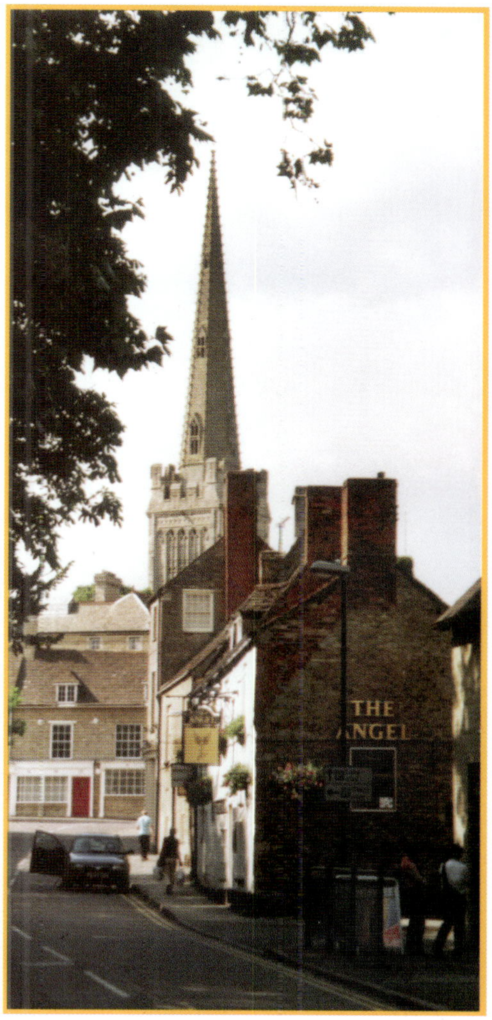

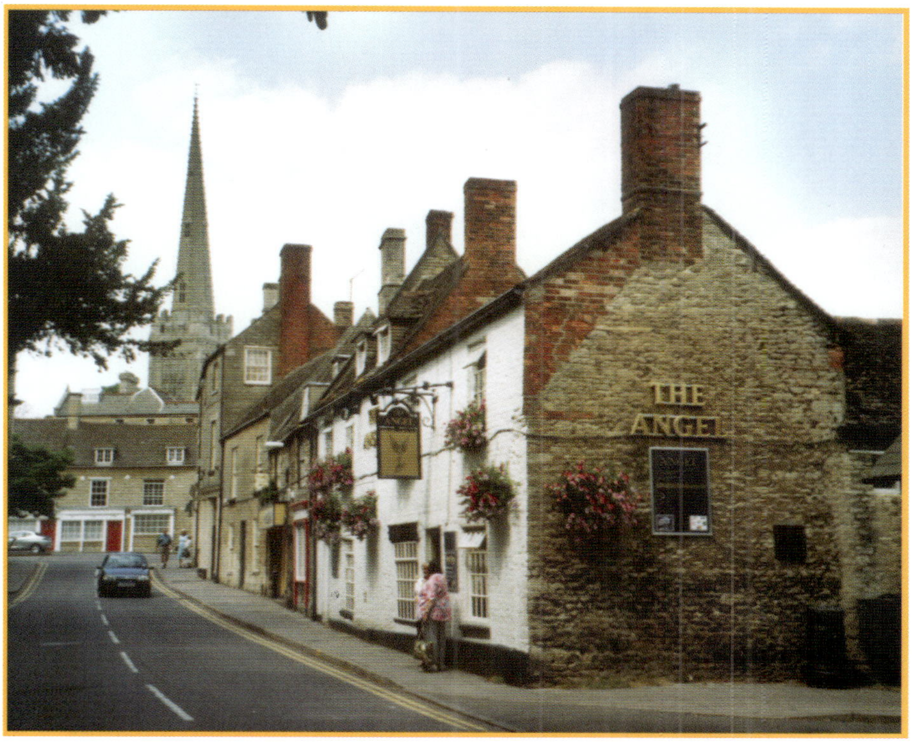

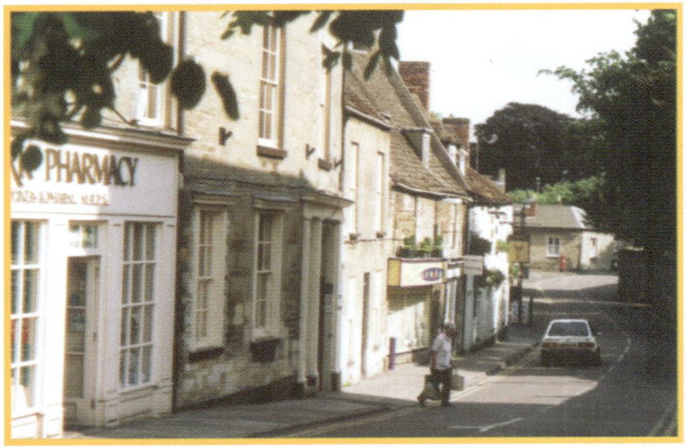

Left, looking down St Osyth's Lane from Oundle Market Place.

Oundle Market is held every Thursday. During the rest of the week it is a place for relaxation. It could be said with some justification, that all roads lead to the Market Place, the centre of the town's life for many centuries. Over forty public buildings in Oundle have been identified as once being 'public houses' and The Nags Head was once situated at number 30 the Market Place and on the corner shown in the photograph below.

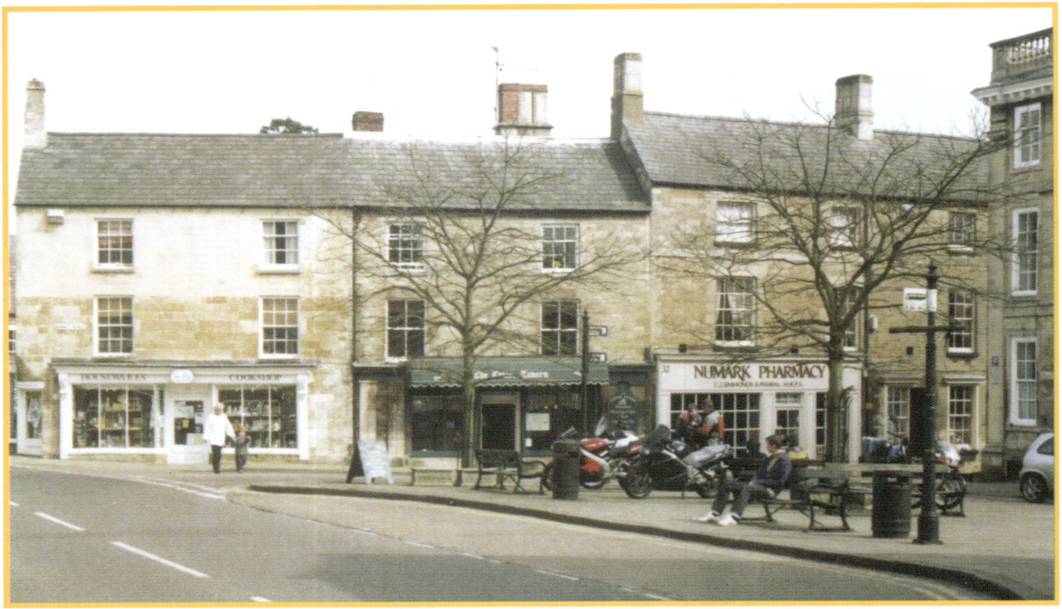

Below, an aerial photograph looking north from the town centre. The old town wall is visible in the centre of the photograph with New Street on the left and North Street on the right.

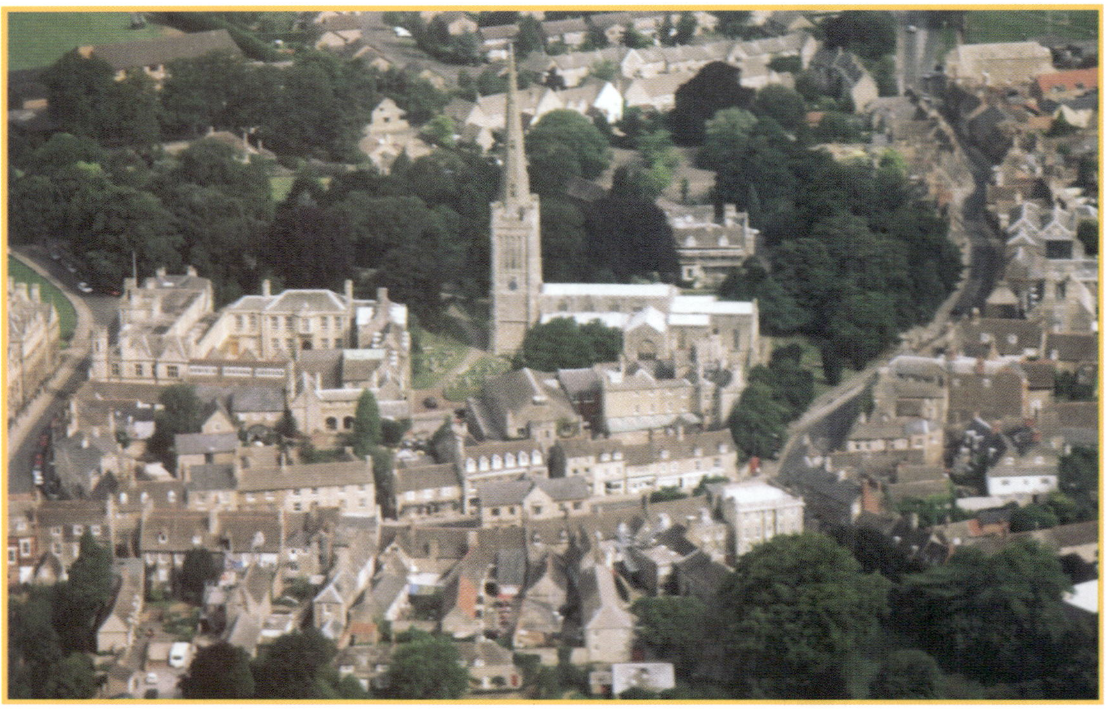

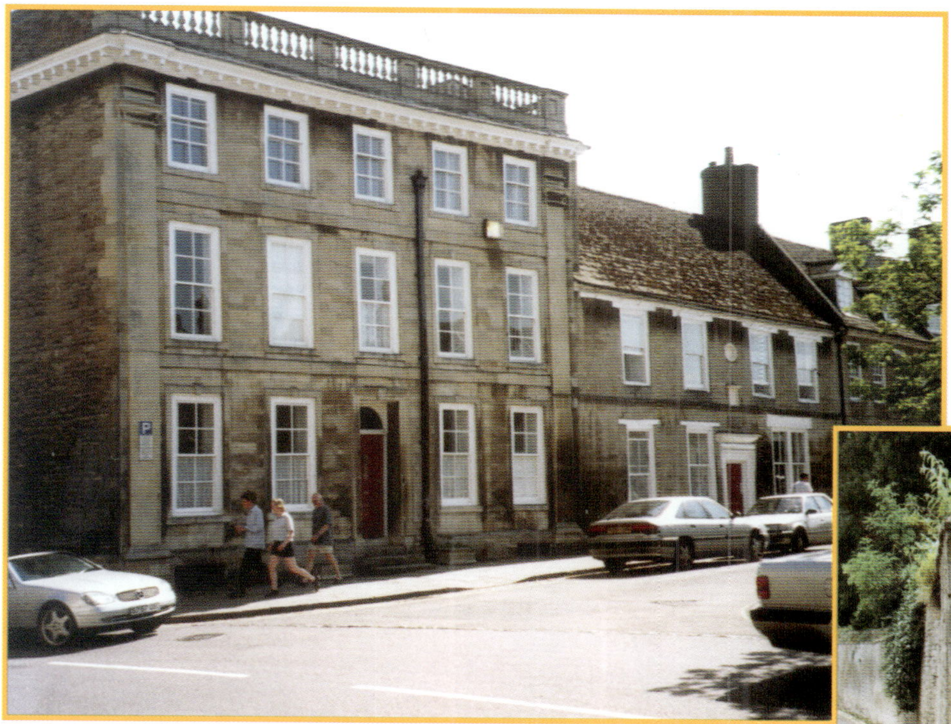

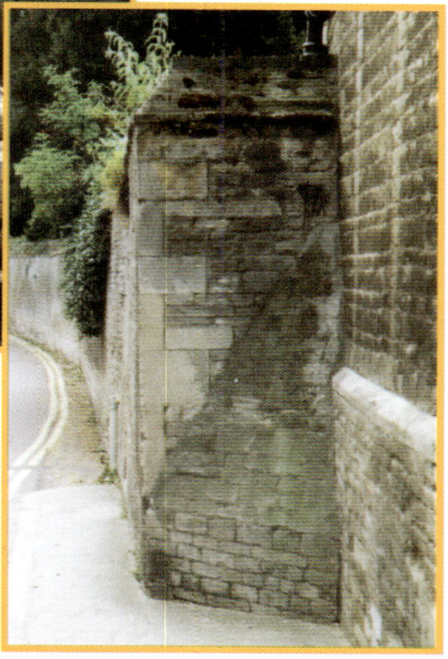

On the corner of the Market Place and St Osyth's Lane stands Bramston House (above), purchased by Oundle School in 1917 and enlarged to include many of the adjoining buildings. The house was originally built by the lawyer Stephen Bramston during the eighteenth century. The front elevation has hardly been altered and the high balustrade completely hides the roof. Around the corner in St Osyth's Lane is a 'splash back'. These were used to fill corners near to public houses in the days before public conveniences were available and to 'prevent nuisances'!

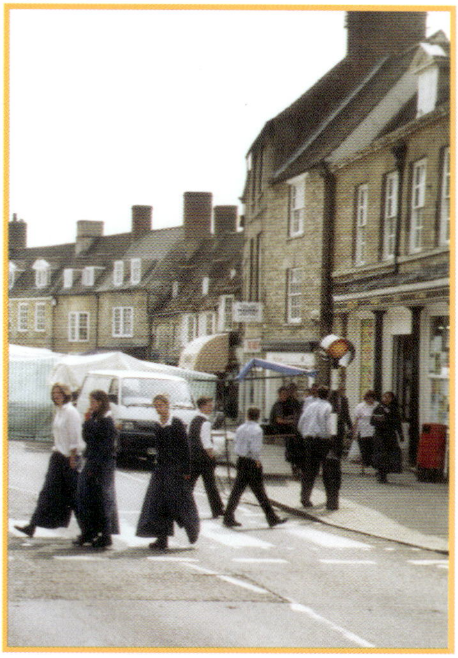

Left, break at Oundle School, Thursday in the Market Place.

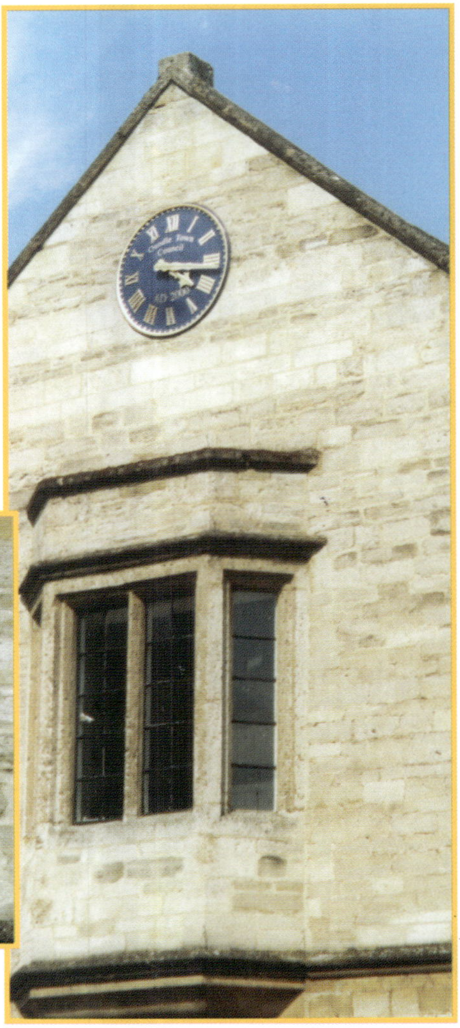

The Town Hall, now converted into shops and offices, standing in the centre of the Market Place was built in 1826 using stone from a church demolished in Barnwell. Oundle's unique sixteenth century octagonal cross and a row of shops were demolished to accommodate the new Town Hall. On the south wall and above the oriel window is the crest of the Watts-Russell family. The clocks were added at the turn of the present century.

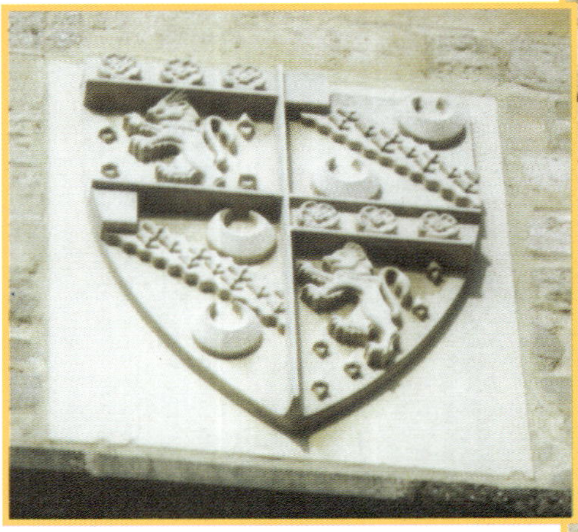

The north side of the Market Place with the unique seventeenth century colonnaded bookshop and also the sports shop (below), are both operated by Oundle School. The colonnaded bookshop projects out on the upper floors thus enabling greater use above the ground floor.

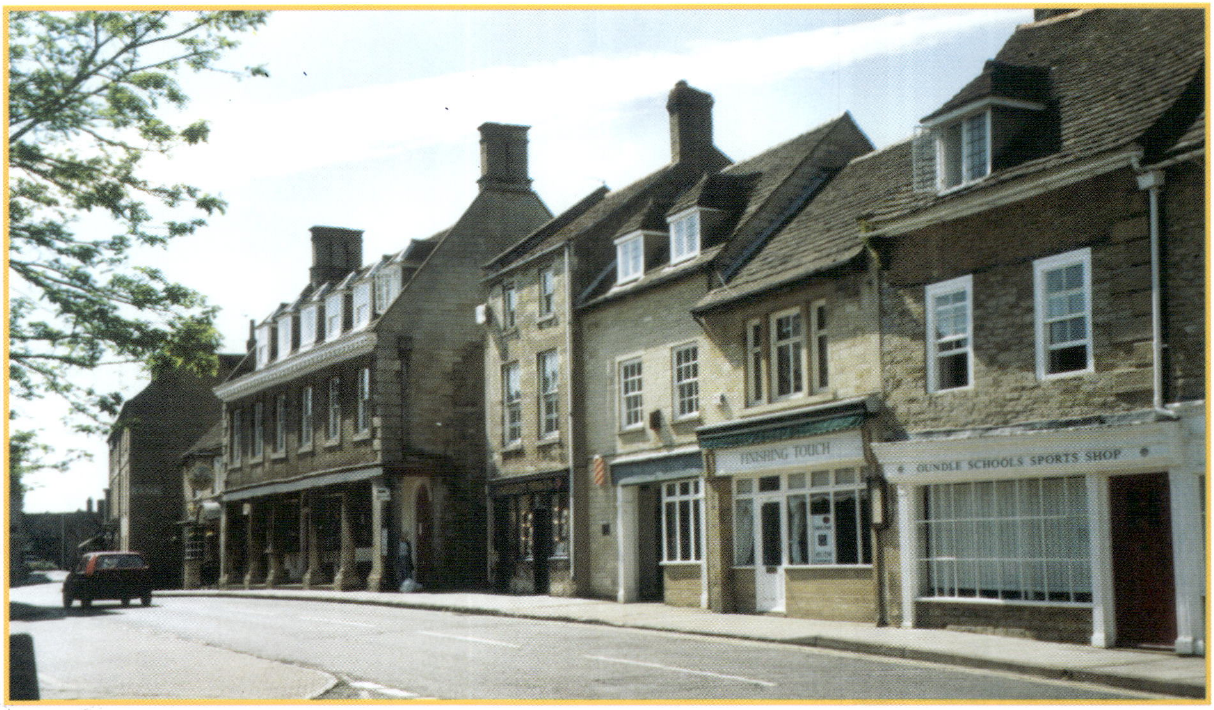

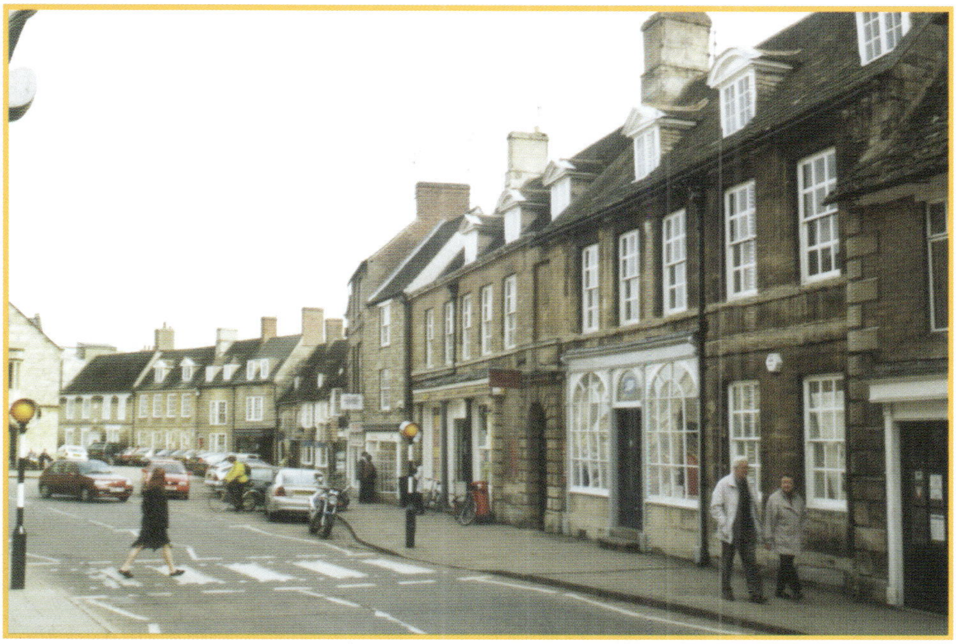

Above, the north side of the Market Place with the Town Hall to be seen just on the left. A busy focal point for traders and shoppers in Oundle. Many of the buildings date from the seventeenth century.

Below, the Rose and Crown - the name has not changed for centuries. The Northamptonshire poet John Clare was billeted here in 1812 when training with the militia. The pub was popular with American servicemen during the Second World War.

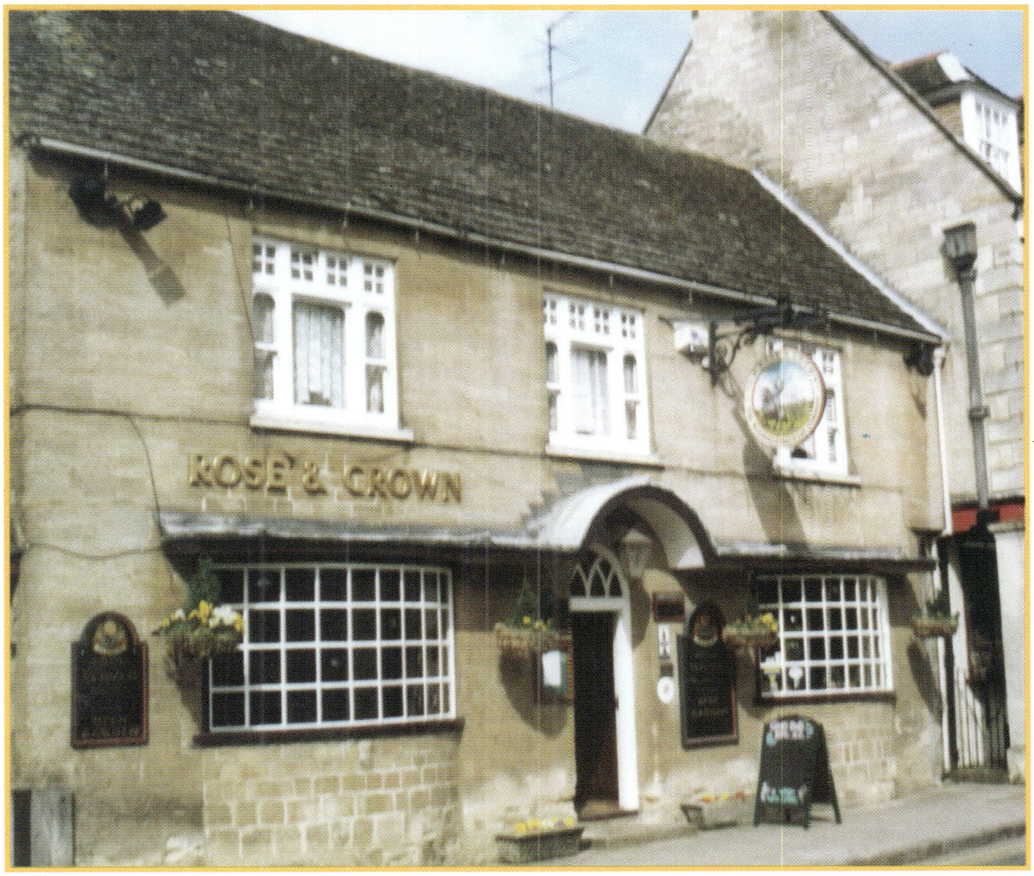

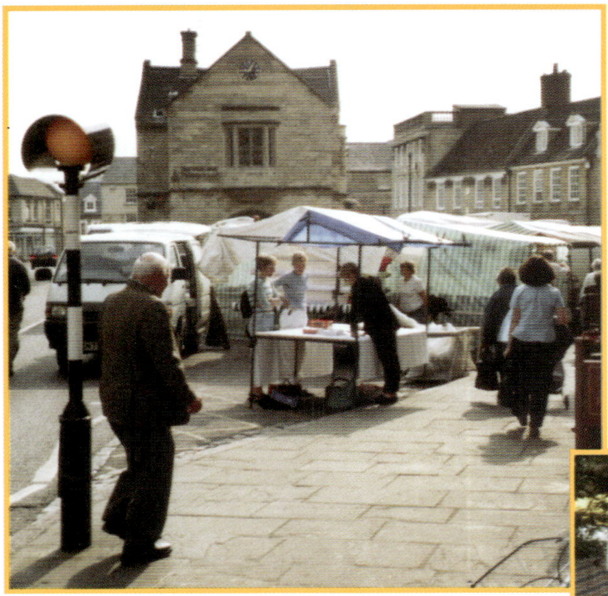

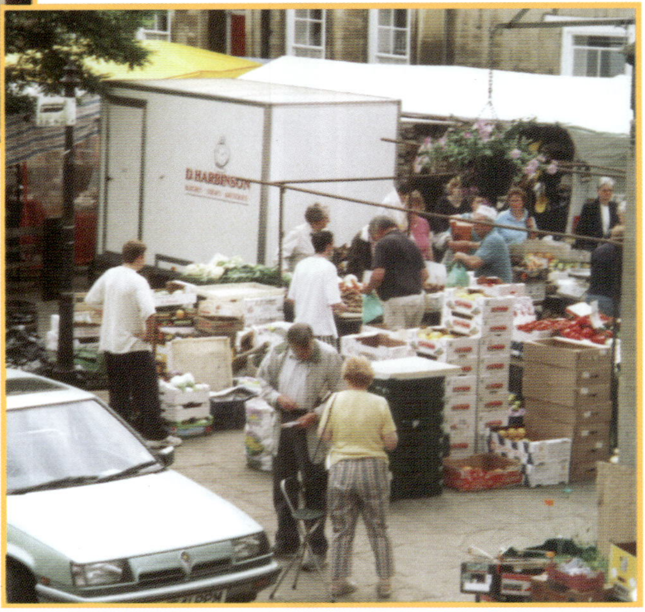

Thursday and Market Day is an important day for the town, bringing both traders and customers from around the area. The market has been established in some form in the town for many centuries, altering to meet the social and commercial needs of the time.

Many stalls do change from year to year but the green grocers and clothing stalls seem ever popular.

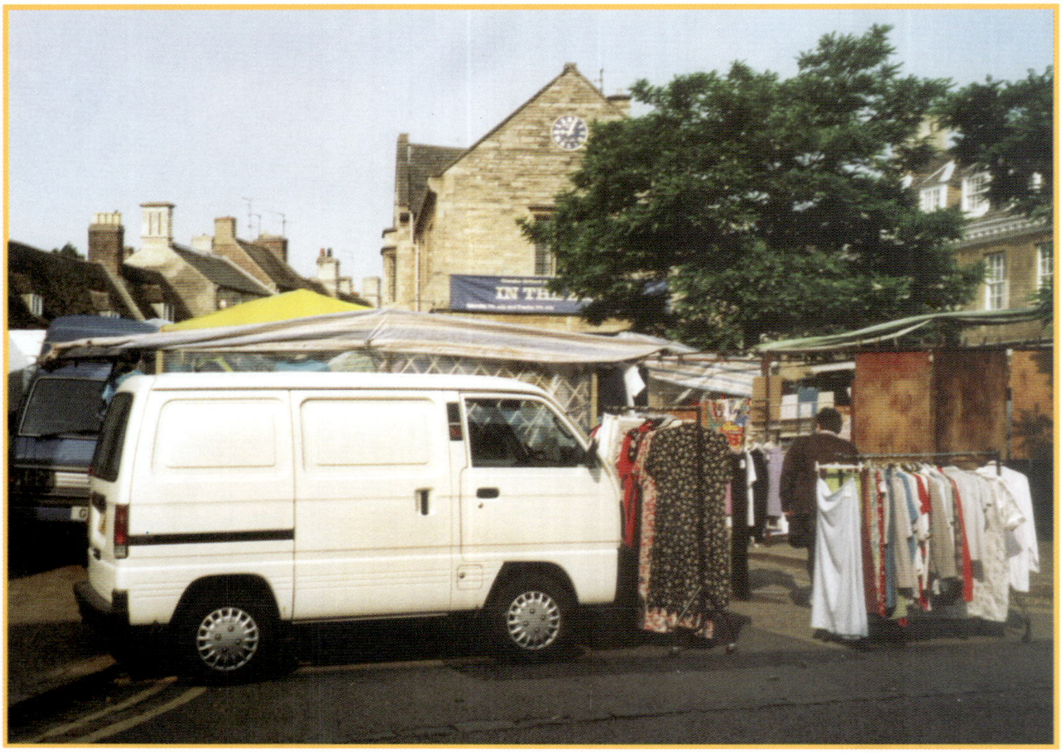

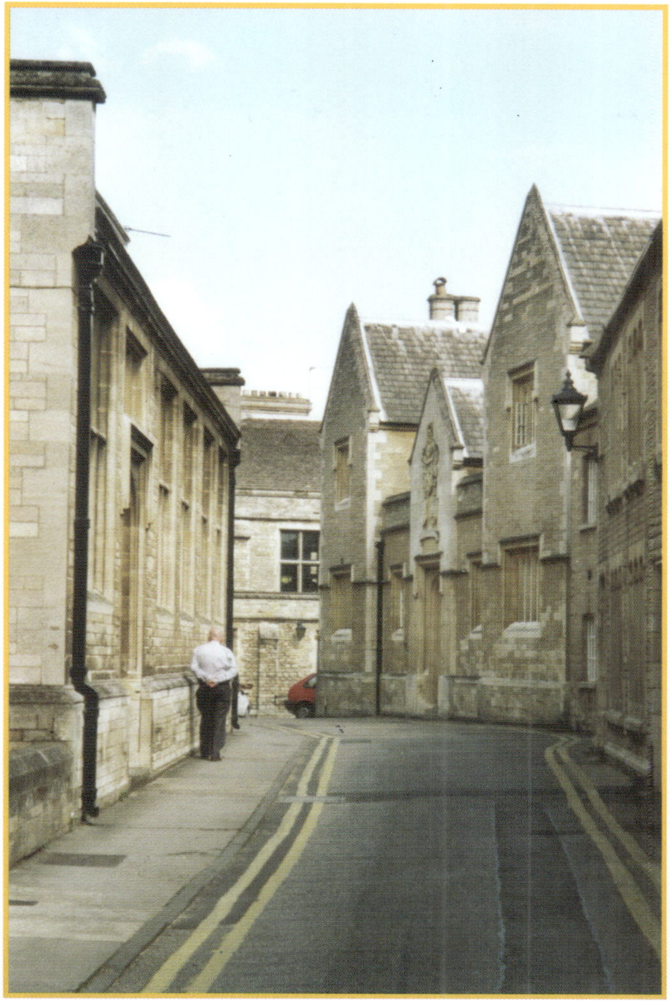

Left, Church Lane showing the present Bursar's Office on the right. The site has had many uses including almshouses and the original brewery of John Smith's, who was a local lad.
Below, is Jericho Lane off the Market Place and one of the many secretive 'back alley' lanes found in Oundle.

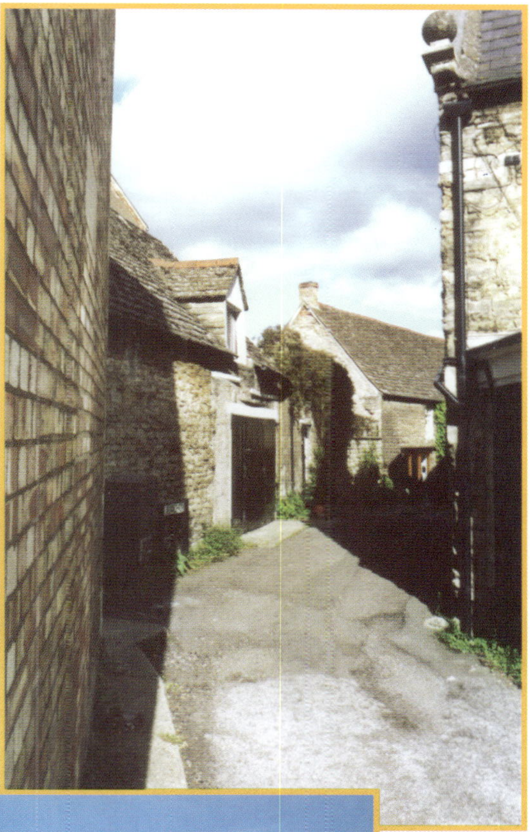

Below, the corner of the Market Place and North Street showing the entrance (behind the white van), to what may be Oundle's oldest street, Jericho, (also picture right).

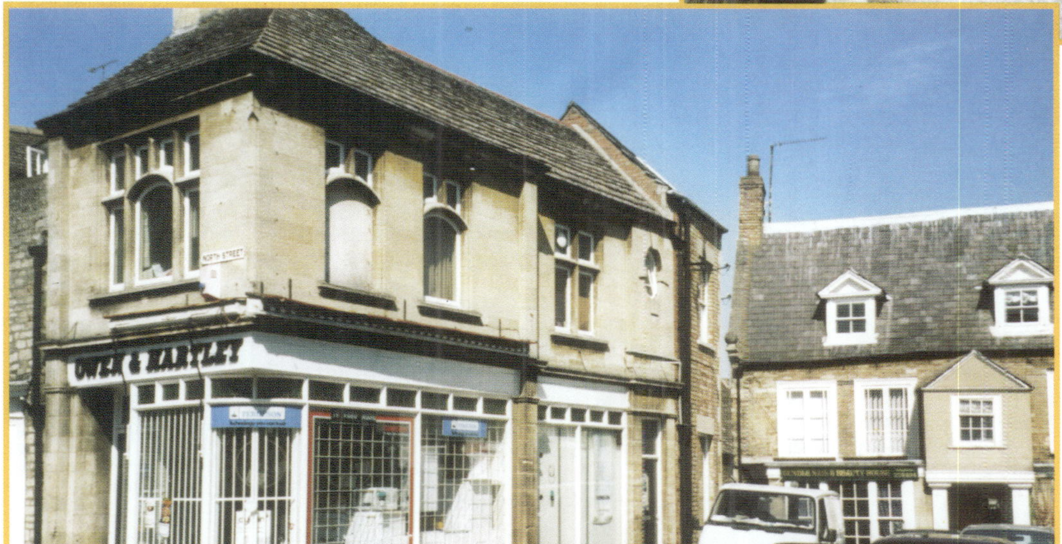

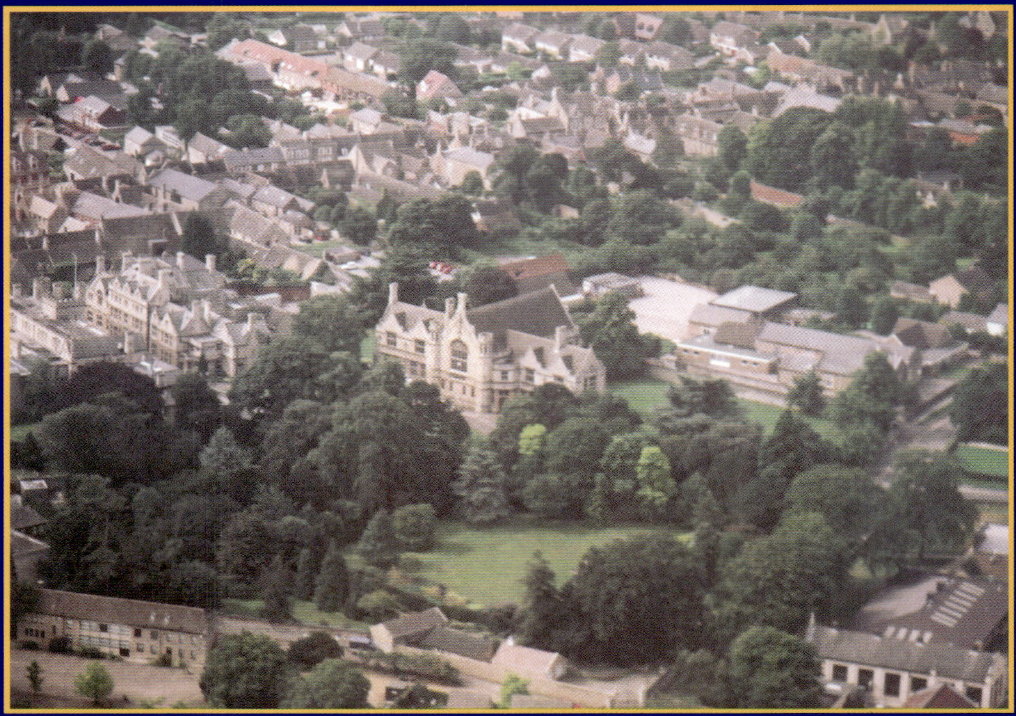

St Peter's Church and Immediate Environs

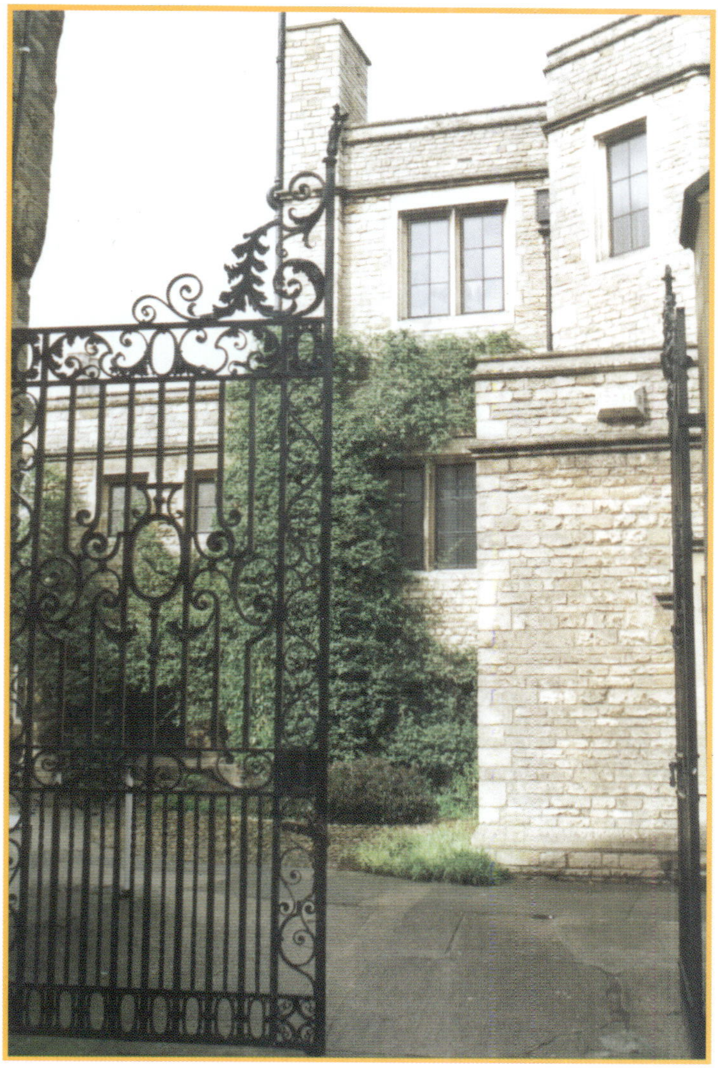

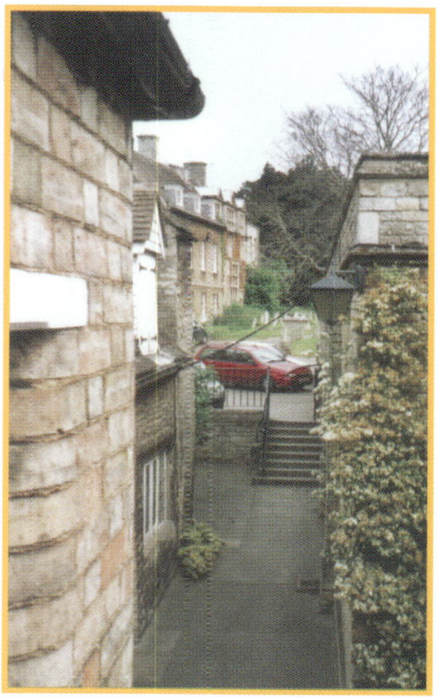

There are many pedestrian thoroughfares and interesting ally ways out of the Market Place. This one is known as 'Bookshop Passage'. Belonging to Oundle School it is kept closed for a few days every year to prevent it from becoming a right of way.

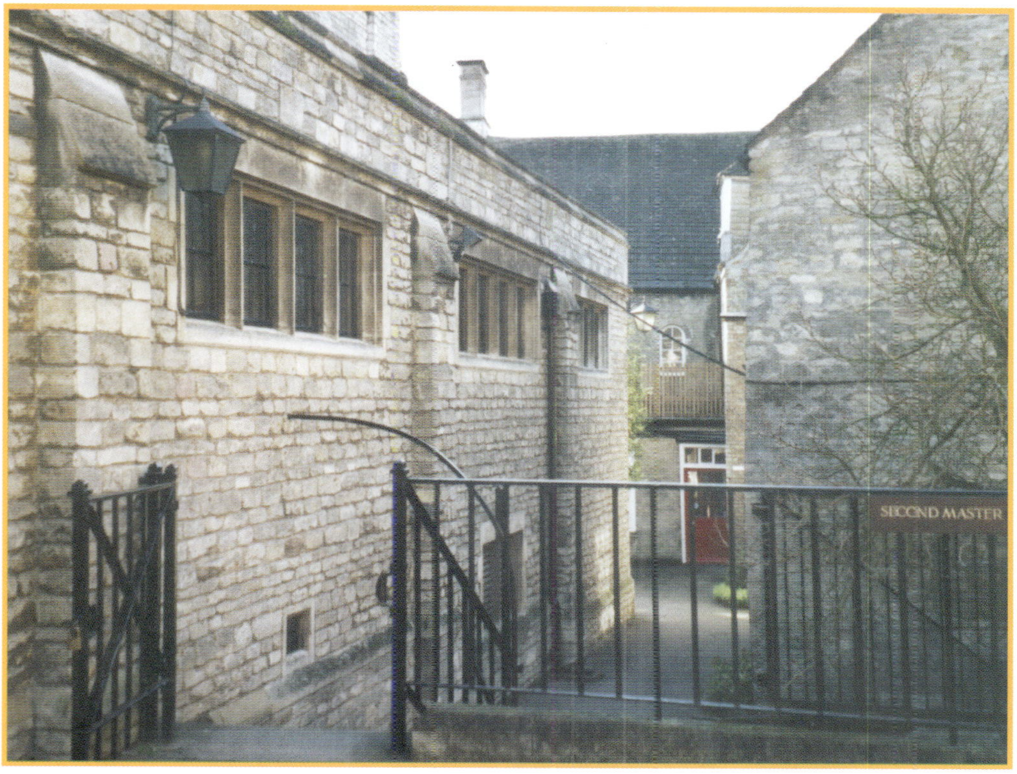

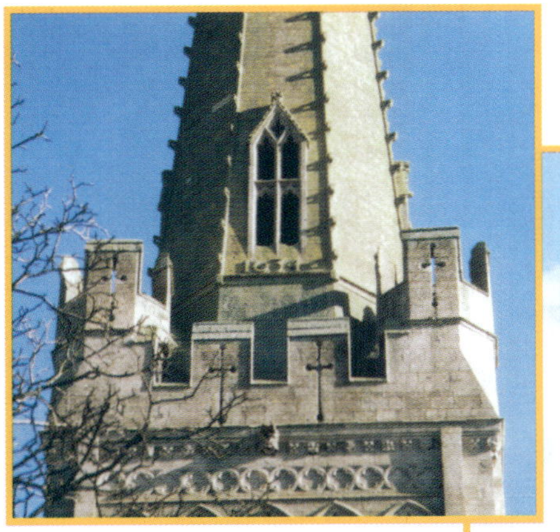

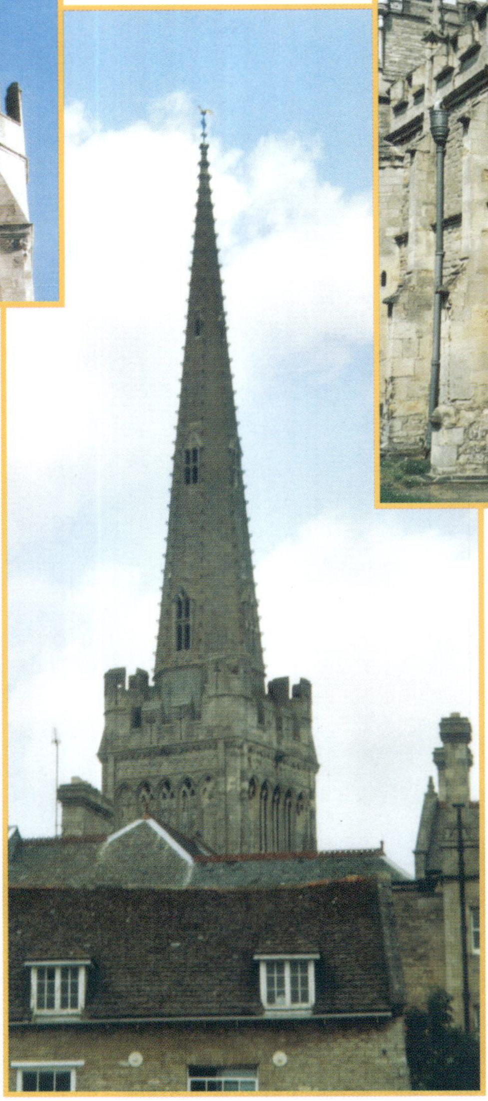

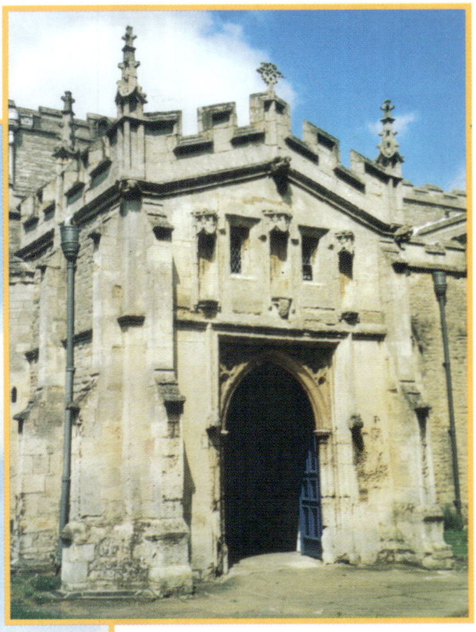

The most prominent landmark, St Peter's Church is set on foundations from at least the eighth century. Most of the building was completed in the middle ages but the spire was started in 1634. Its crocketted design has tempted the occasional schollboy to climb it! On one such occasion the schoolboy was given a thrashing and a shilling when he descended.

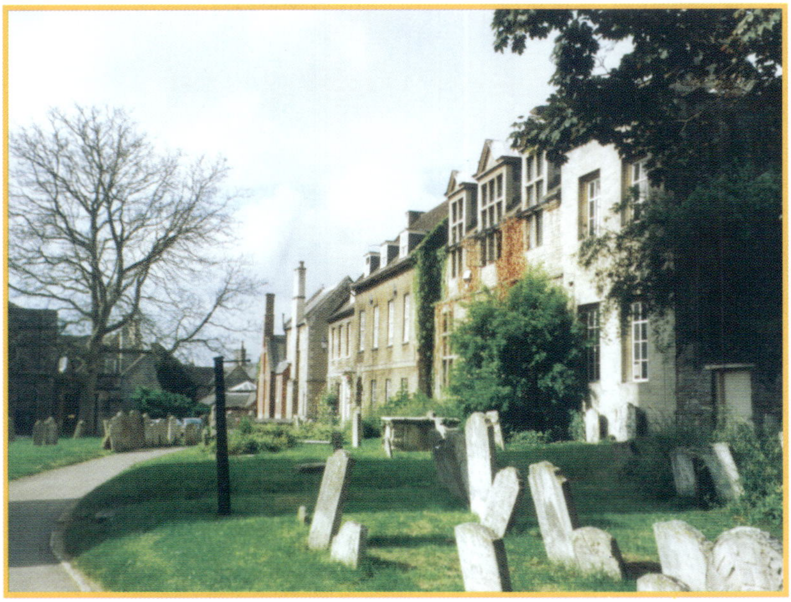

The western side of the churchyard (left) is also the eastern side of the Oundle School cloisters. The walnut tree on the left of the photograph has now been cut down!

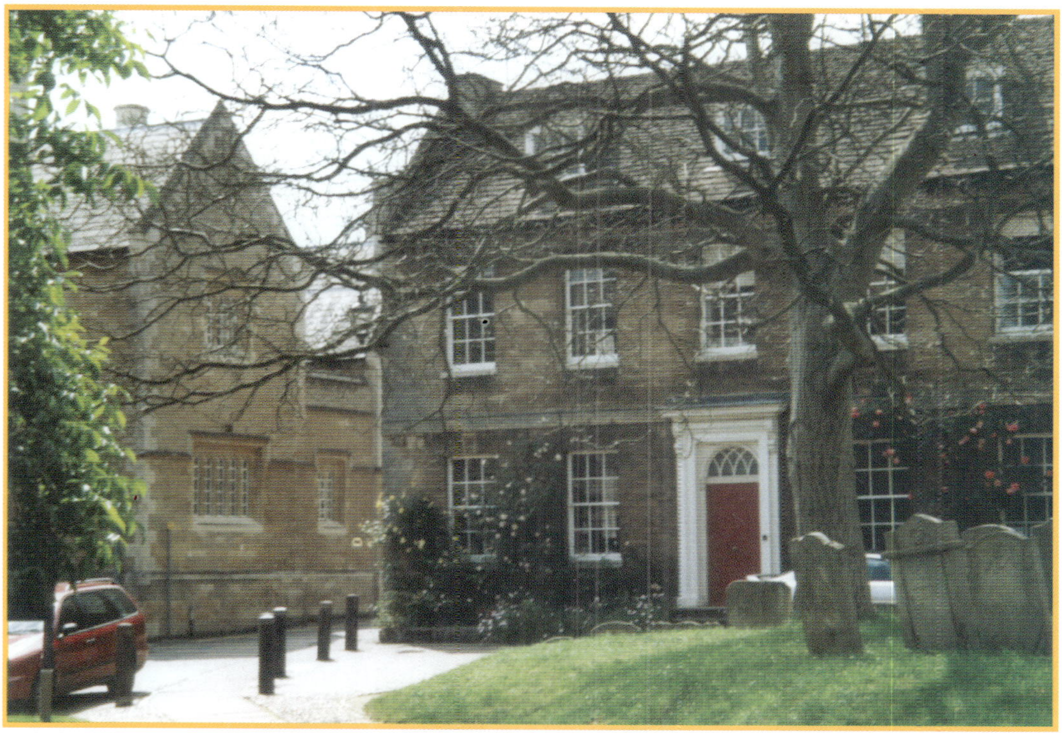

Above, the Bursar's House on the left and situated on the corner of the churchyard was built in 1763 for the new headmaster Samuel Murthwaite and any boarders he could find! Desparate times perhaps as there were only ten boarders recorded in the register! The new house cost £366 to build.
The photograph below shows the same building with one of the entrances to the cloisters.

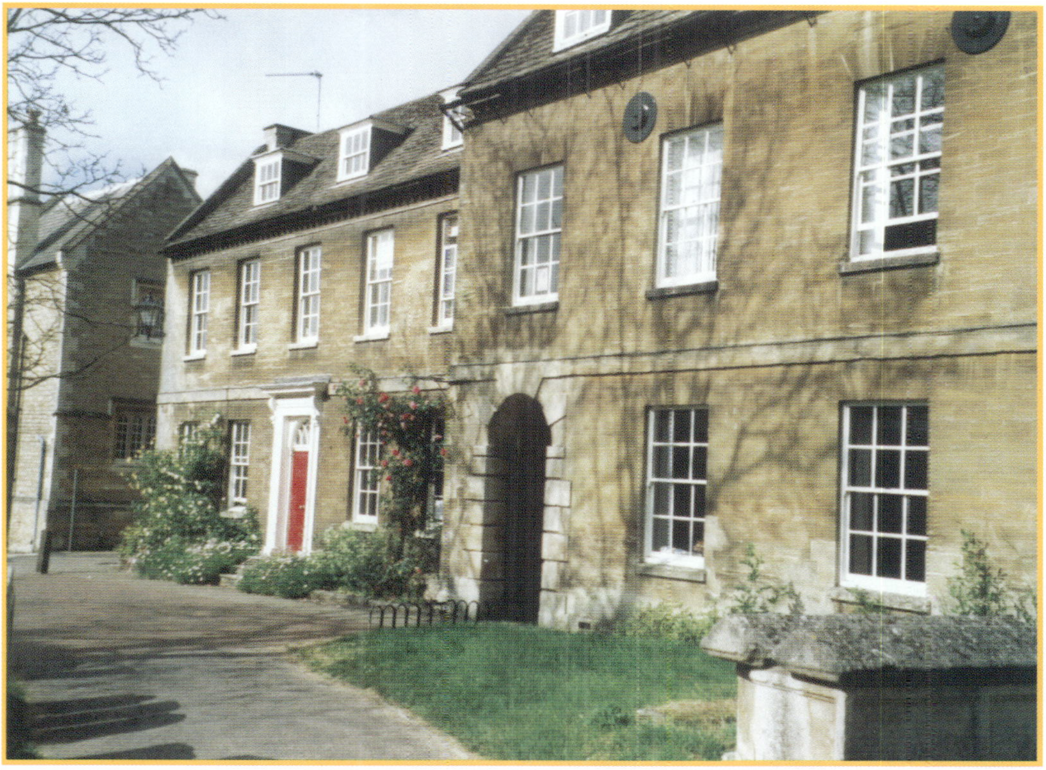

Laxton School, below, was the beginning of Oundle Public School, following the bequest of Sir William Laxton, former Lord Mayor of London in 1556 and 'local boy'. He instructed in his will that the former guild-house should be acquired and used as a grammar school with accommodation for 'seven poor honest men'. The guild house stood in the churchyard on the site of the current Laxton School building. The current building was completed in 1855.

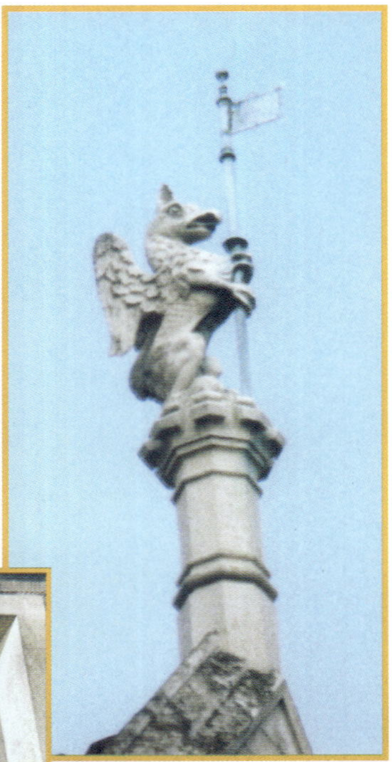

The tablet (right) on the east wall once stood over the main entrance to the old school. The coat of arms link Sir William Laxton, the founder, with the Grocers' Company and the City of London. and the inscribed plate in Hebrew, Latin and Greek is not a message in triplicate. The Latin records the benefactors and beneficiaries; the Greek says how much the beneficiaries benefitted and the Hebrew says how blessed is the benefactor as a result. The flag held by the winged phoenix flies from the top of the building. In the foreground in spring a cross is marked out by daffodils.

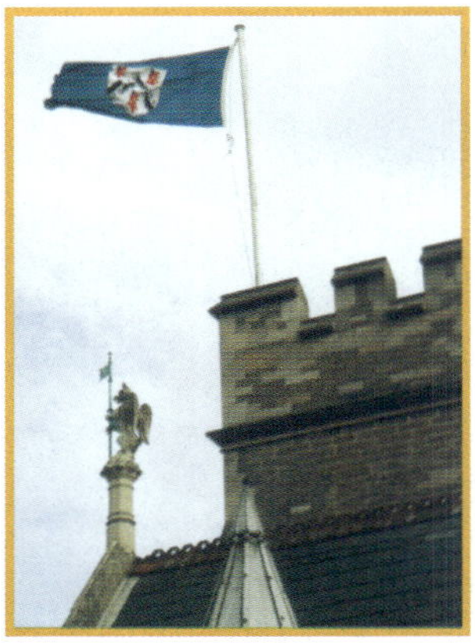

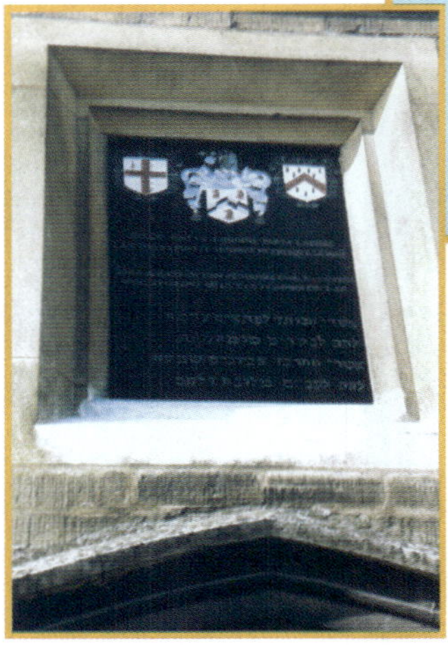

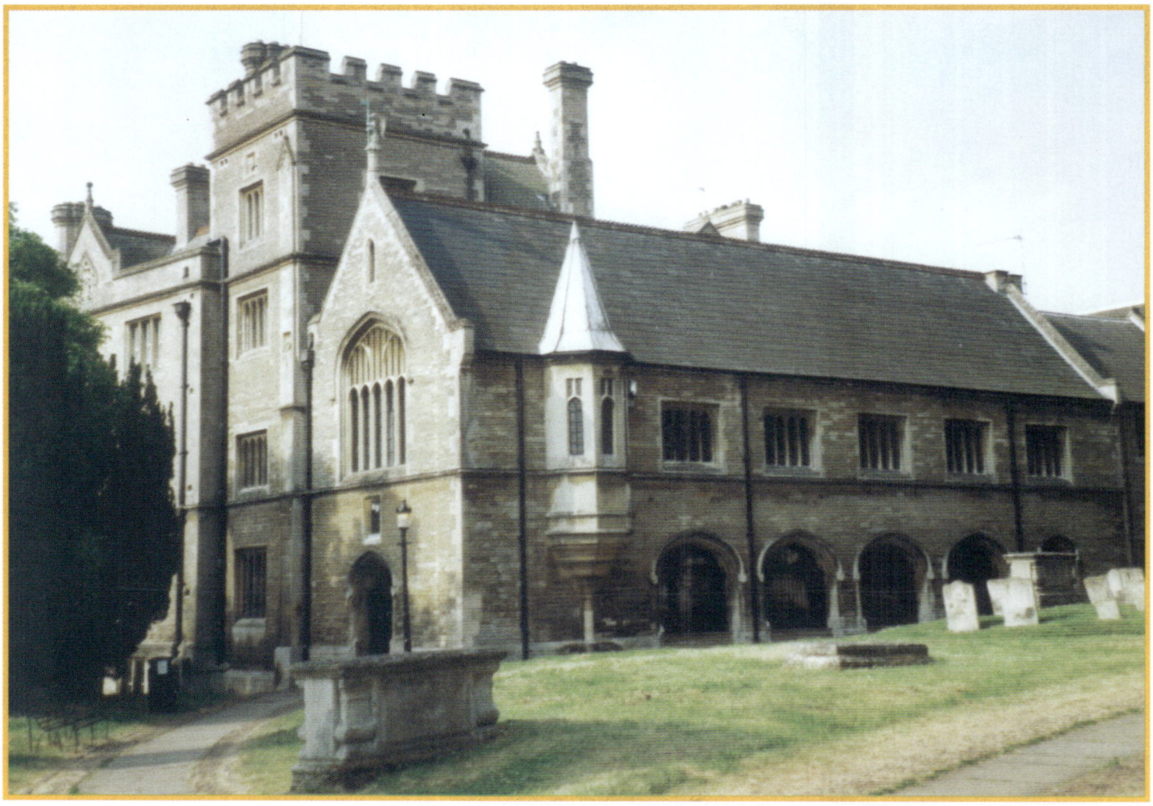

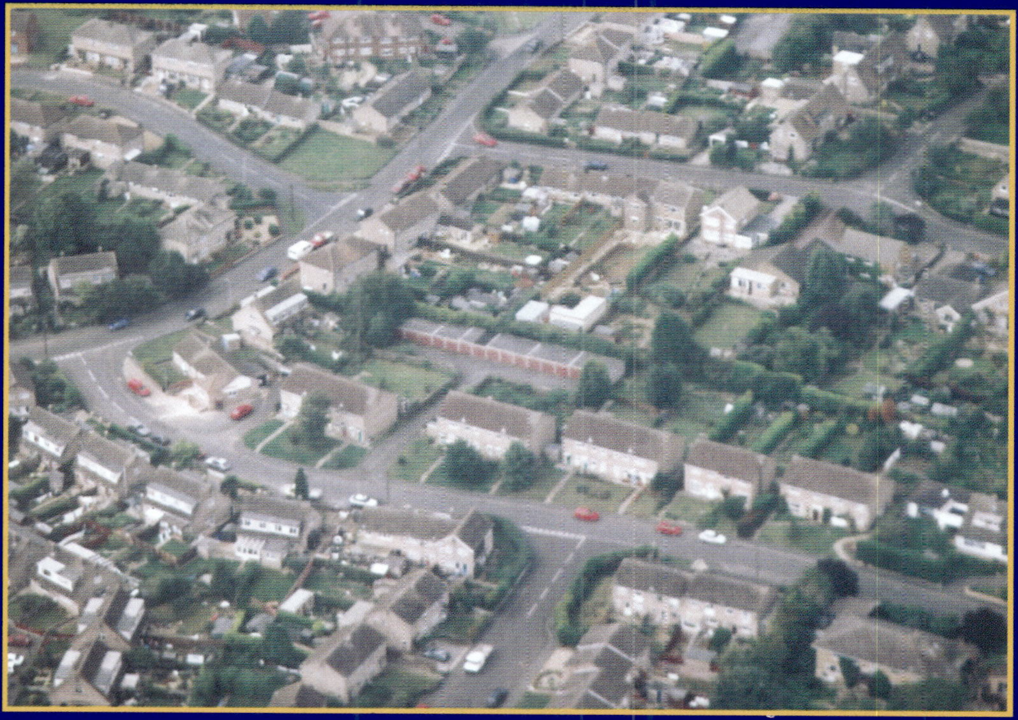

Central and North Oundle

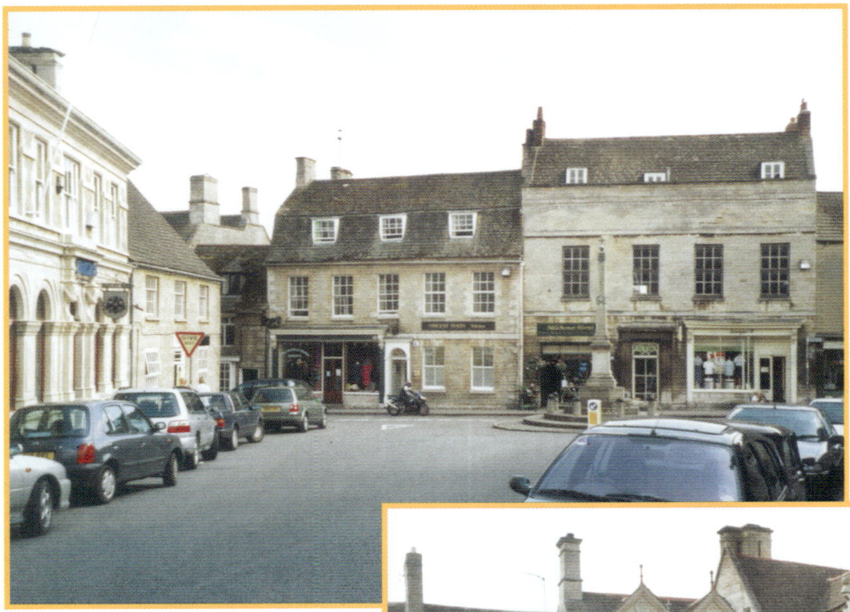

The War Memorial was erected after the First World War, prior to this the site was occupied by a large water pump.

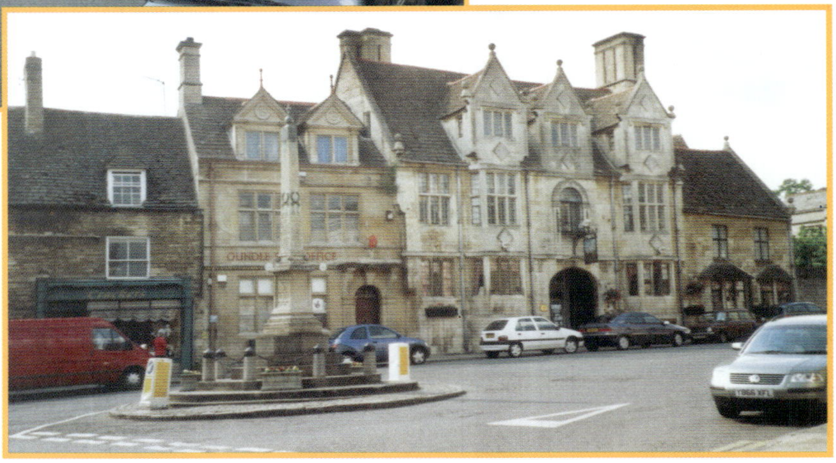

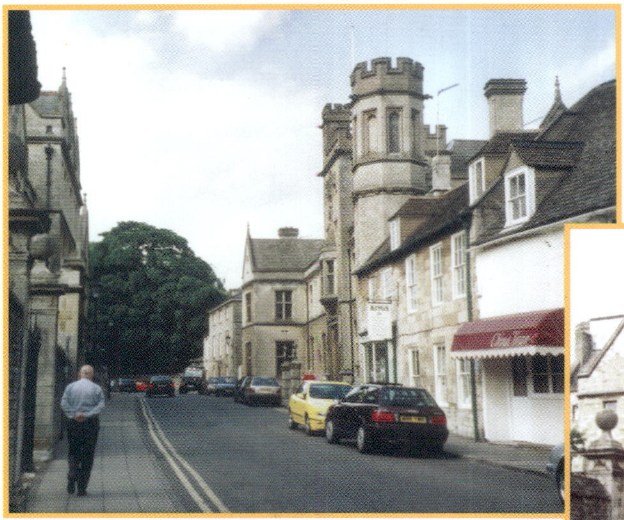

New Street the site of many of Oundle's important buildings. The Talbot Hotel rebuilt in 1626 but retaining many of its previous characteristics, including a medieval back range with an open passage or gallery. Rumour has it that the superb staircase came from Fotheringhay Castle. also to be seen are The School House Study Rooms, The Cloisters and, out of sight, the Great Hall.

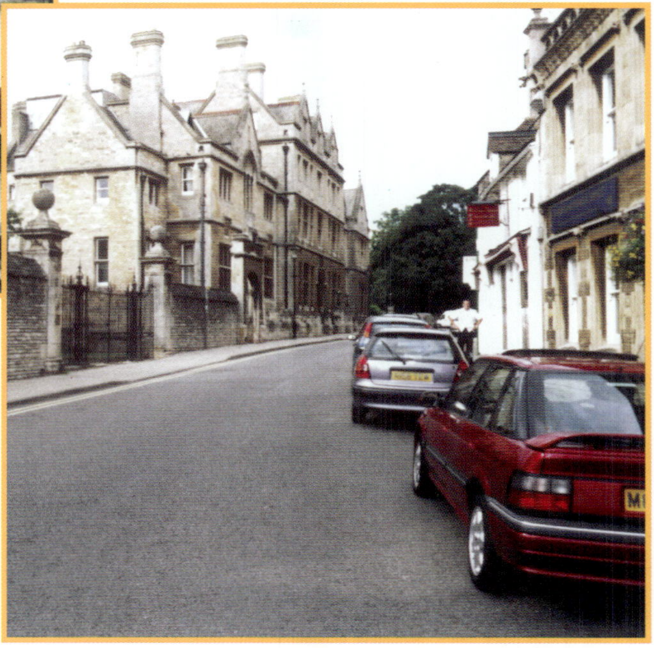

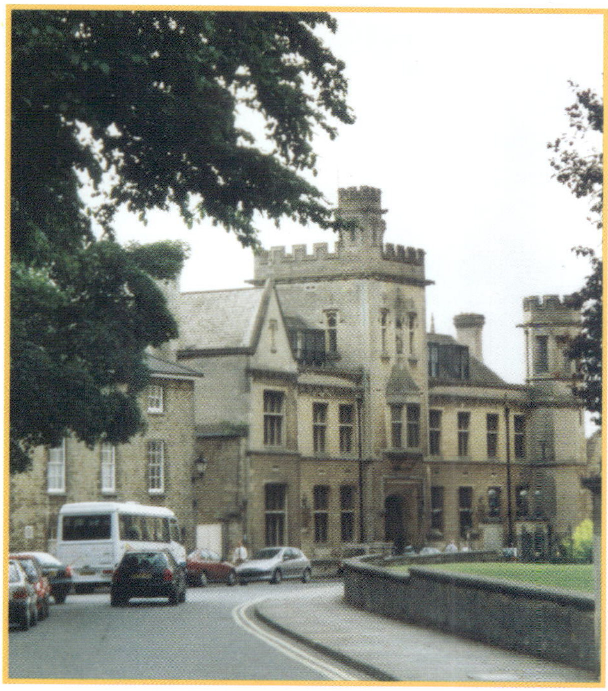

Glapthorn Road towards the south. St Peter's vicarage is nearest left and the Oundle Schol Cloisters beyond. The Great Hall is opposite.

Below, The Talbot Study Rooms.

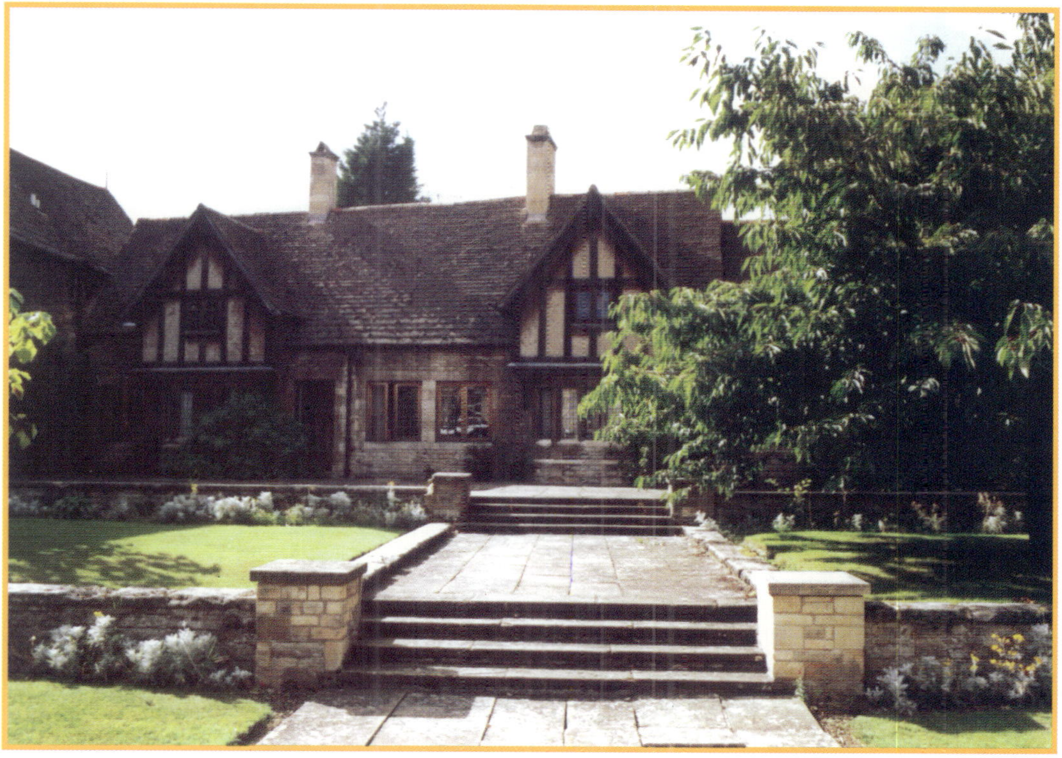

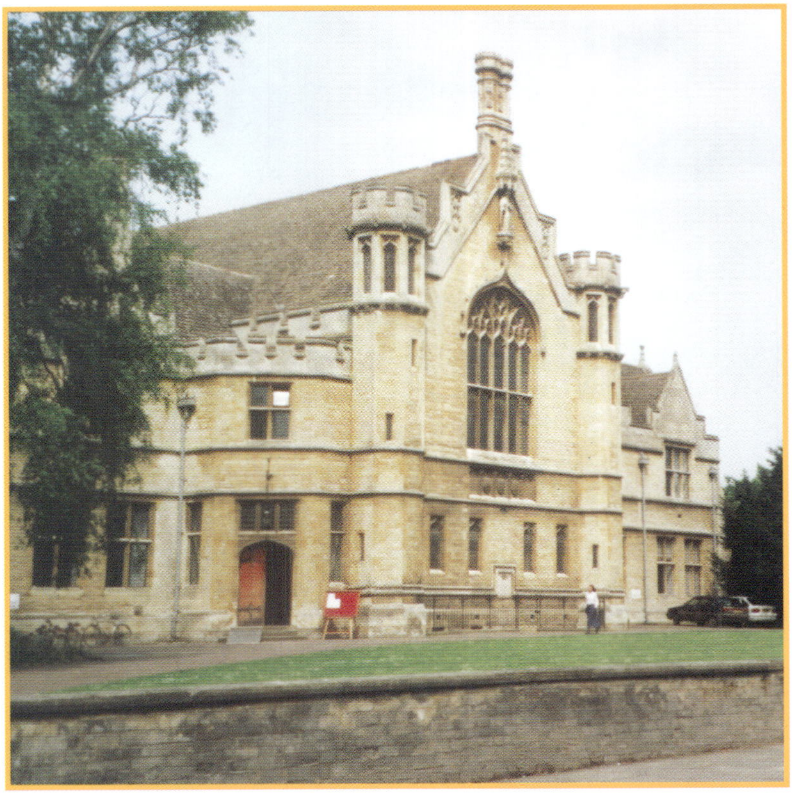

Oundle School's Great Hall was built in 1908. The imposing building has under gone several changes to accommodate an increasing number of pupils.

The present Headmaster's and Admissions Offices are in the north wing.

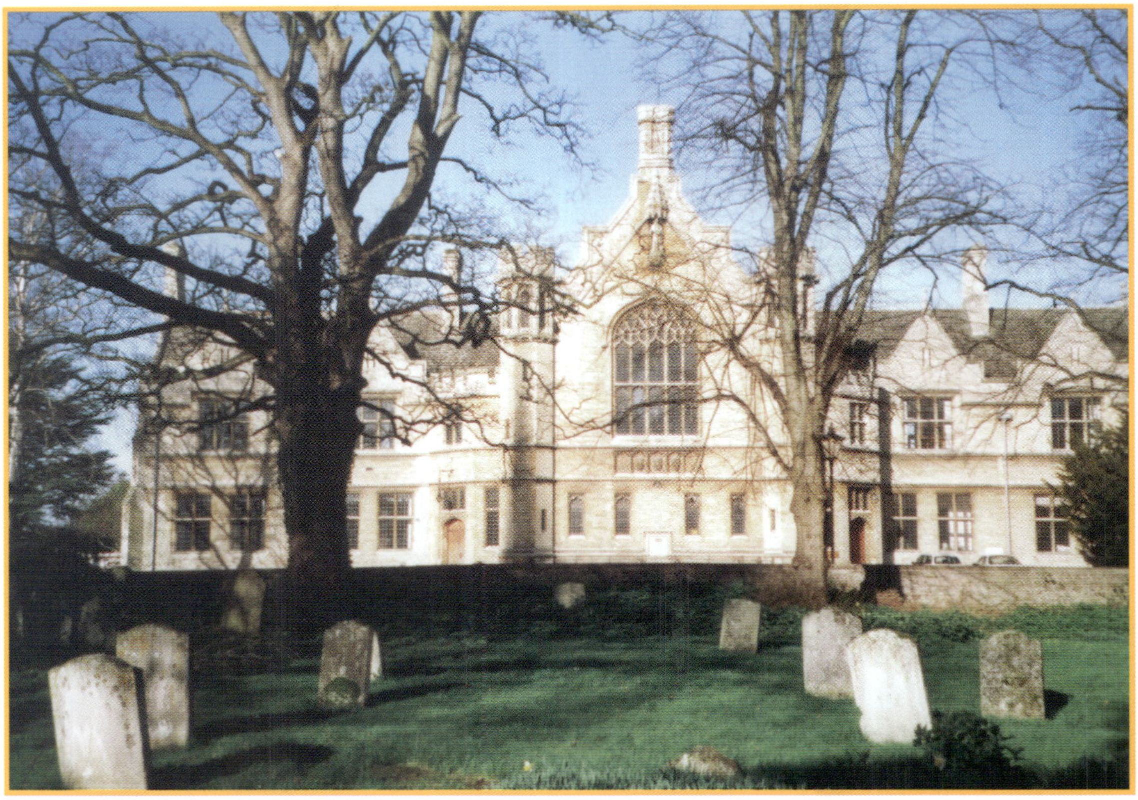

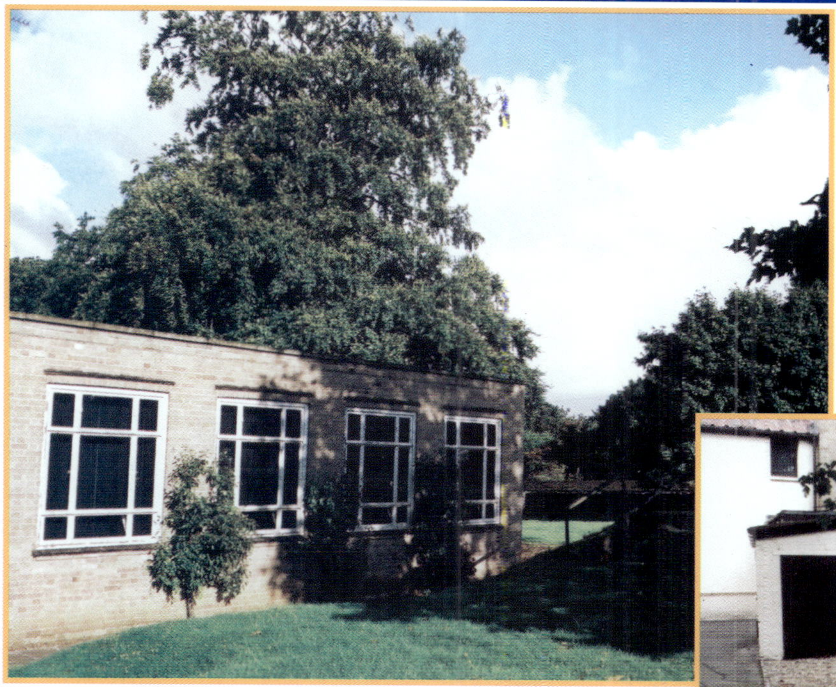

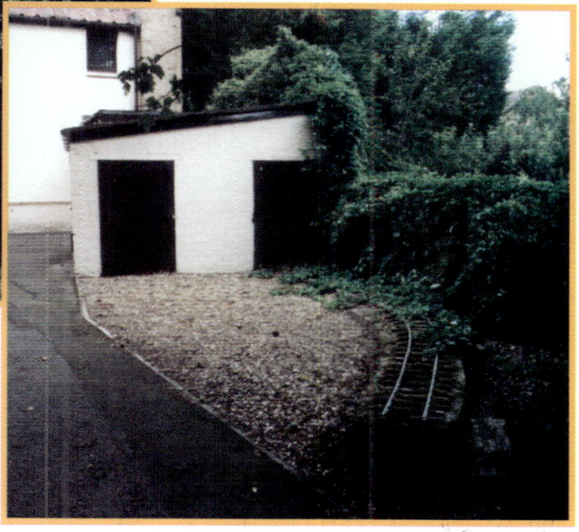

The Oundle School chemistry block in Glapthorn Road, the site of countless experiments. To the right is the entrance to a wartime air raid shelter and just visible in the shadows (below) are the intertwined serpents adorning the building. Above right are the Oundle School workshops and now a disused miniature railway engine sheds.

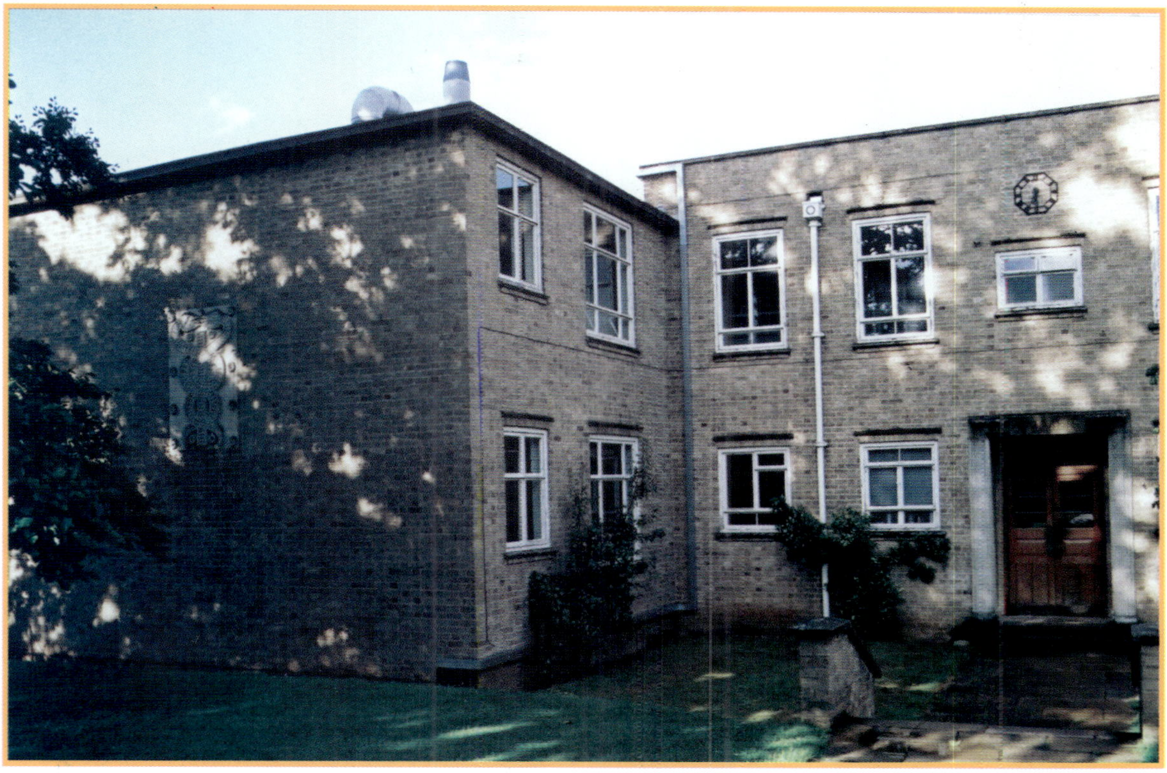

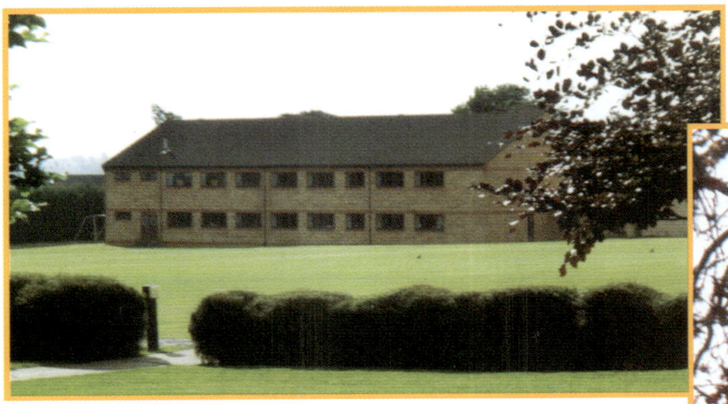

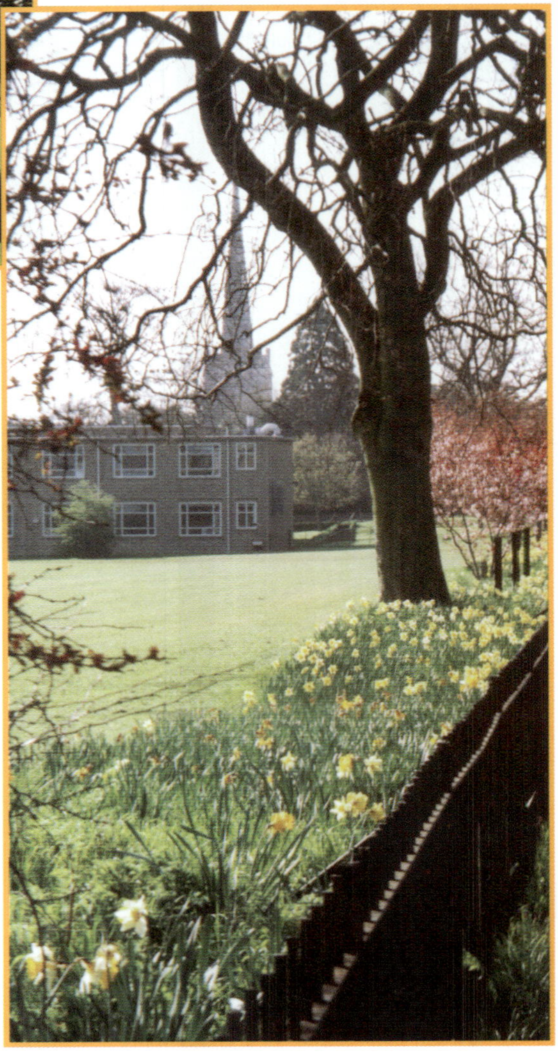

Oundle School buildings are wide spread across the town. Above the workshops and right the chemistry laboratories and a lovely sight of Home Close in the spring, showing off their magnificent daffodils. Below the Sir Peter Scott building housing the Mathematics and Physics Departments and with the Yarrow on the right of the photograph. Sir Peter Scott was an Old Oundelian. Oundle School owns many aristocratic looking buildings around the town and Yarrow was given to the school by Sir Alfred Yarrow, in memory of his son Eric who was killed at Ypres in 1915. This gallery is now used as a venue for exhibitions by School staff and pupils and other local artists.

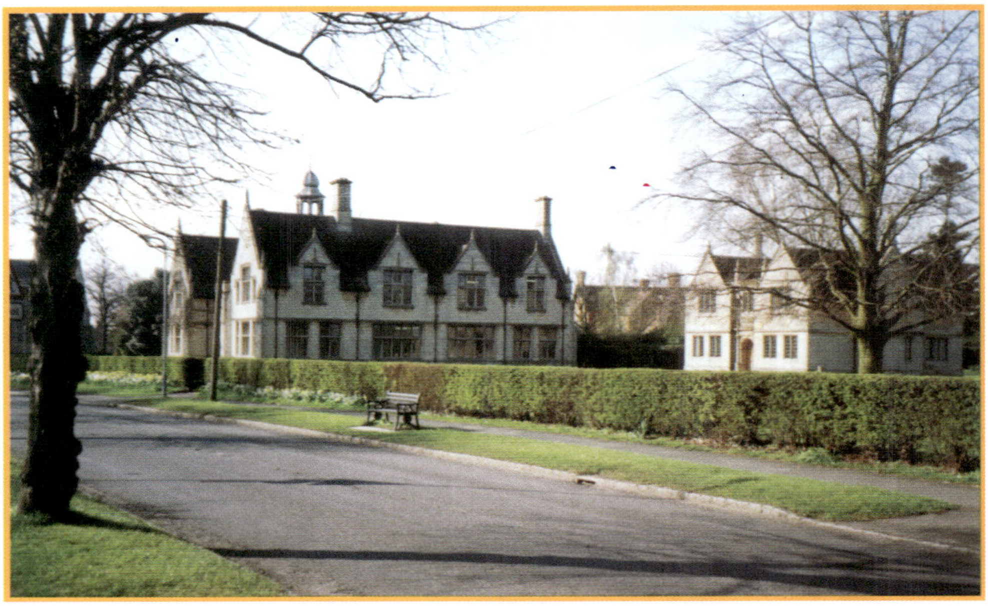

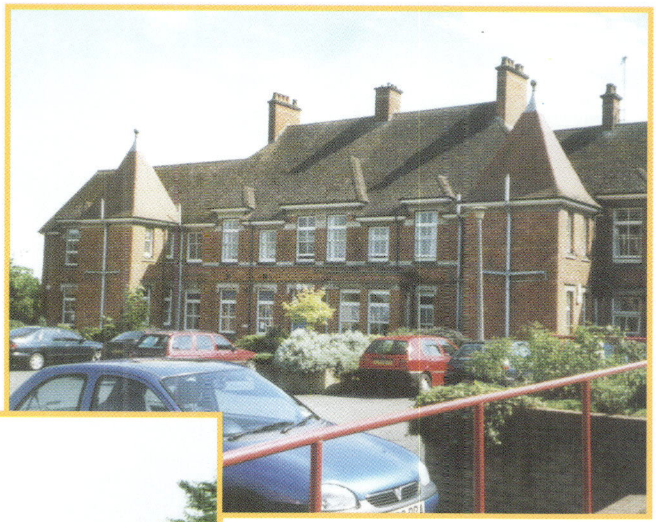

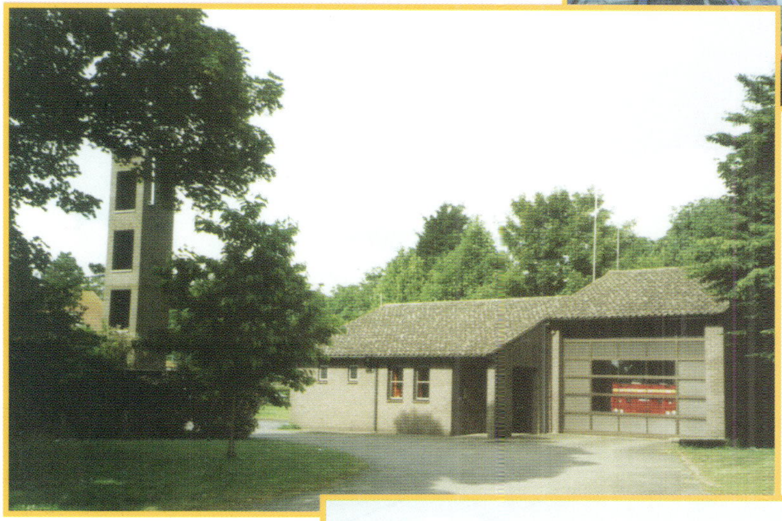

Municipal buildings concentrated in Fletton Way off Glapthorn Road. In descending order these are the Citizens Advice Bureau, the Fire Station, the Library and the Health Centre.

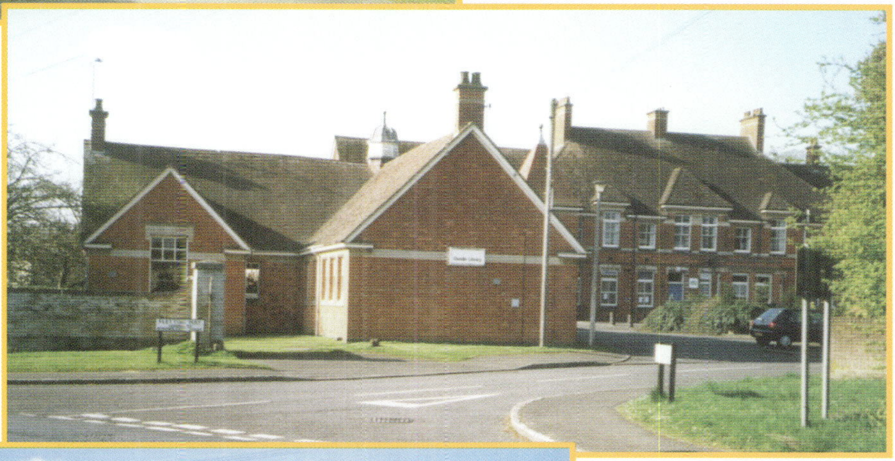

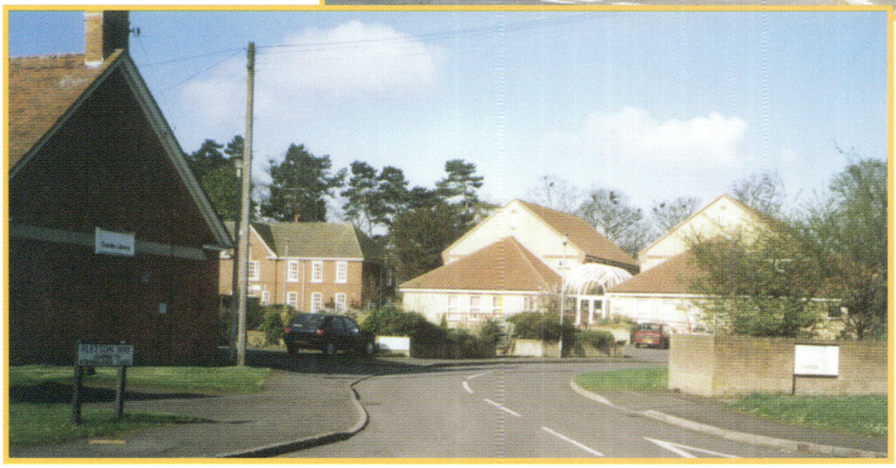

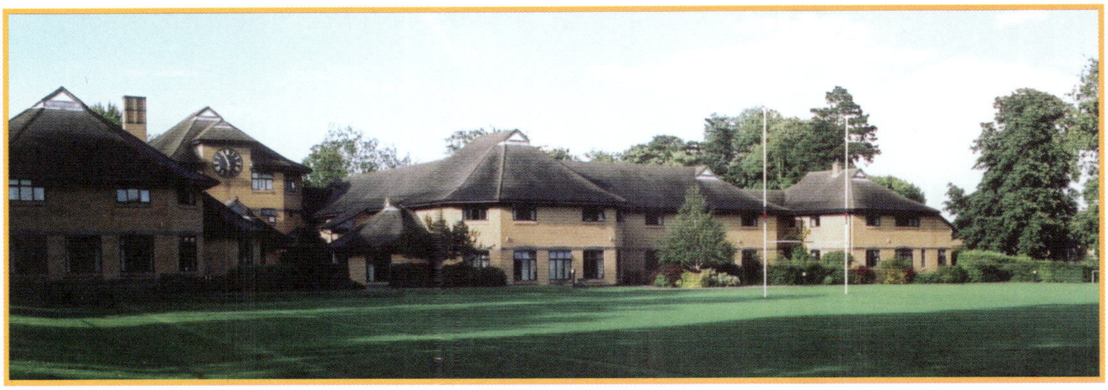

Open spacies are abundant all around Oundle and here the students at Oundle School wake up to a brand new day surrounded by trees, daffodils in spring, bird song and an environment conducive to learning. This is not always the case but Wyatt and Kirkeby houses (above), built in the 1990's to accommodate the female pupils and Sanderson and Dryden (below), converted in the late twentieth century, again to accommodate the girls certainly benefit from these surroundings.

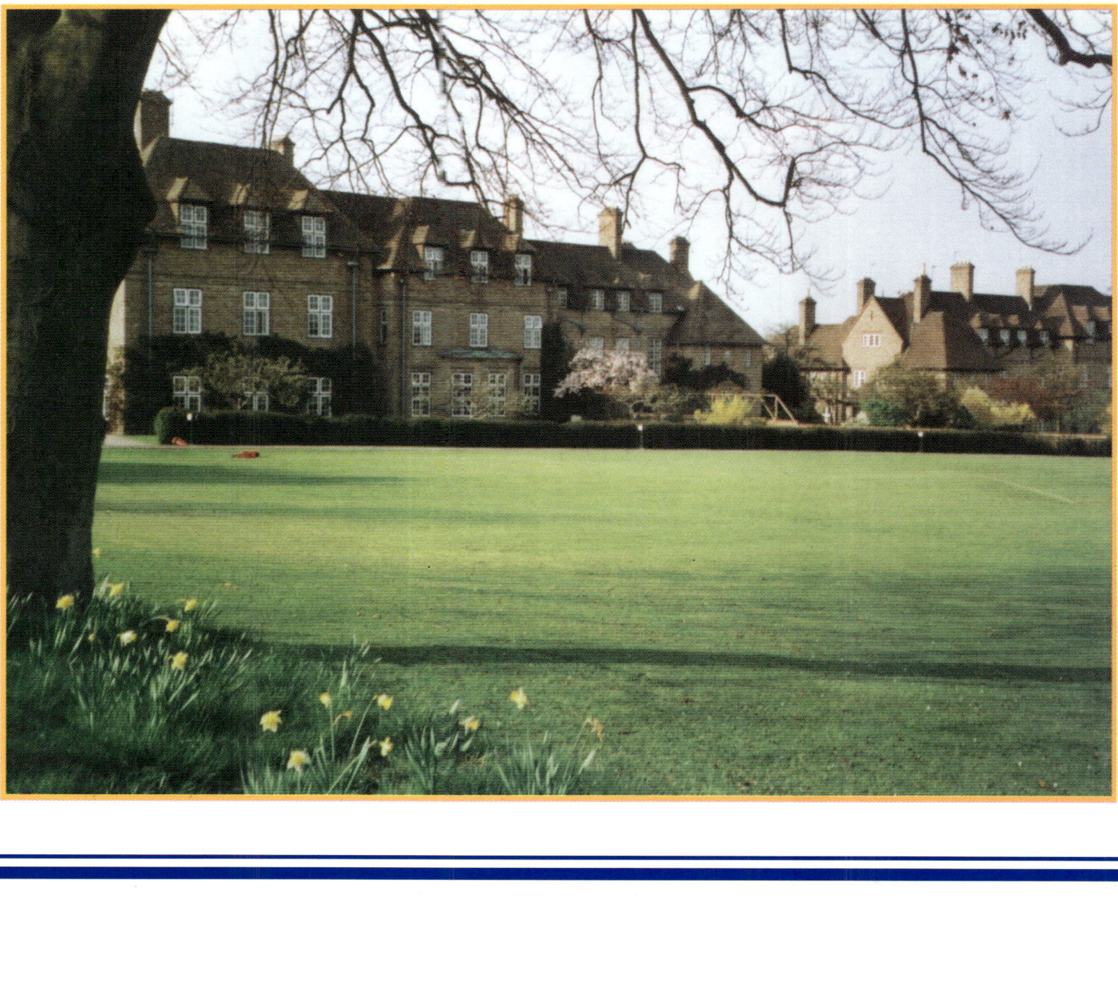

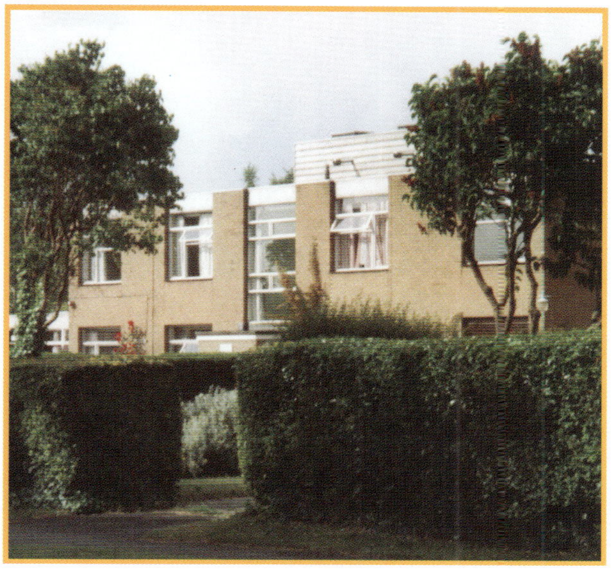

Glapthorn Road is the main thoroughfare coming into Oundle from the north. Three buildings along the route include: Abbot House Residential Home (left), The Old Oundle Workhouse Chapel (below) and at the foot of the page the Oundle School Laundry block.

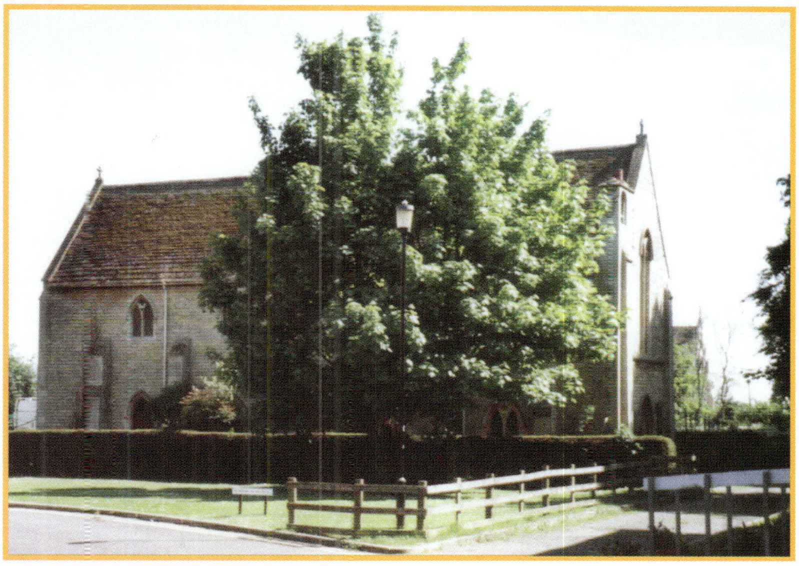

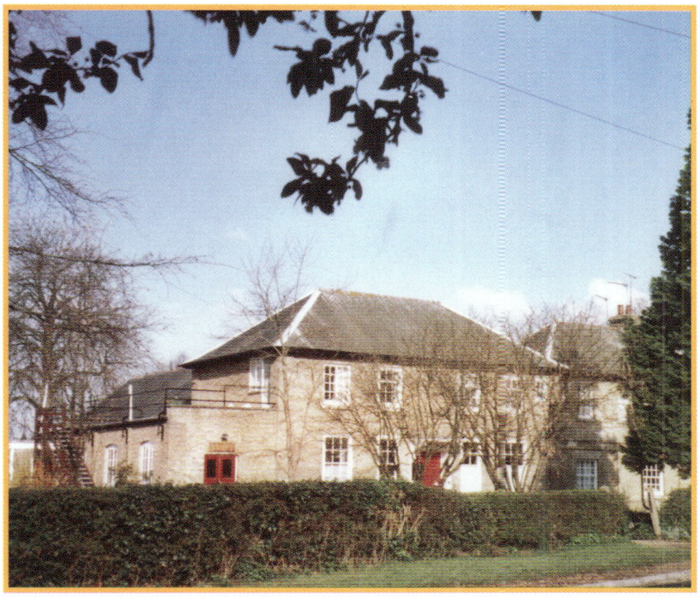

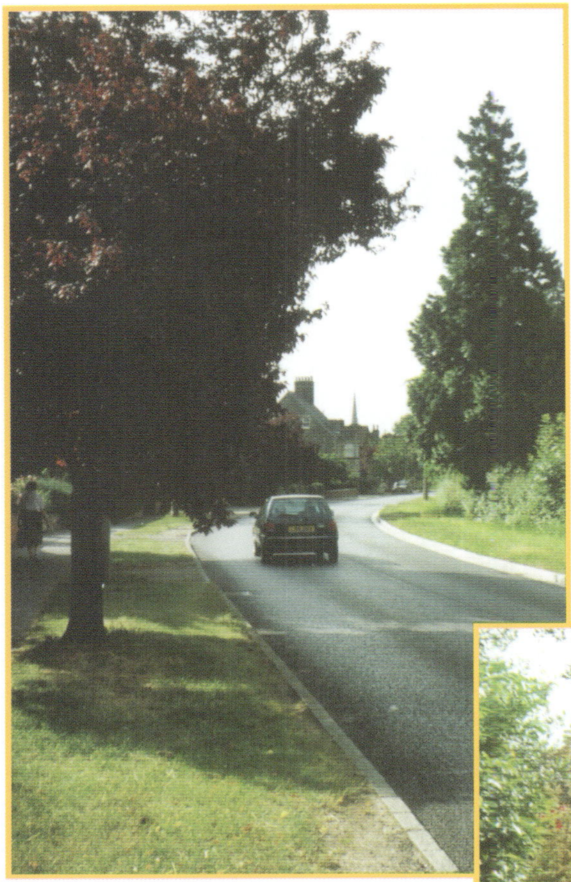

Much of Glapthorn Road on the western side is playing fields belonging to Oundle School and although there are housing developments to the east and a new development at the top on the west there is still a feeling of openness as is adequately demonstrated by these photographs.

Left, looks south along the road towards the town centre.

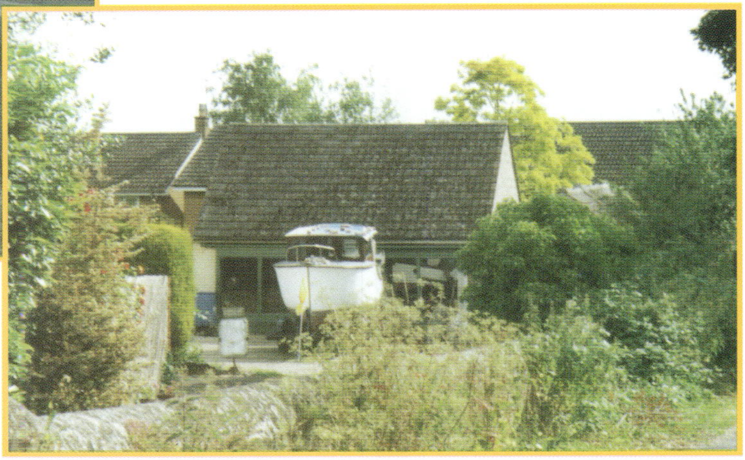

Mill Garage (right), in Glapthorn Road lies on the site of an old mill.

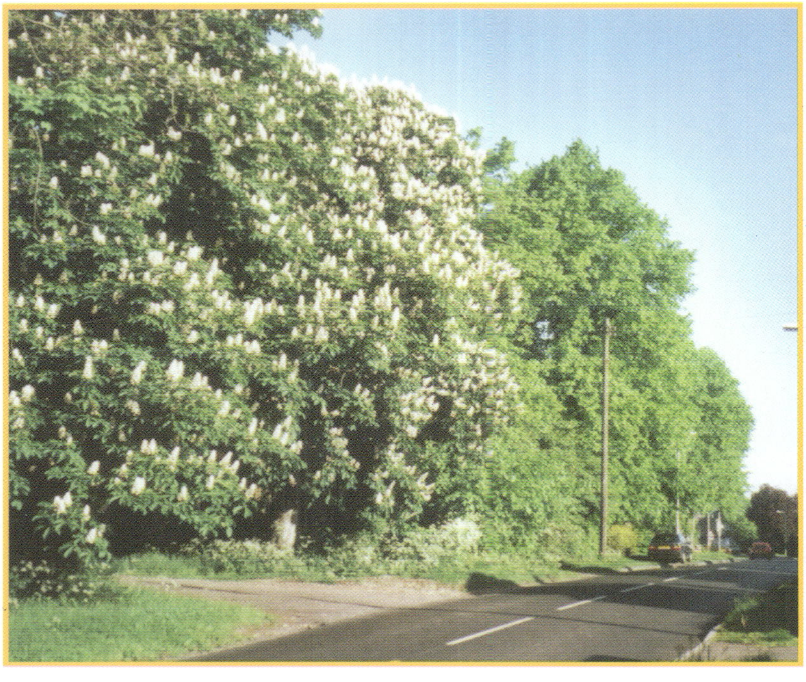

Left, Glapthorn Road looking northwards from the junction with Cotterstock Road.
Being close to the top of the road, open countryside begins to appear.

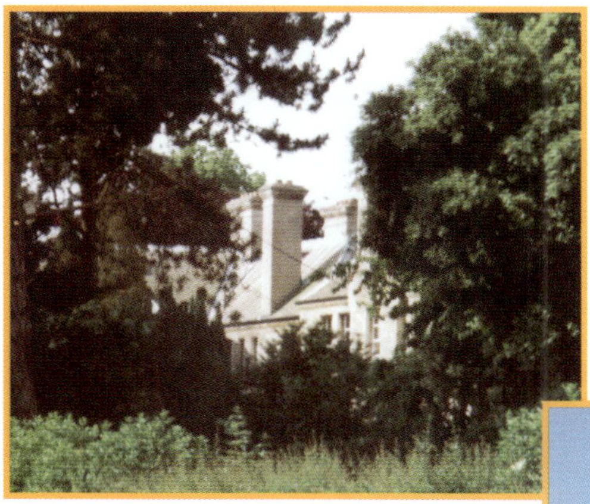

Further photographs along the Glapthorn Road reveal; left, the outline of Oundle School's old sanatorium, and below, The George Public House at the junction of Glapthorn Road and Cotterstock Road.

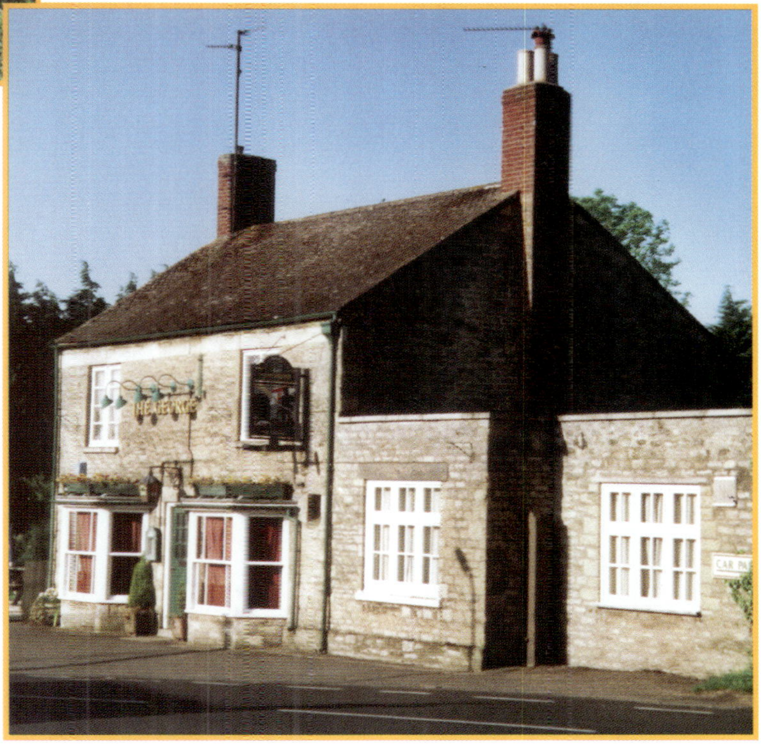

Further new development include Below, the new Pavilions housing estate at the top of Glapthorn Road on the edge of the town and still under construction in 2001.

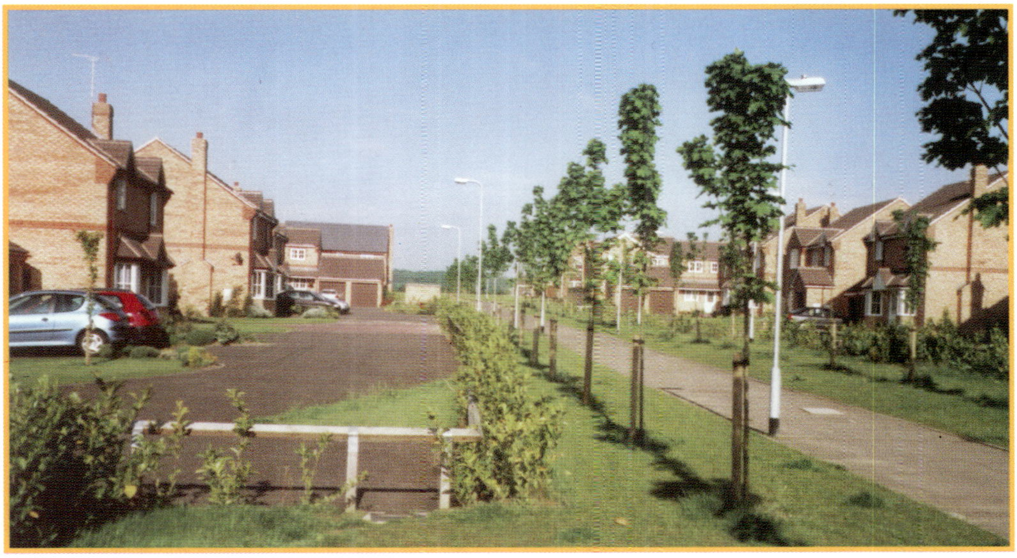

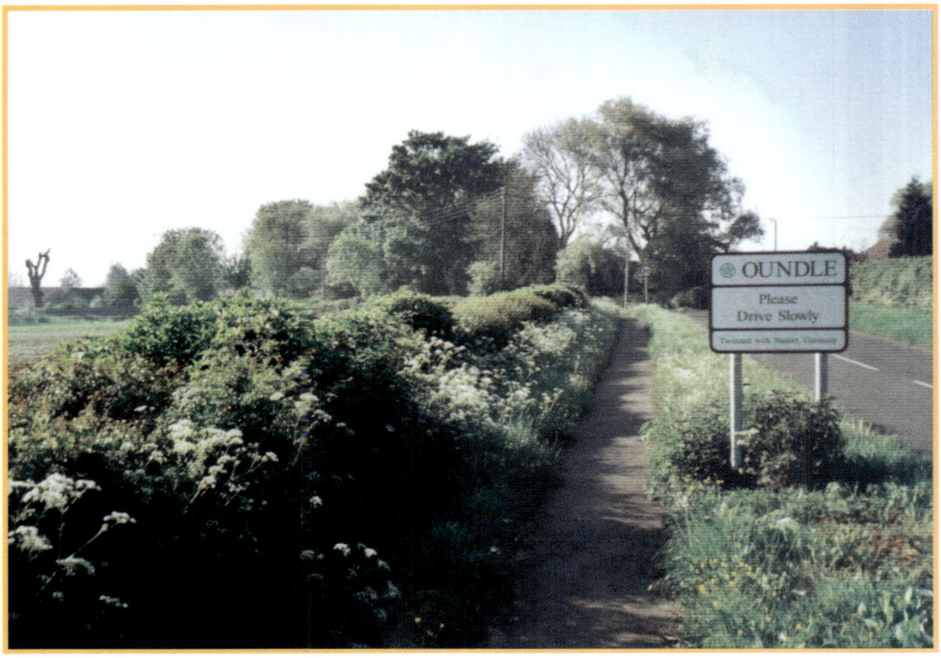

A further entrance to Oundle from the north passes the County Council Middle School and the photograph above shows the entrance to the town along the Cotterstock Road.

Along the Glapthorn Road the stone on the right marks an important source of water. Dated 1849 it reads;

THIS SPRING
IS THE PROPERTY OF THE
OUNDLE BOARD OF GUARDIANS
WHO HAVE THE RIGHT OF
ENTRY FOR REPAIRING IT
AND THE PIPES WHICH PIPES LIE
IN DIRECT LINE FROM
THIS TO THE
TANK NEAR THE ROAD
1849

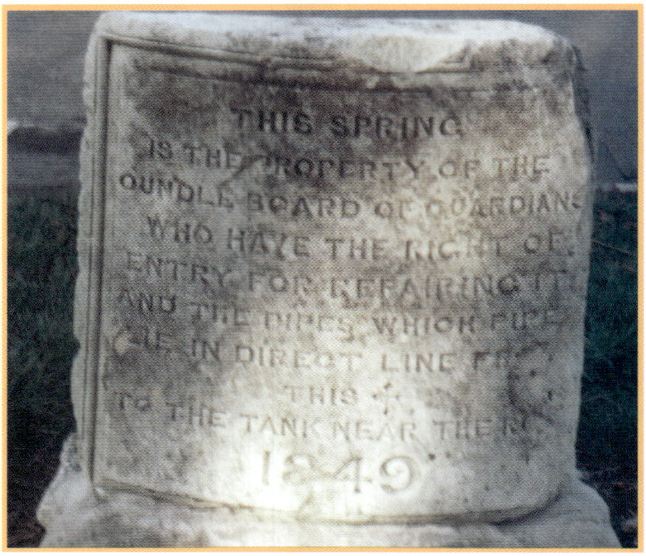

Below, a panoramic view of Oundle with St Peter's Church spire ever dominant and looking south east across the Nene Valley towards Ashton and Polebrook.

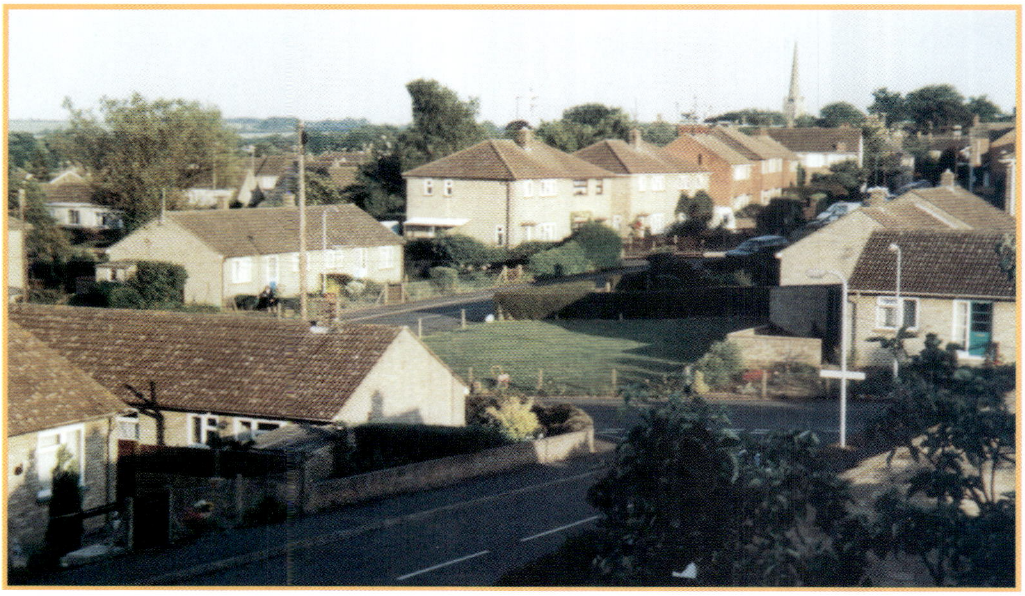

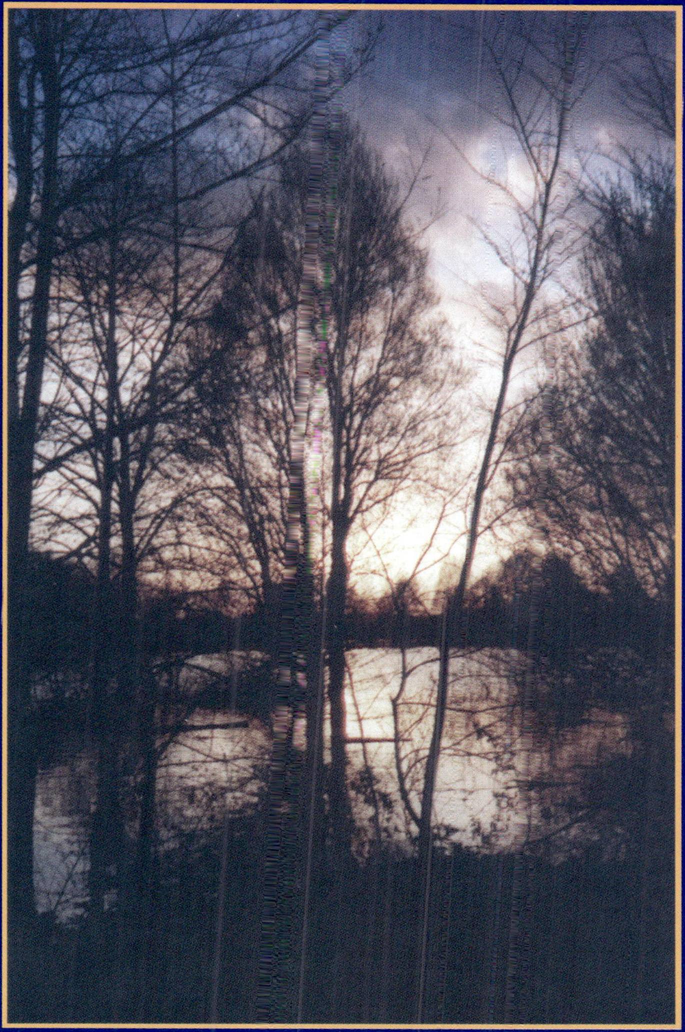

WESTERN OUNDLE

Right, Oundle Methodist Church. A foundation stone at the foot of the wall is dated 1939.

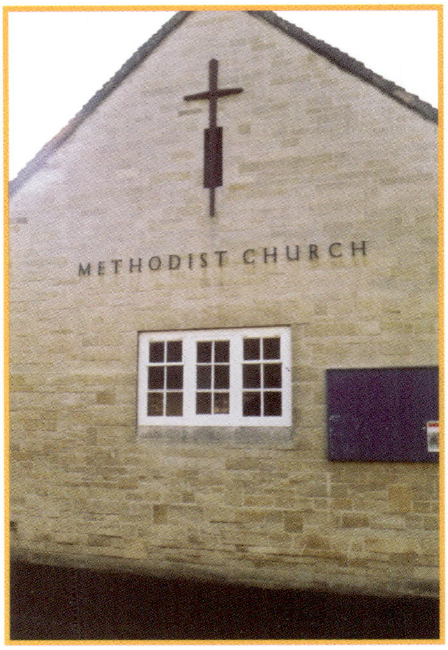

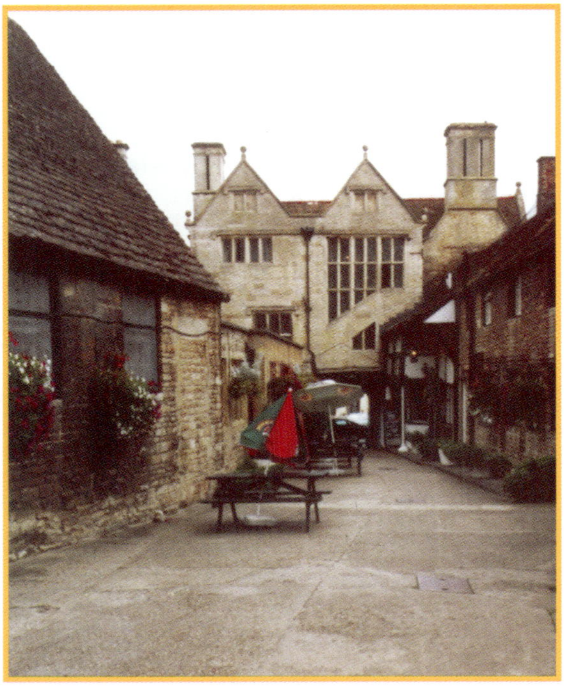

Two photographs, left and below, show the rear of the Talbot Inn, one of Oundle's most famous hostelries. Earlier called The Tabret and famous for its connections with Fotheringhay Castle. At the far end is the carriageway under the main seventeenth century buildings and above is the great window crossed by the famous staircase. Drummingwell Lane, running at the back of the Talbot has the famous Drumming Well. no longer visible but it is under the road opposite the Talbot Inn yard and is said to reverberate when great events are at hand. Opposite the Talbot and standing on the corner of the Market Place and New Street was The Swan public house. Standing on the site of the Moot Hall it was the place in the early 1800's where coaches to London would leave three times a week. Adjacent to The Talbot and further along New Street was The Turks Head, Barnes Brewery was also nearby and brewed for twenty years from 1864 to 1884. Both buildings are now owned by Oundle School.

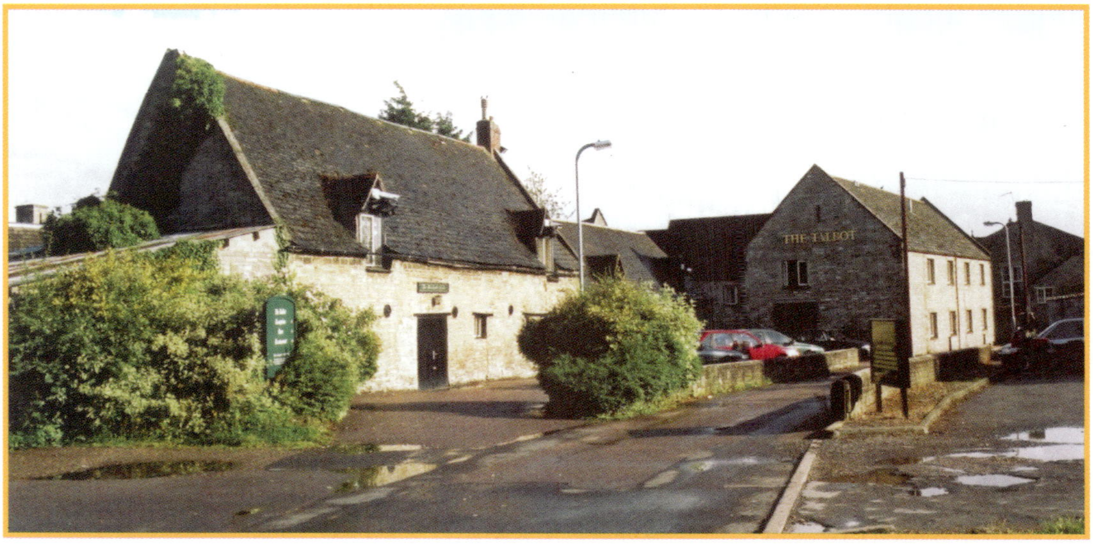

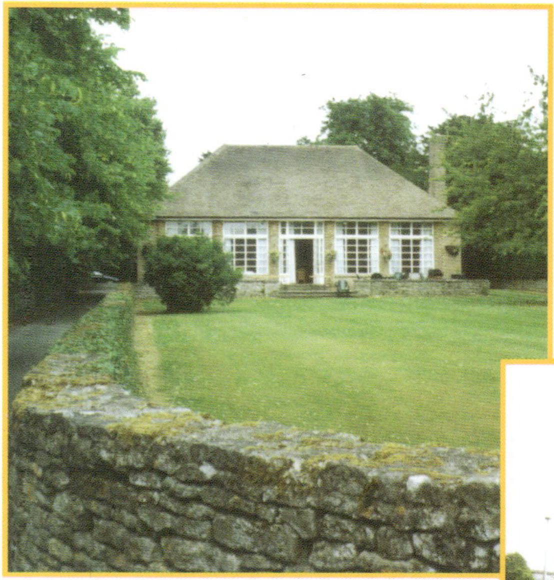

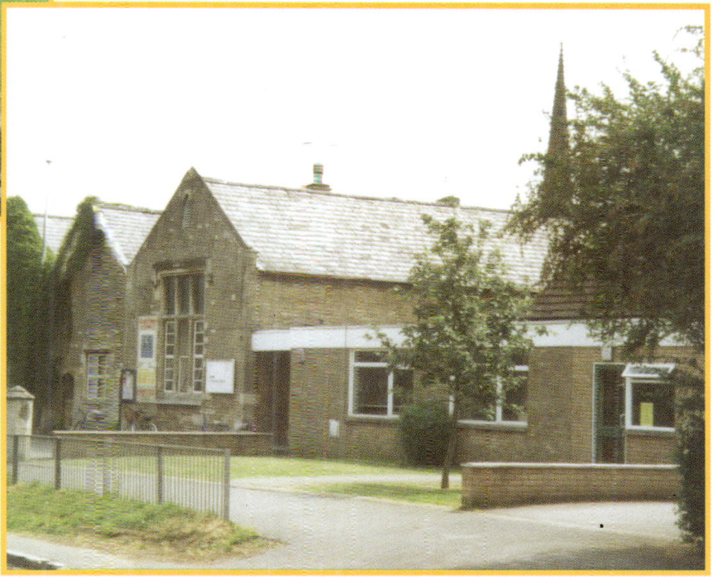

Milton Road and the site of Oundle School's Common Room (above), and Oundle County Primary School (right).

Below is an aerial view showing Bellamy Road (bottom left), winding its way to join Cotterstock Road near the top of the picture.

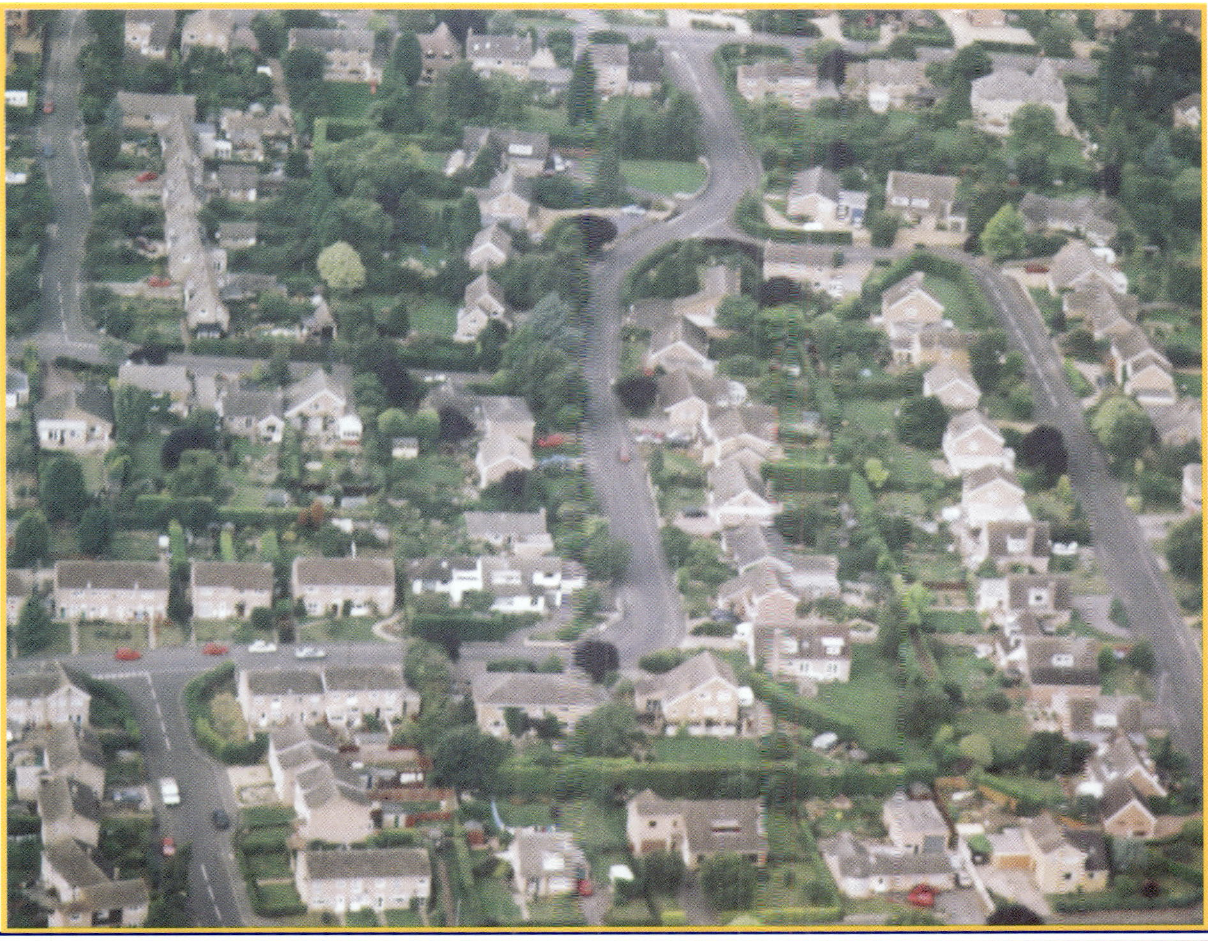

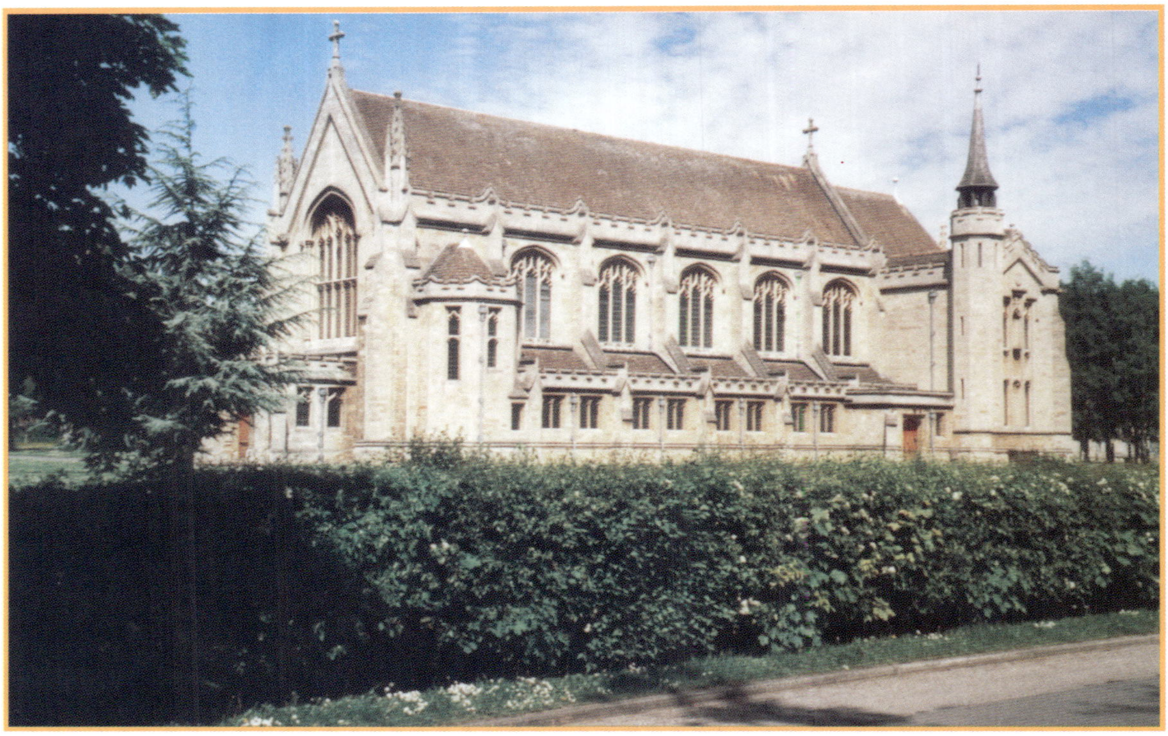

Two views of Oundle School's Memorial Chapel, consecrated by the Bishop of Peterborough in November 1923 and a memorial to Oundle School's dead in the First World War. Beautifully and spaciously situated amongst lawns and flower beds this can be a lovely, quiet and peaceful area only a few minutes walk from the hustle and bustle of the Market Place. The photograph below shows the east end with the stained glass window by John Piper and the famous statue on the lawns with the inscription, "*Here am I send me*."

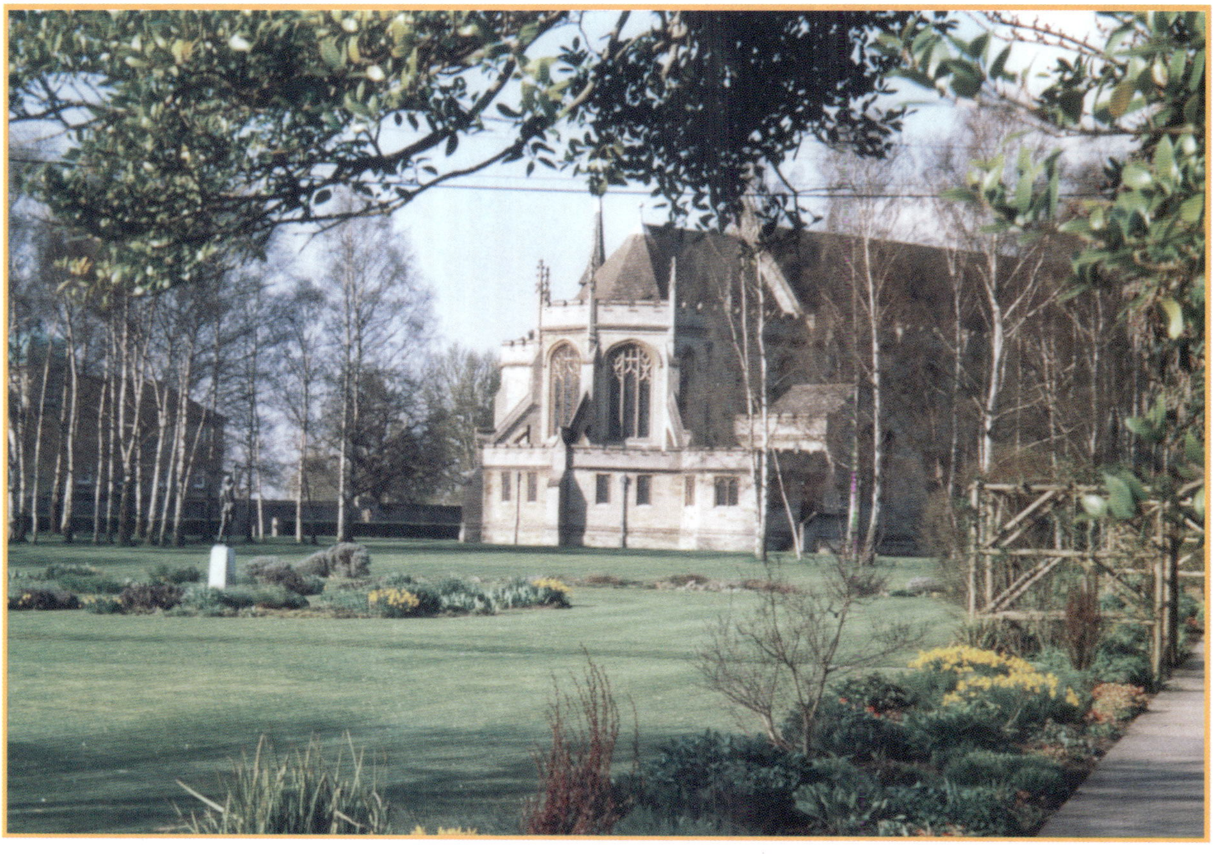

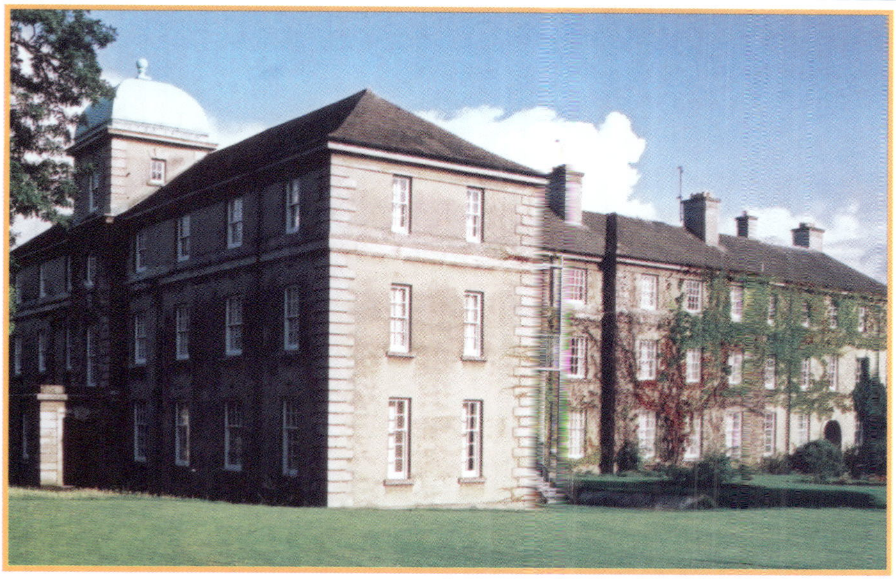

Again in lovely surroundings, St Anthony House one of the boy's boarding houses of Oundle Public School.

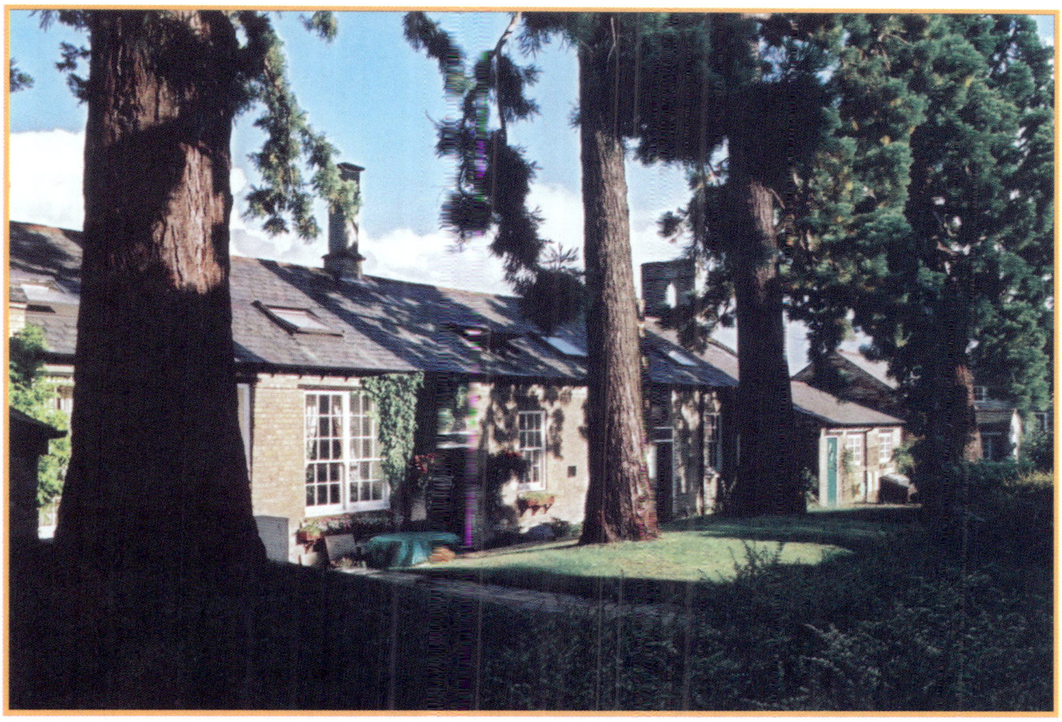

Above, the old British School, see the bell tower through the trees and right, the new Spurlings development off Milton Road.

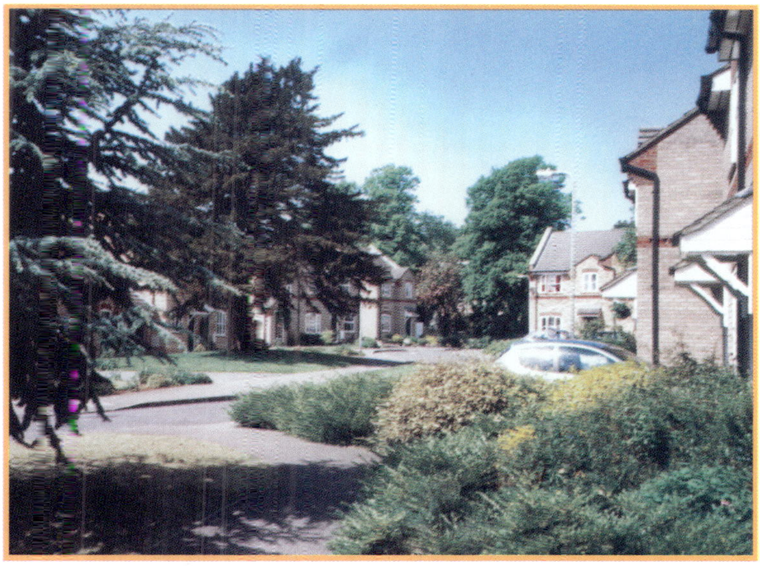

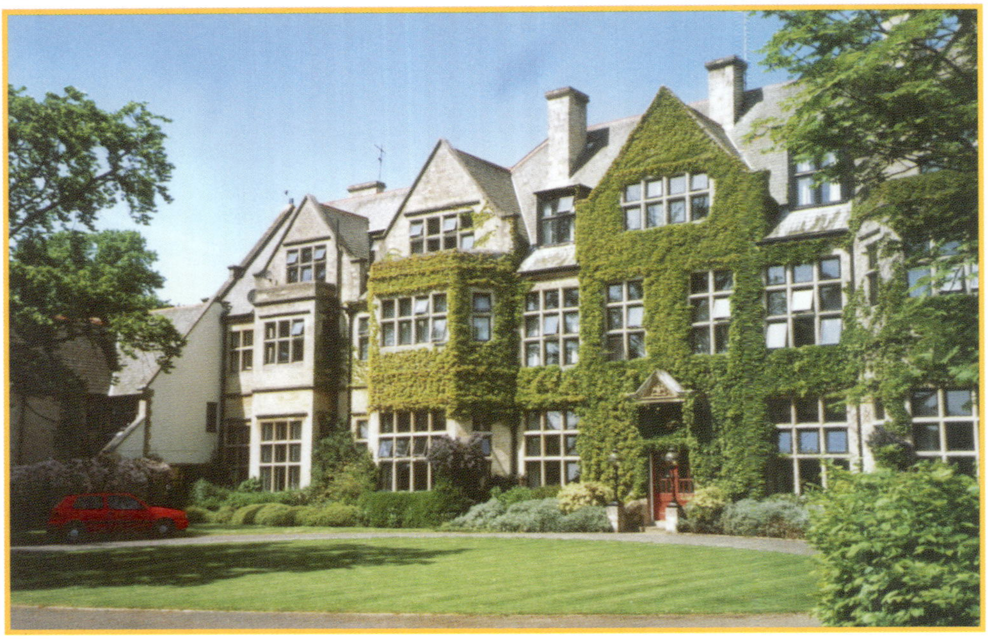

Above, Fisher and Crosby Houses, Fisher known formerly as Laxton House. Dr Fisher was Headmaster from 1922 to 1945 and during his time and since, very highly thought of and respected.

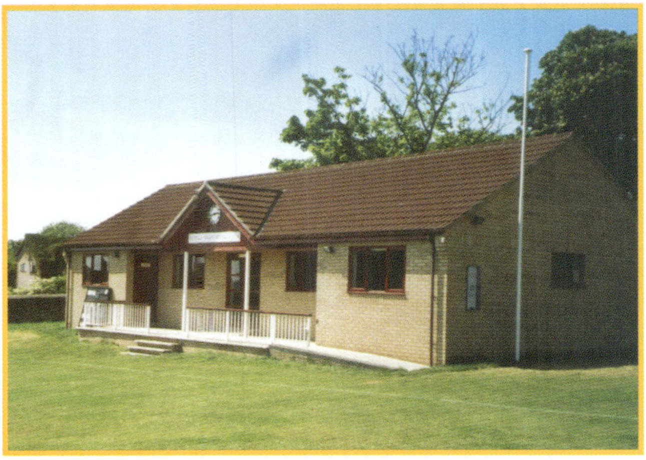

Right is the new cricket pavilion in Milton Road and the home of Oundle Town Cricket Club.

Below, further boarding houses of Grafton and Sidney.

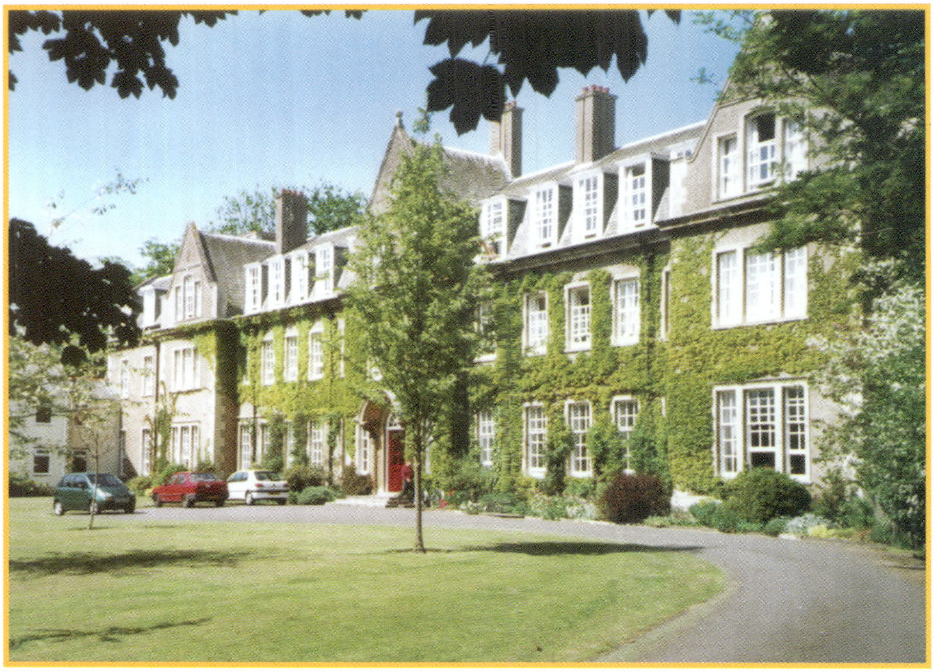

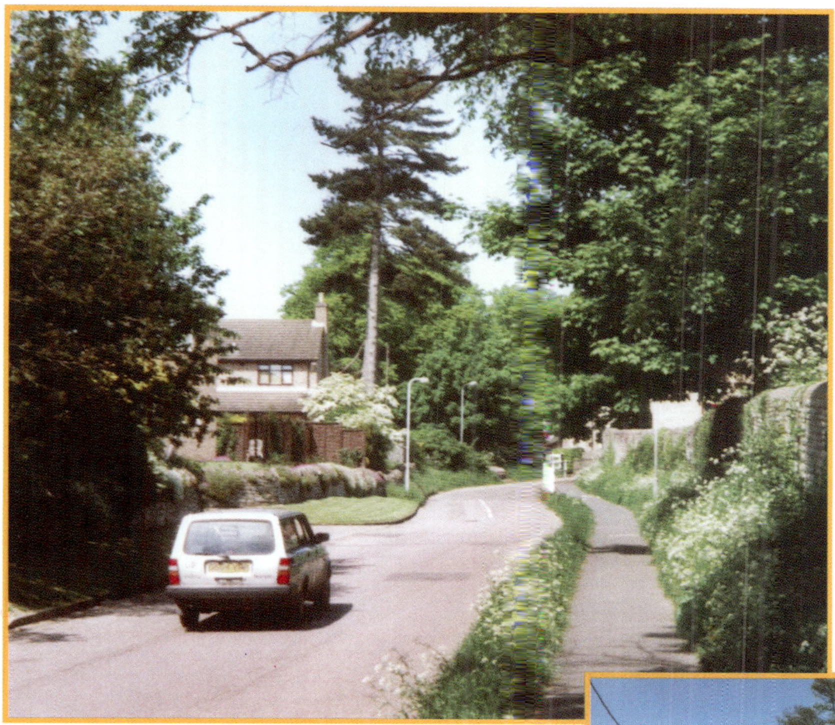

Left, the junction of Benefield Road and Milton Road with the small recent development of St Ann's Court emerging through the trees.

Below, the old Grove Service Station soon to be demolished.

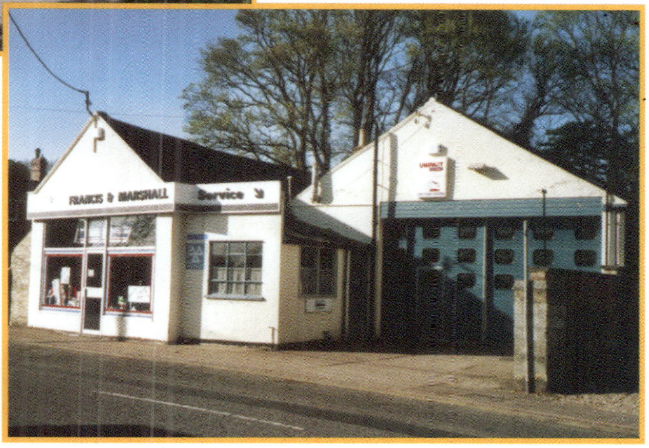

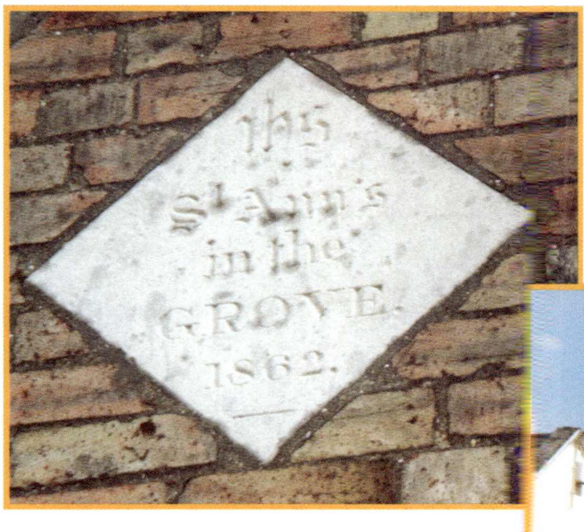

Above, the commemorative stone on the former St Ann's Chapel on the left of the Francis and Marshall building and right, the Oundle Drill Hall and the Catholic Church.

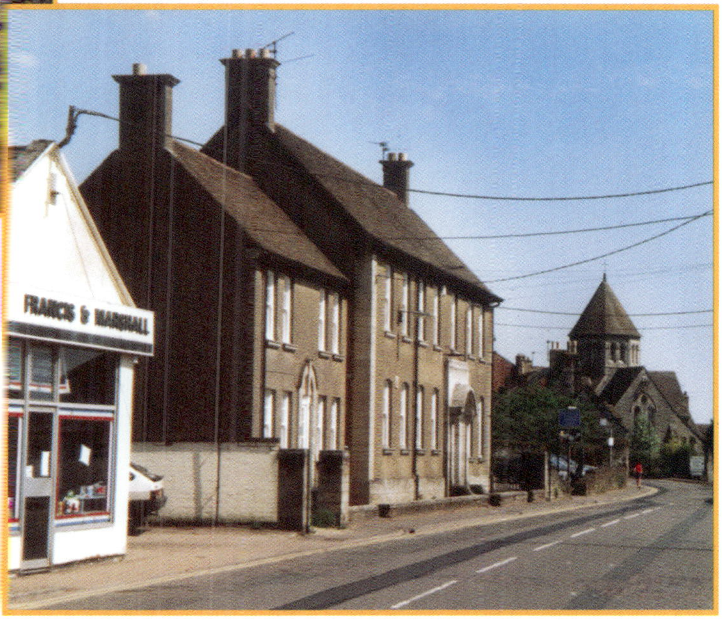

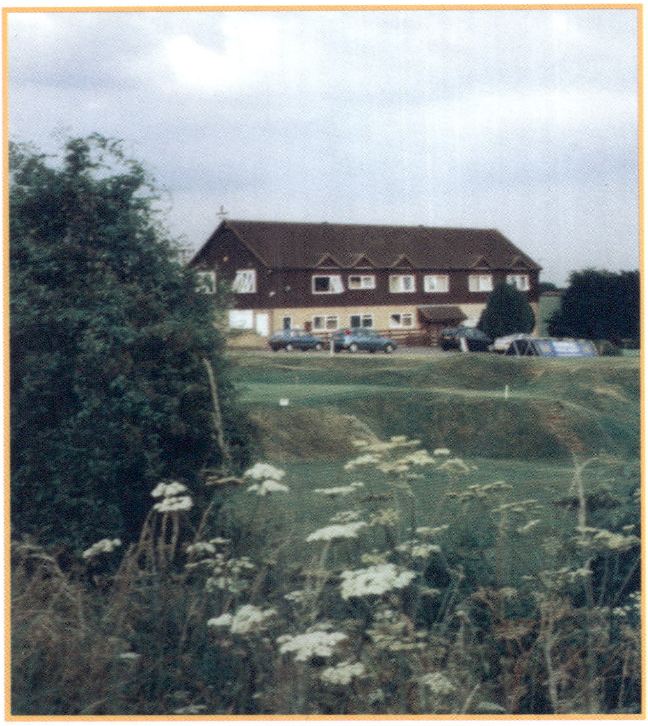

Three photographs along the Benefield Road.

Above, The 'Nineteenth Hole' of Oundle Golf Club.

Right, the western gateway to Oundle.

Below, western Oundle from the footpath between Benefield Road and the Stoke Doyle Road.

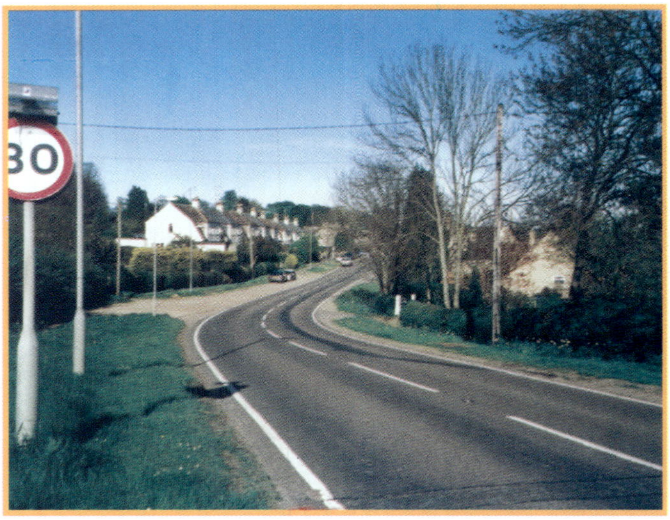

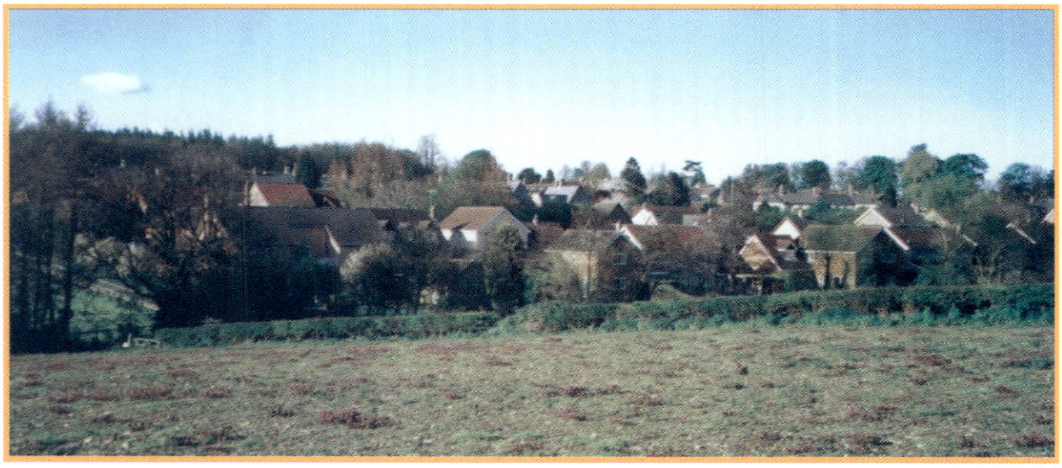

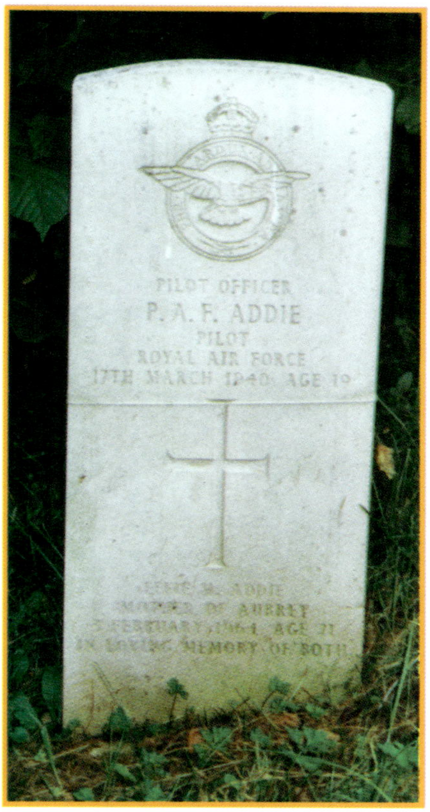

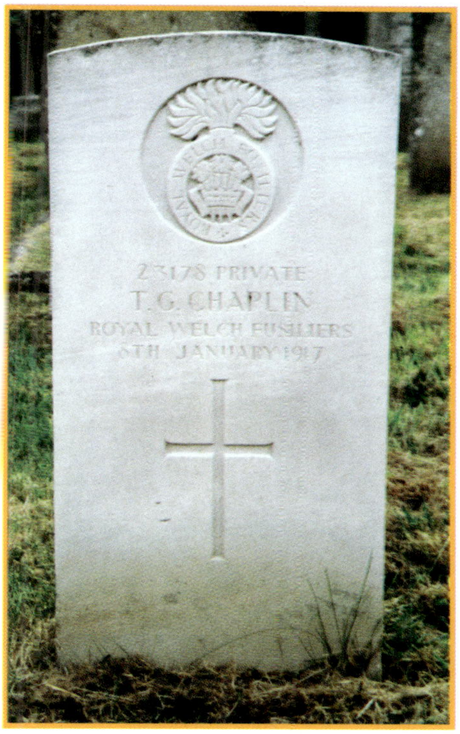

Oundle Cemetery and Chapel below, and above and left war graves from the two wars. Throughout the country there are war graves, some unknown, but many men and women in the services who lost their lives locally and were buried in nearby cemeteries. On the left is the grave of a pilot from World War Two and on the right a fusilier's from the First World War.

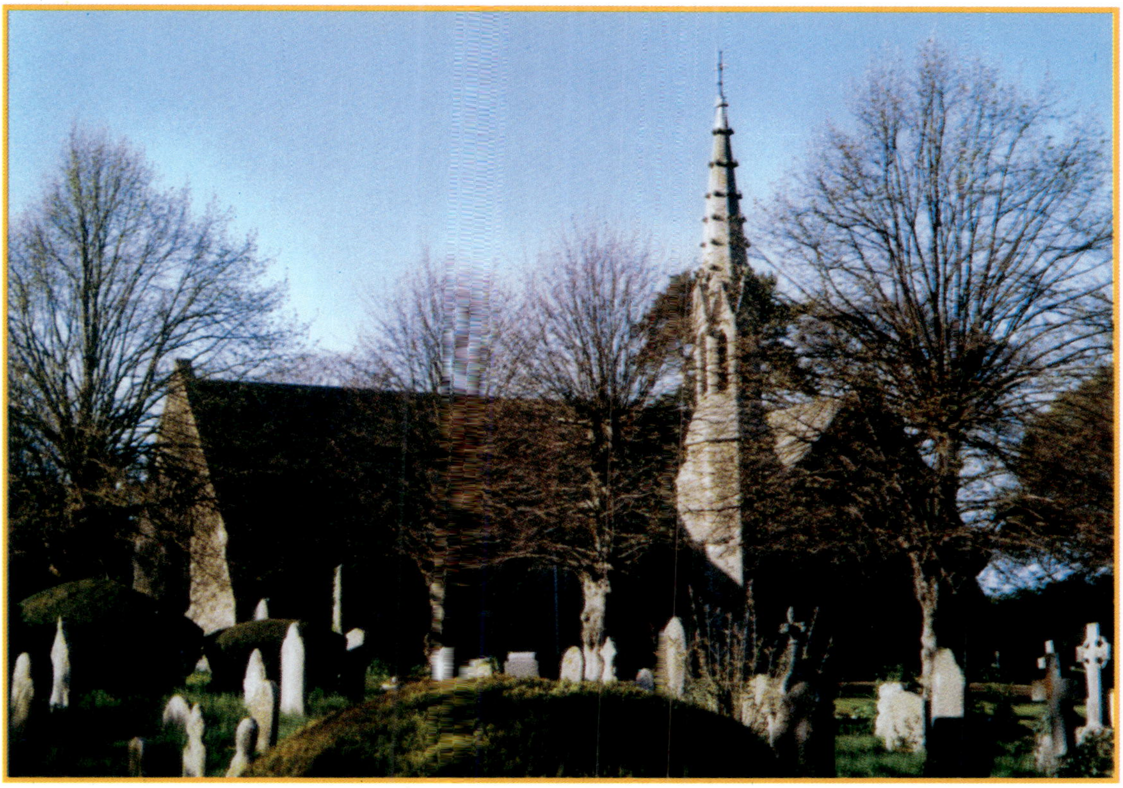

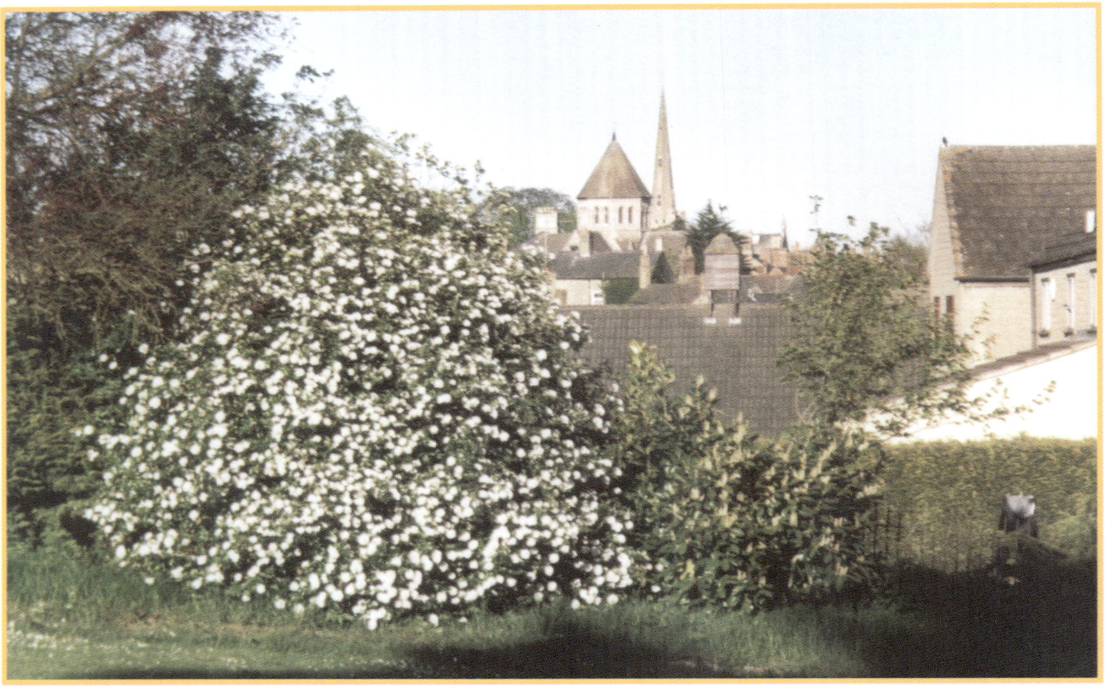

Above, looking from the cemetery towards Oundle the Catholic and Anglican churches dominate the sky line.

Below an aerial view of Warren Bridge Estate on the Stoke Doyle Road, with the cemetery in the bottom left hand corner.

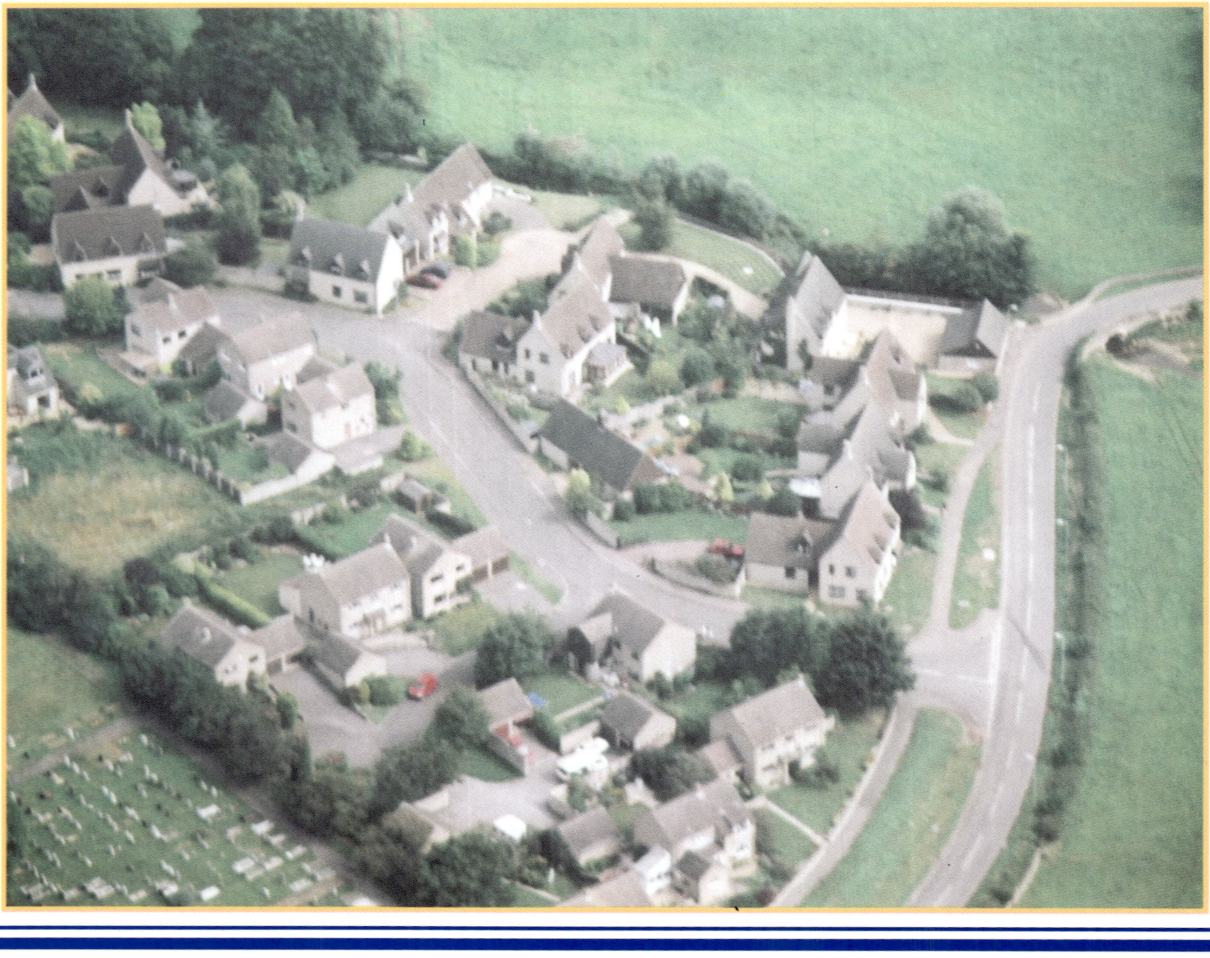

Further views along the Stoke Doyle Road, again the skyline is dominated by the two churches, the Anglican church and its spire and the round Catholic church.

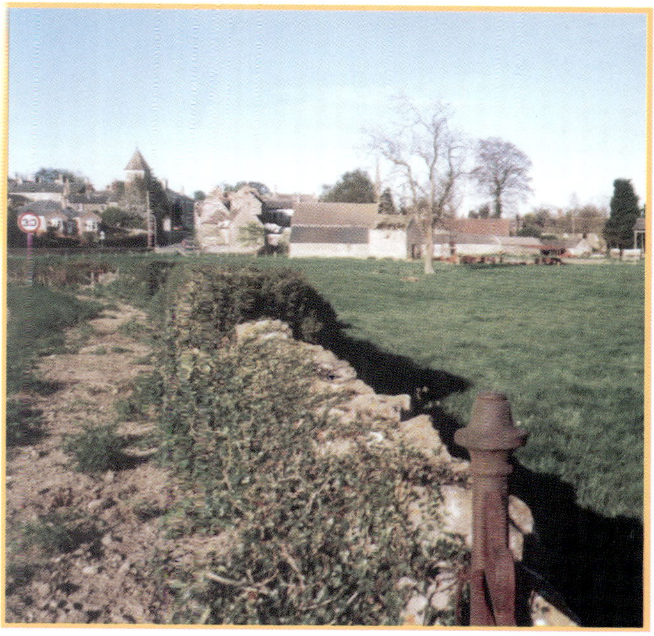

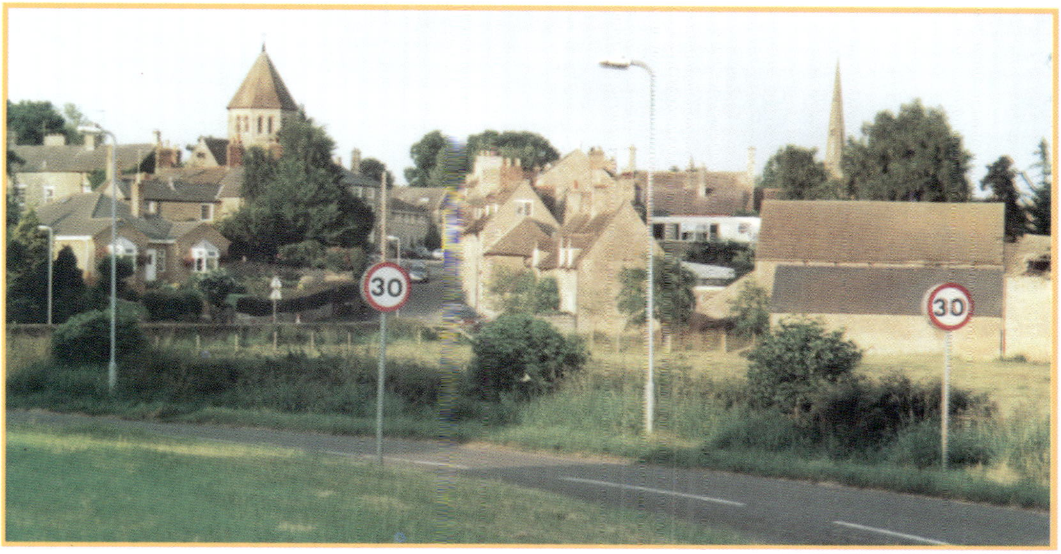

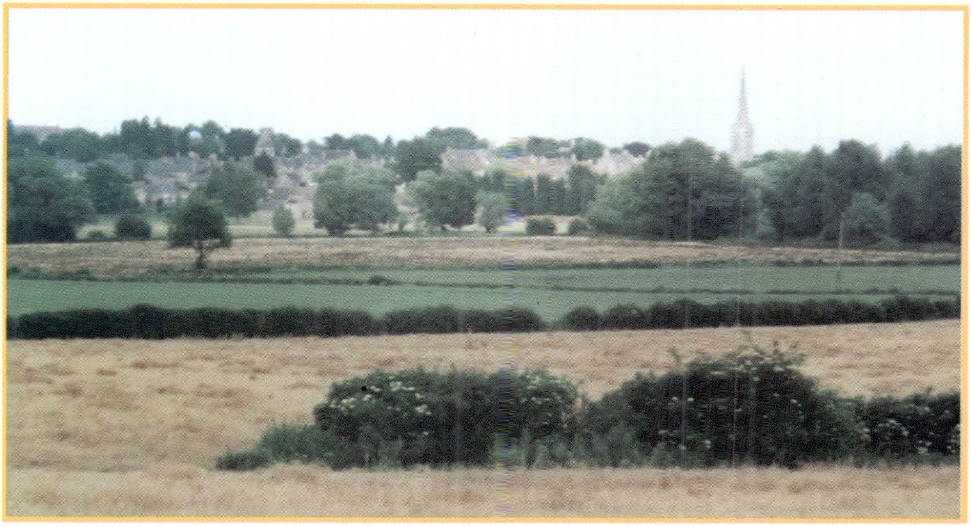

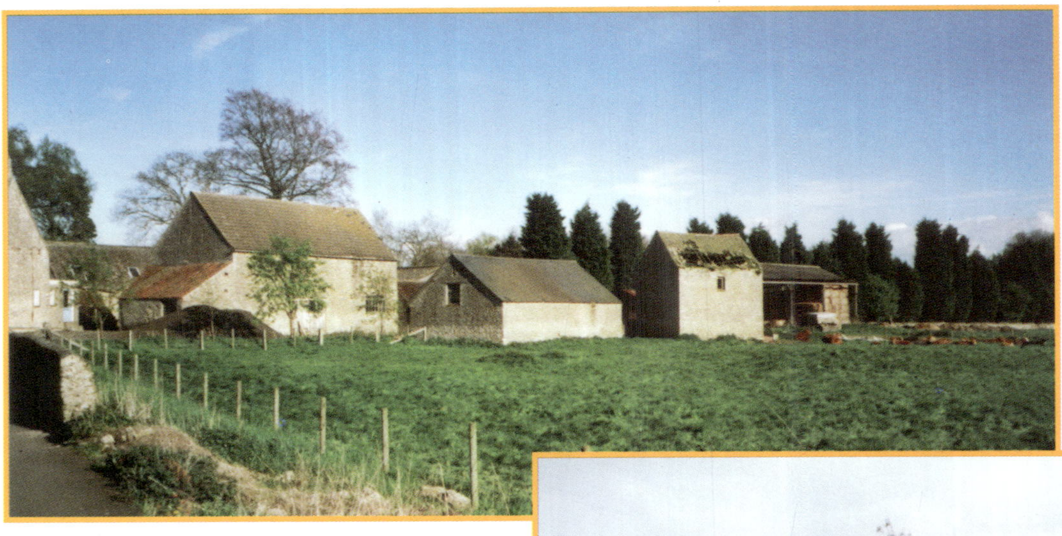

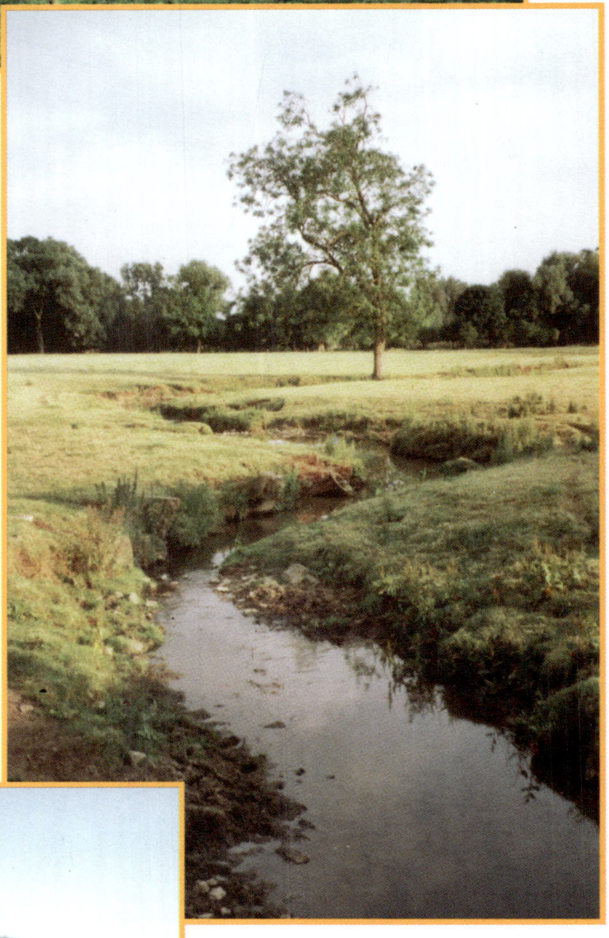

Views along the Stoke Doyle Road.
Above, the farm adjacent to New House.

Right, the Lyveden Brook, one of the many tributaries of the River Nene. It runs from Lyveden off the Harley Way, passing under Warren Bridge before reaching the Nene.

Below, a surge of water flattened the adjacent wall in the Easter floods of 1998 having previously flooded properties in the Warren Bridge Estate.

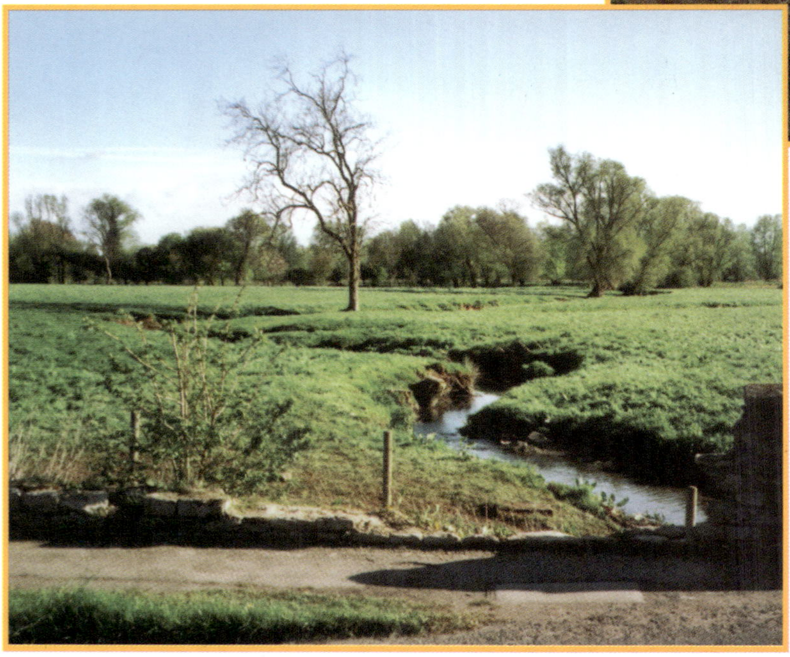

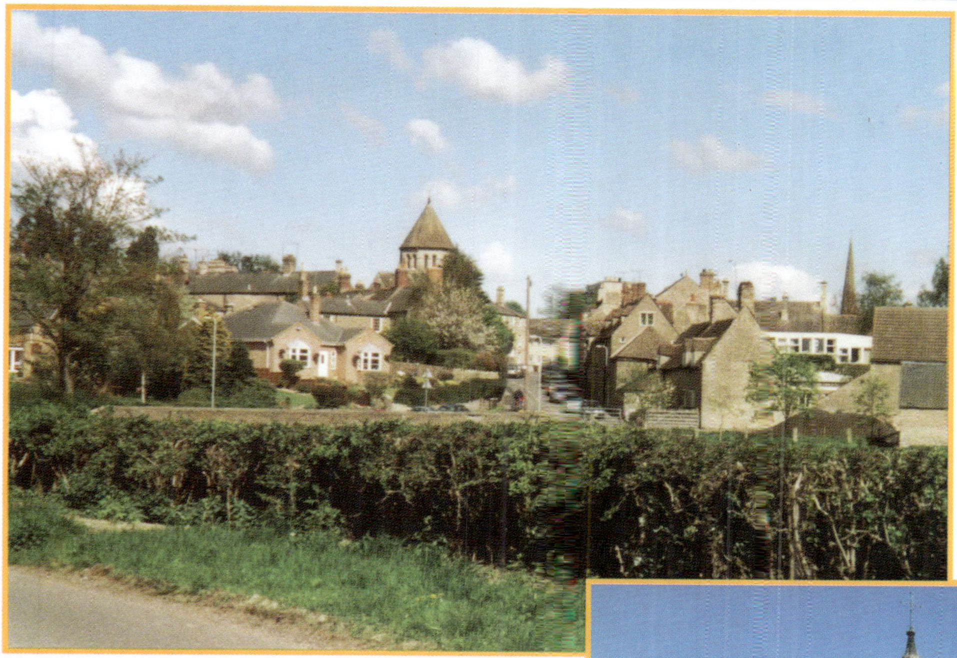

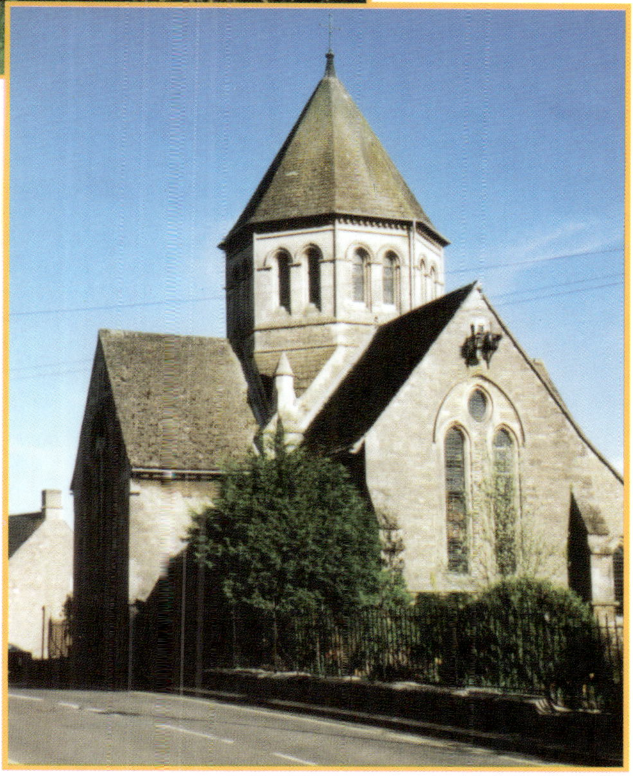

The south western approach to Oundle along the Stoke Doyle Road passes the cemetery to the north and grazing land to the south on the flood plain of the River Nene. The Roman Catholic Jesus Church is in a prominant position at the junction of Benefield Road, West Street and Stoke Hill. The church was built in 1878-79 by the Watts-Russells who were Lords of the Manor.

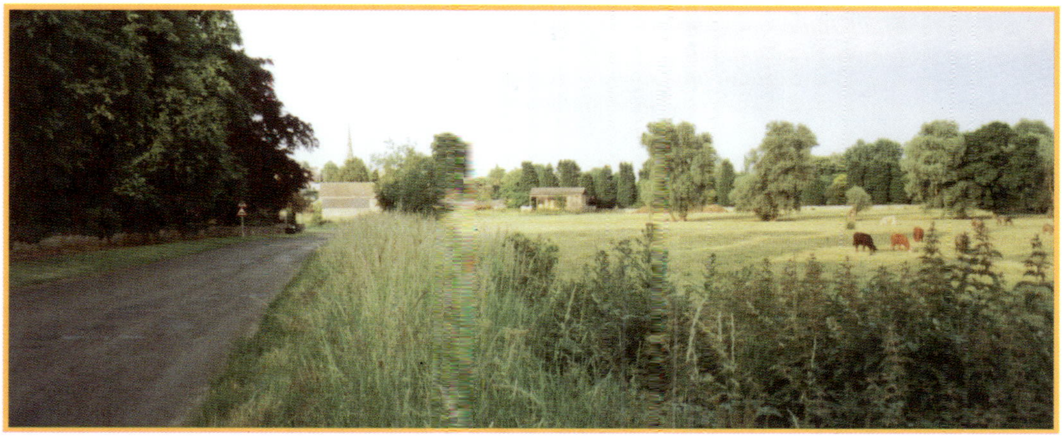

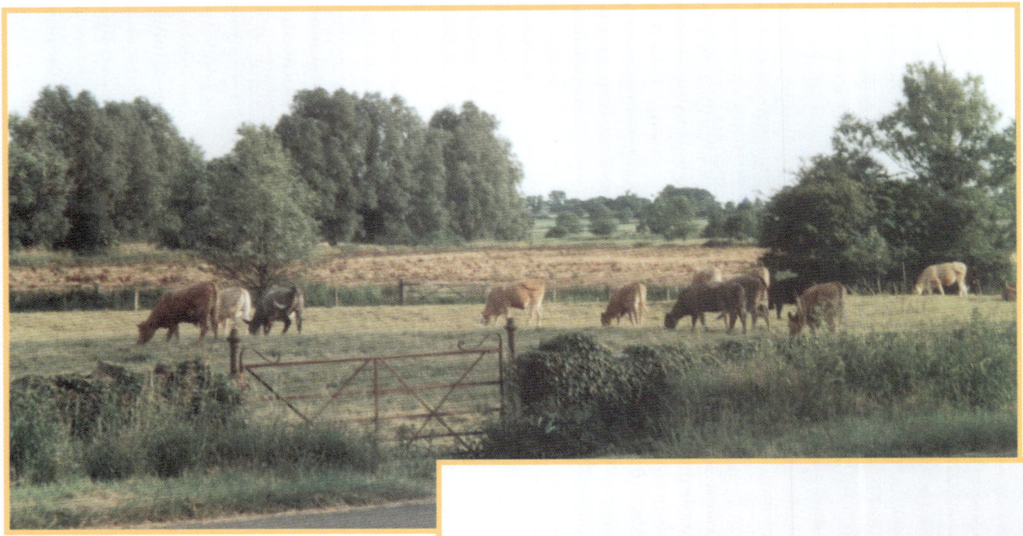

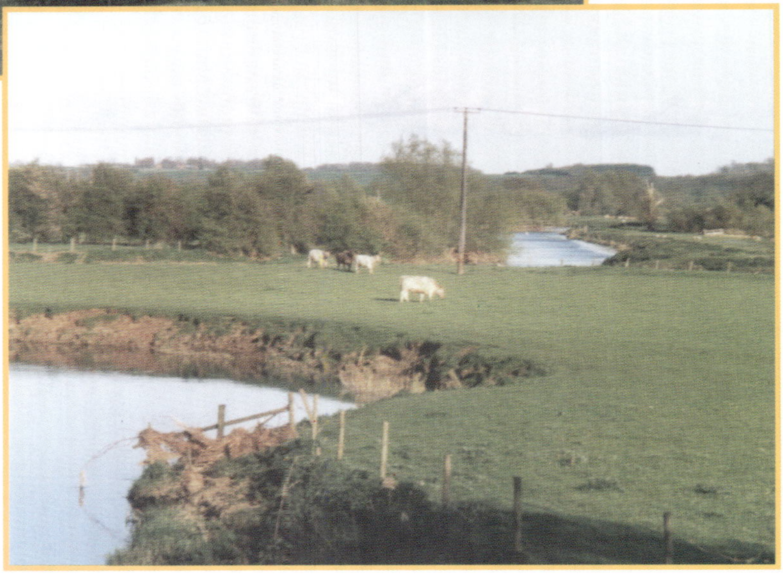

Cattle are an important part of the agrarian economy of the area and both photographs show farmland alongside the meandering River Nene close to South Bridge.

The aerial shot below shows Benefield Road towards Clifton Drive and Warren Bridge.

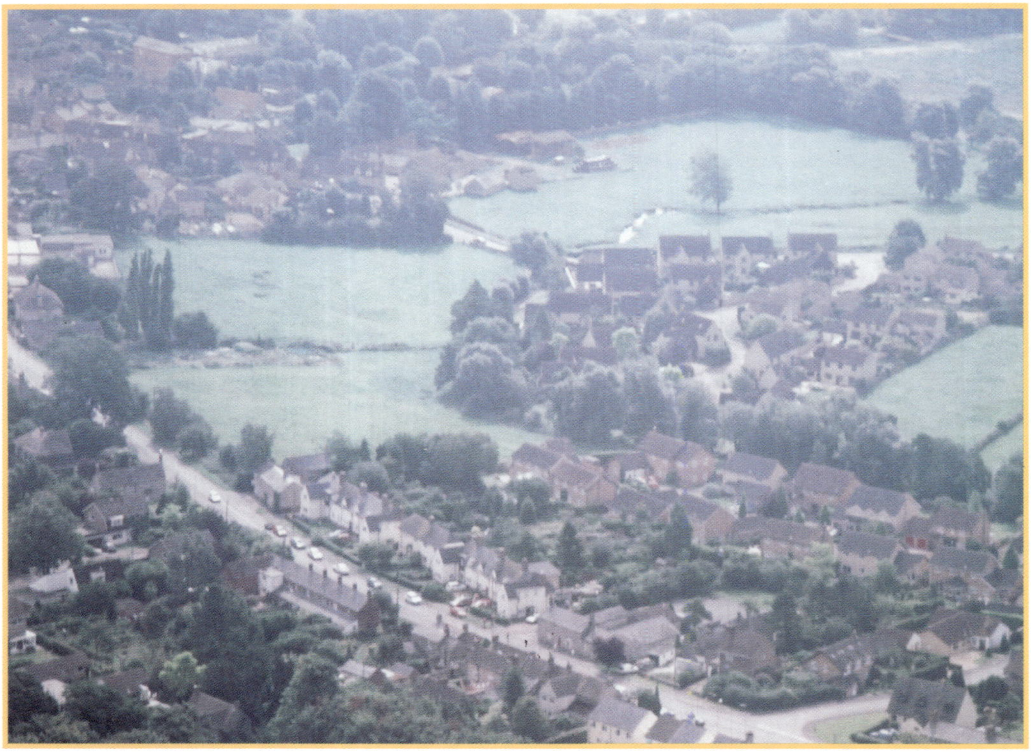

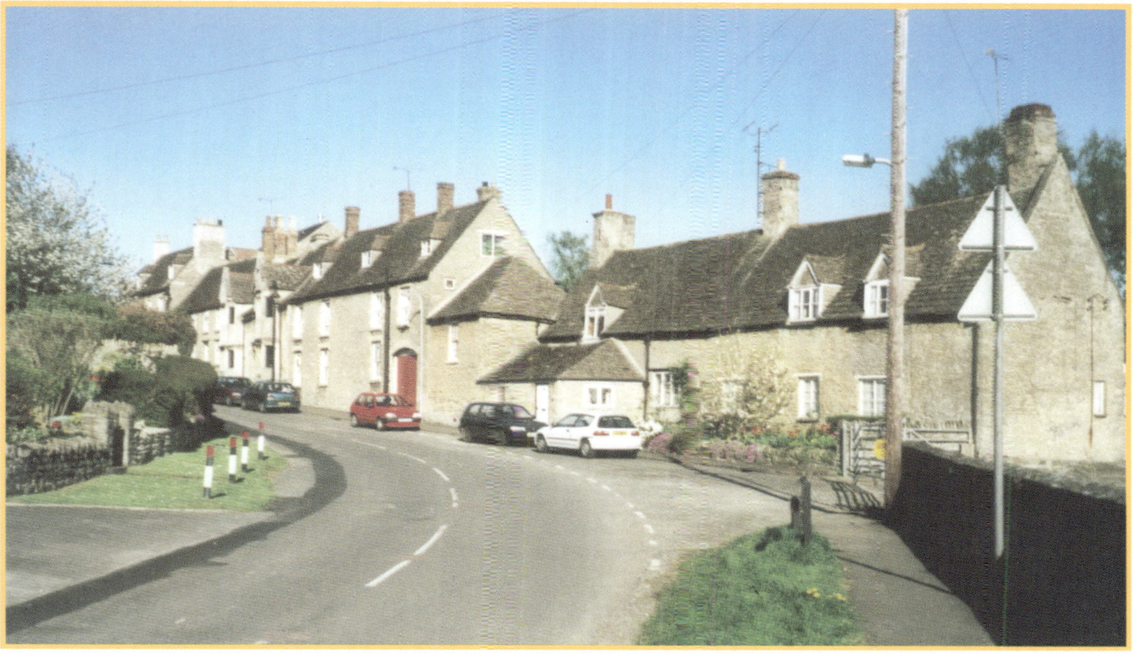

Above, Stoke Hill with Oundle School's New House at the top. One date stone on New House carried a 1640 date but the building is thought to be of earlier origin as inside there is a medieval doorway.

Below, the Old Court House and Registrar's Office, now including Oundle Museum and a number of business units and office accommodation.

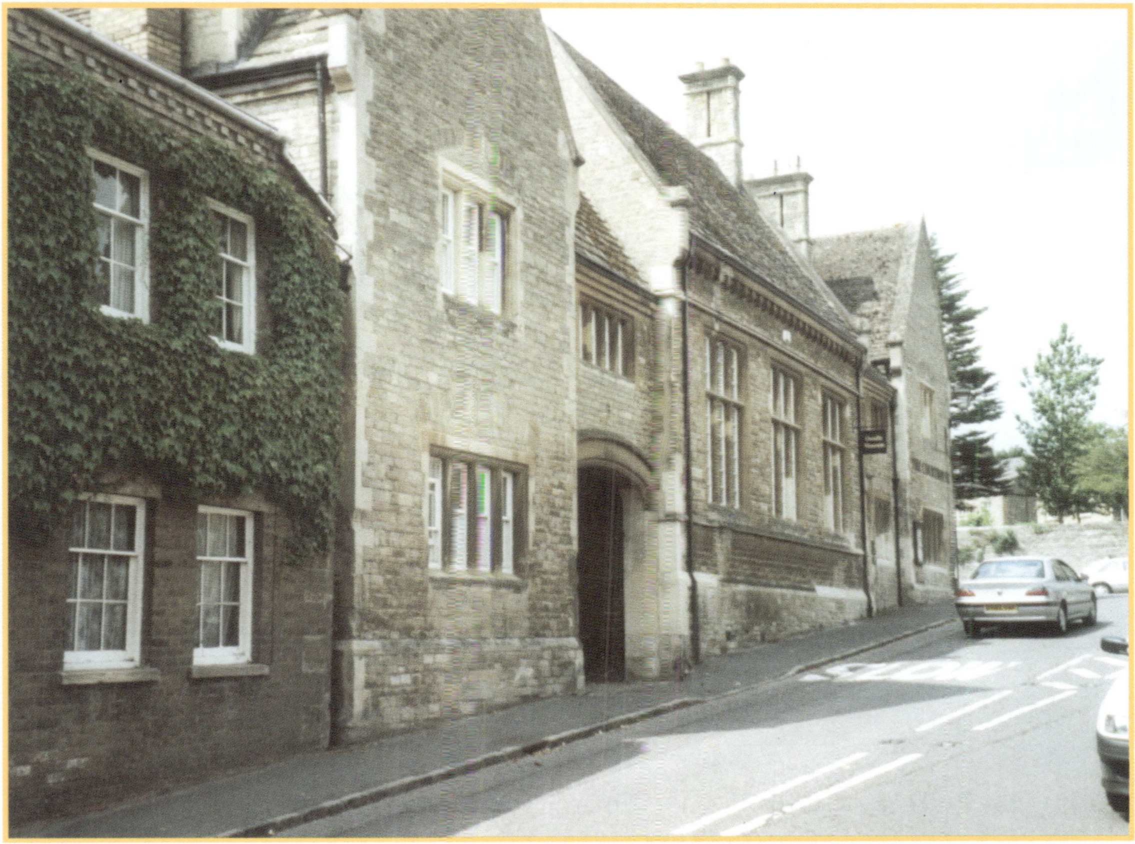

Below, buildings at the junction of West Street and Benefield Road include 'Old Laxton' and 'Cottesmore'.

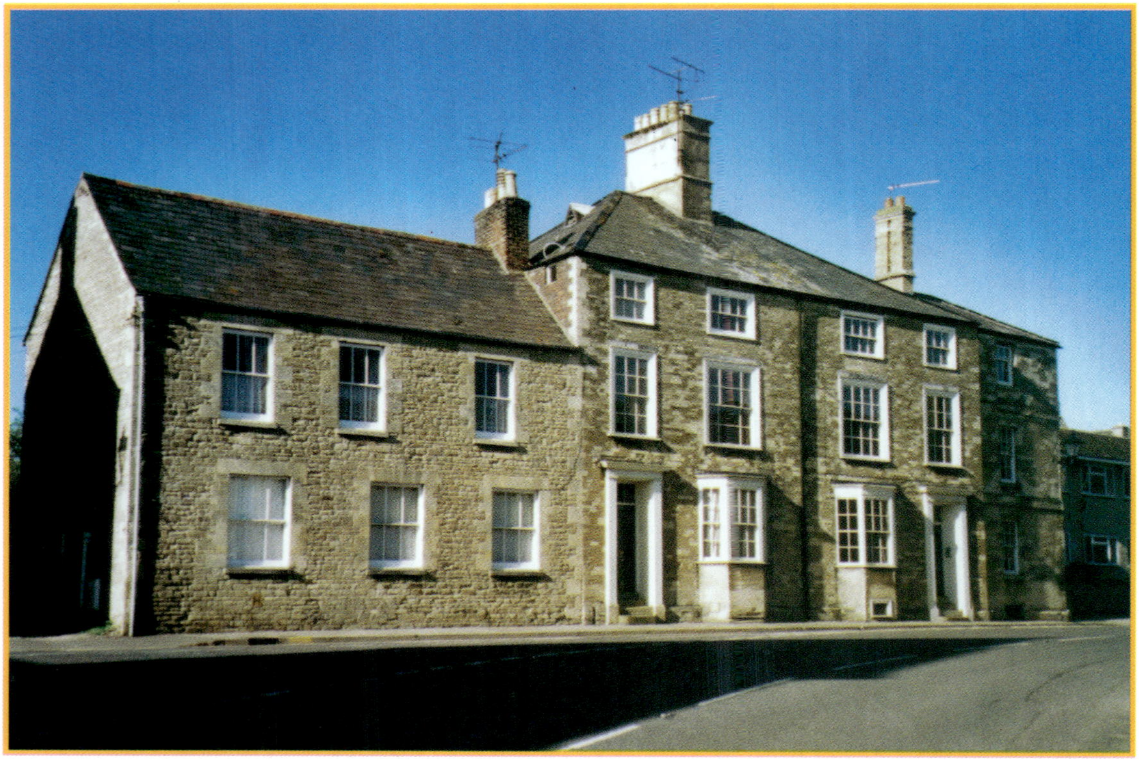

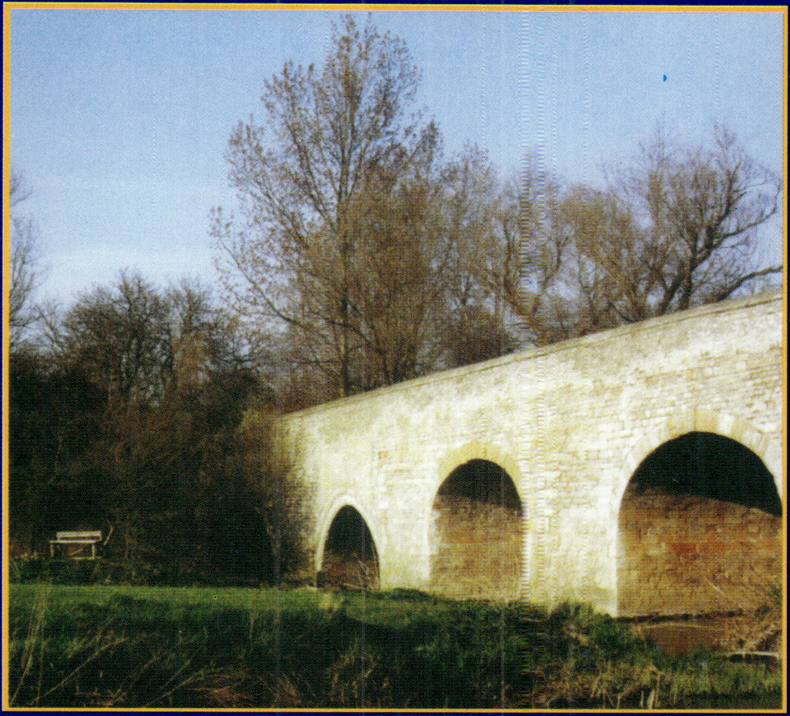

South Oundle

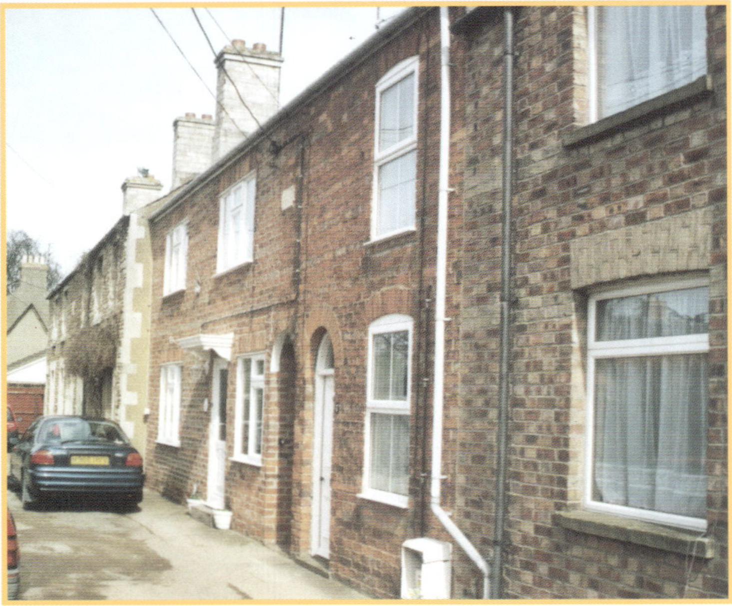

Oundle has a wide variety of Victorian terraced houses as the property in Bassett's Place (left) demonstrates` and St Osyths Lane (below).

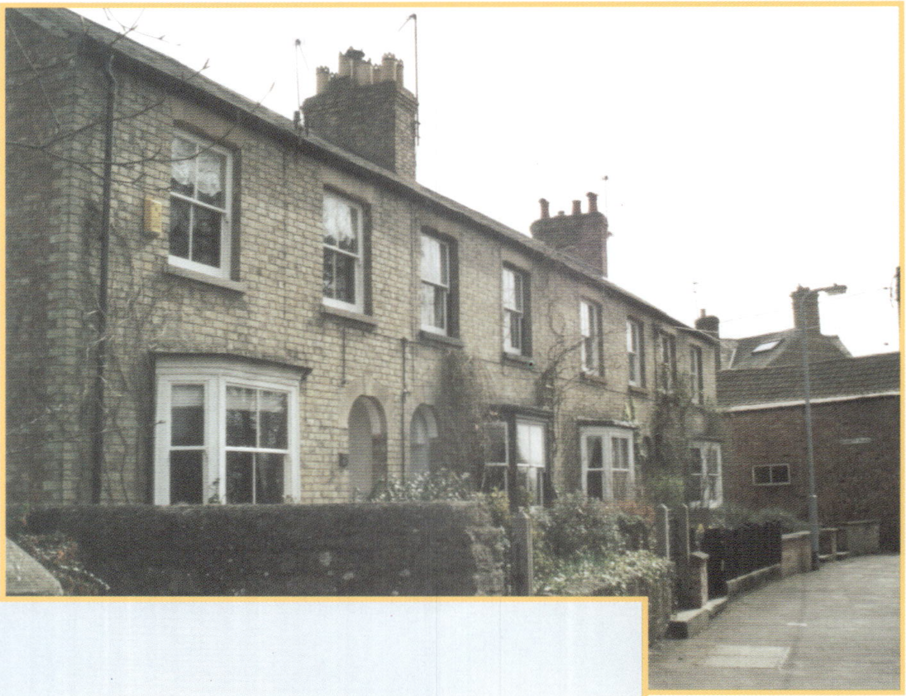

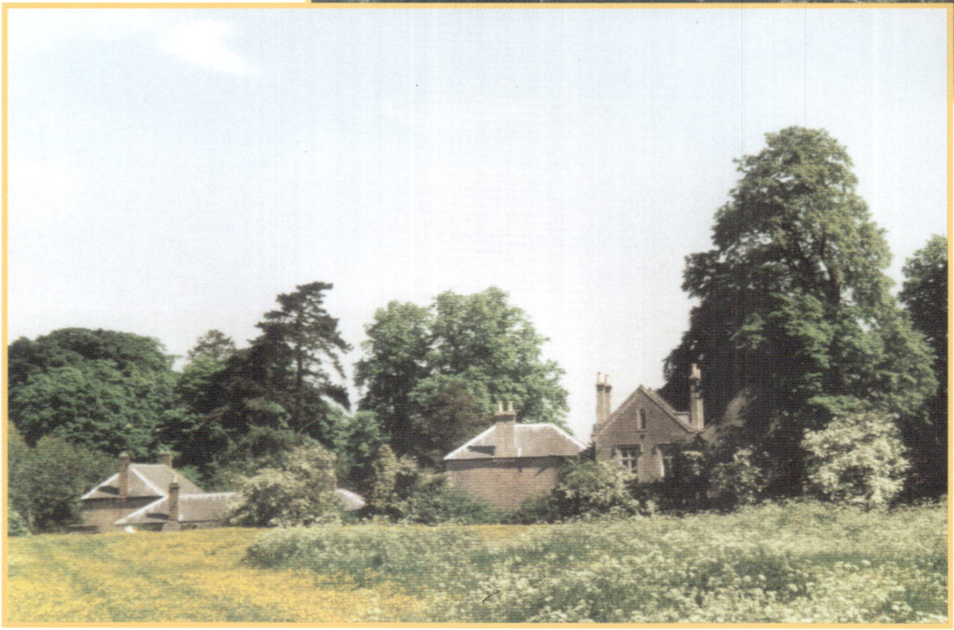

Left, Grazing land looking from Herne Road towards the Ashton Estate.

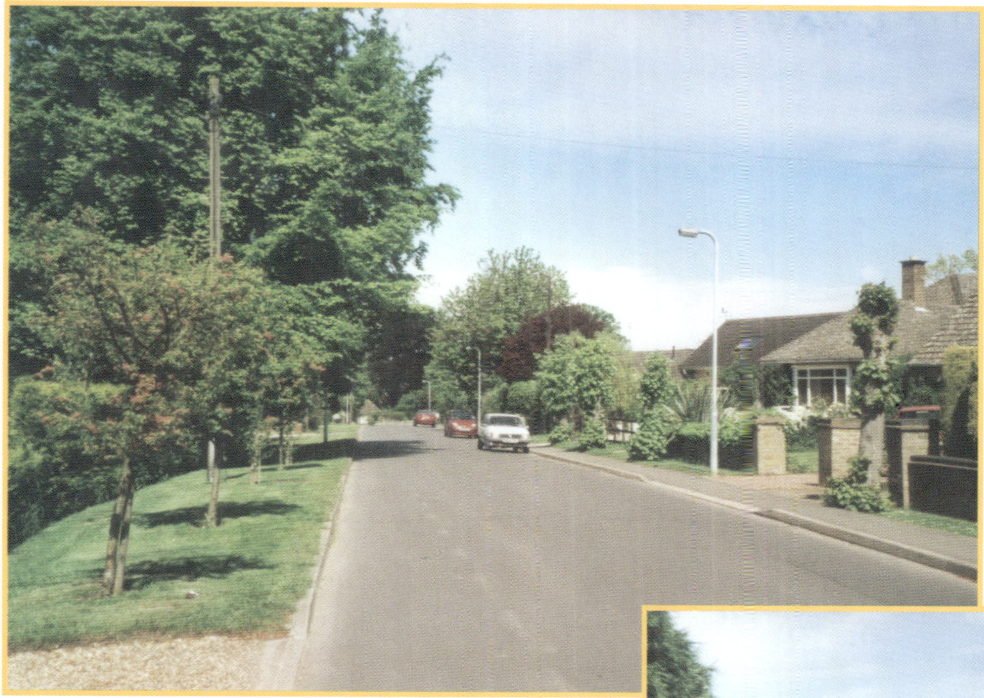

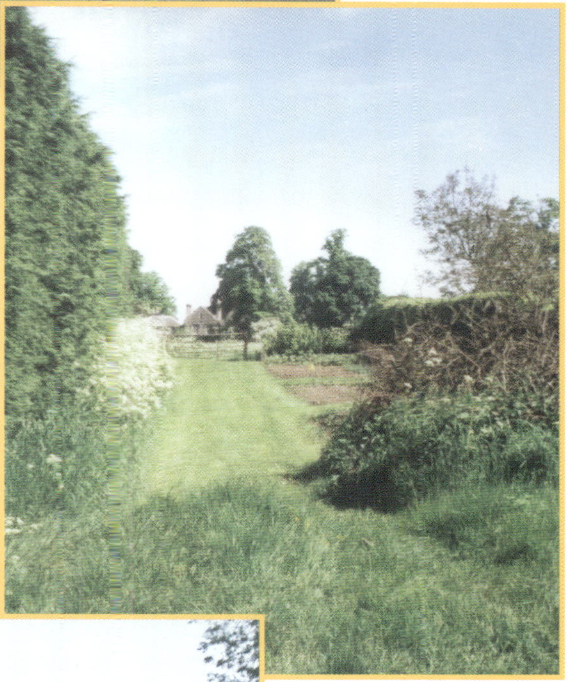

Above and right Herne Road on a summer's cay.

Below, Cheremy Grange, Oundle's Residential Home, which is operated by Mr Bandula Chandraratna and his wife. Bandula has gained considerable fame due to novels published around the turn of the twenty first century - 'Mirage' and 'An Eye for an Eye'.

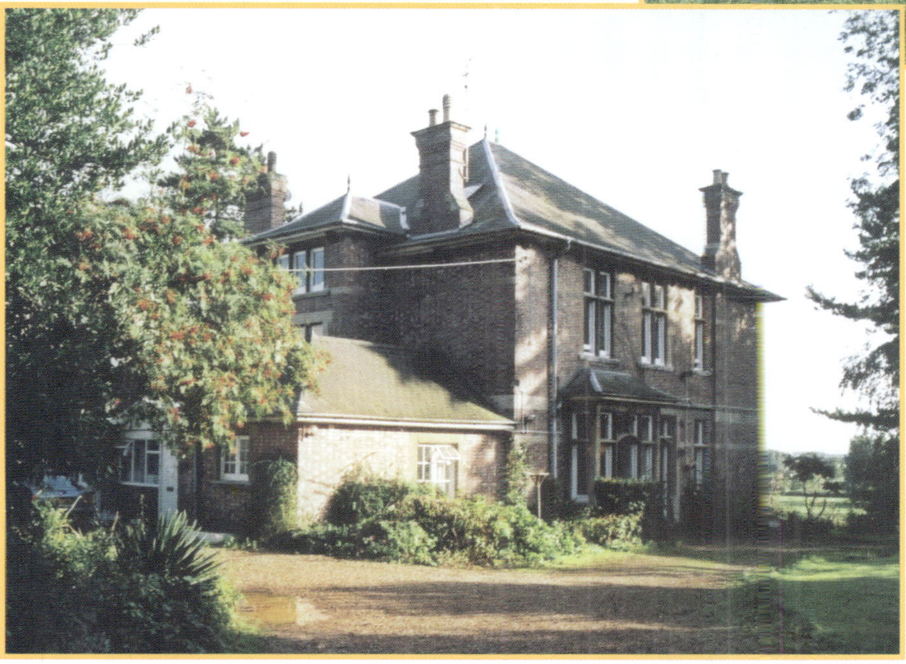

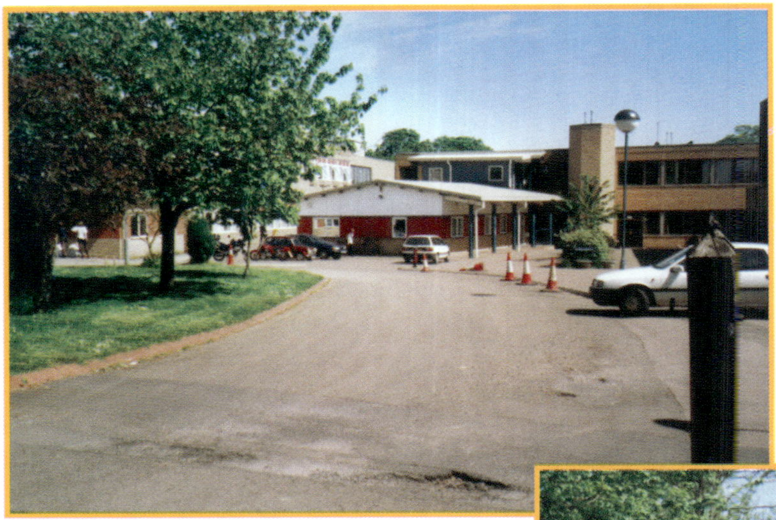

Prince William School, Herne Road. The large comprehensive school caters for children from a radius of at least eight miles. Prince William lived at Barnwell Manor with his family from the 1950's to the 1970's. He was tragically killed when his aircraft G-AWOG crashed during an air race. As a memorial to him the area comprehensive school has been named after him and his name also lives on in the housing estate which surrounds Prince William Road, on the western outskirts of the town.

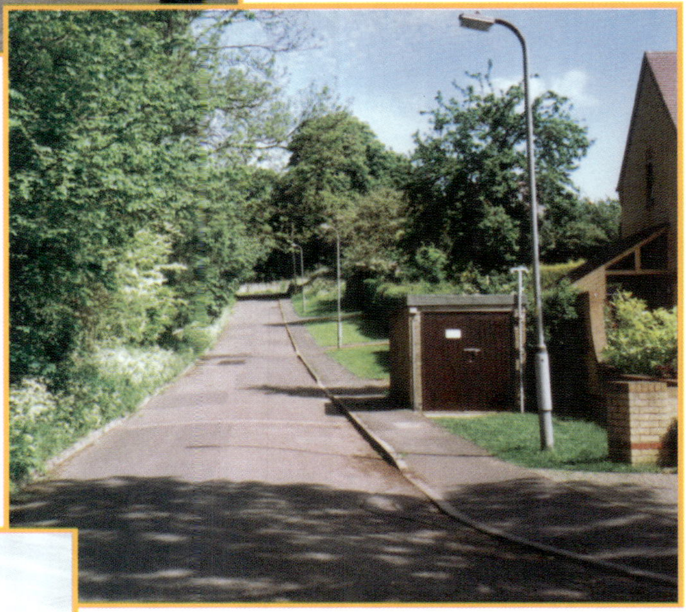

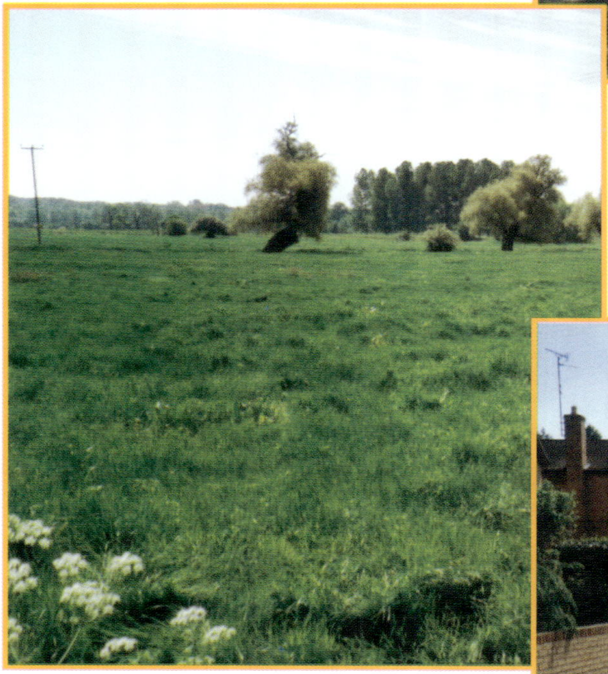

Above, Bassett Ford Road off Herne Road and South Road leads down to the fields and flood plain (left) alongside the River Nene.

During the Easter floods in 1998 the entire area was under water as was the adjacent Riverside Close (below).

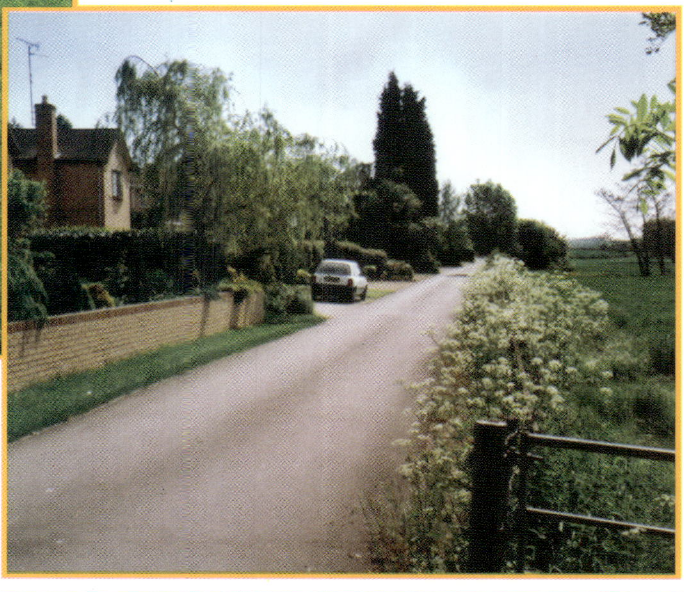

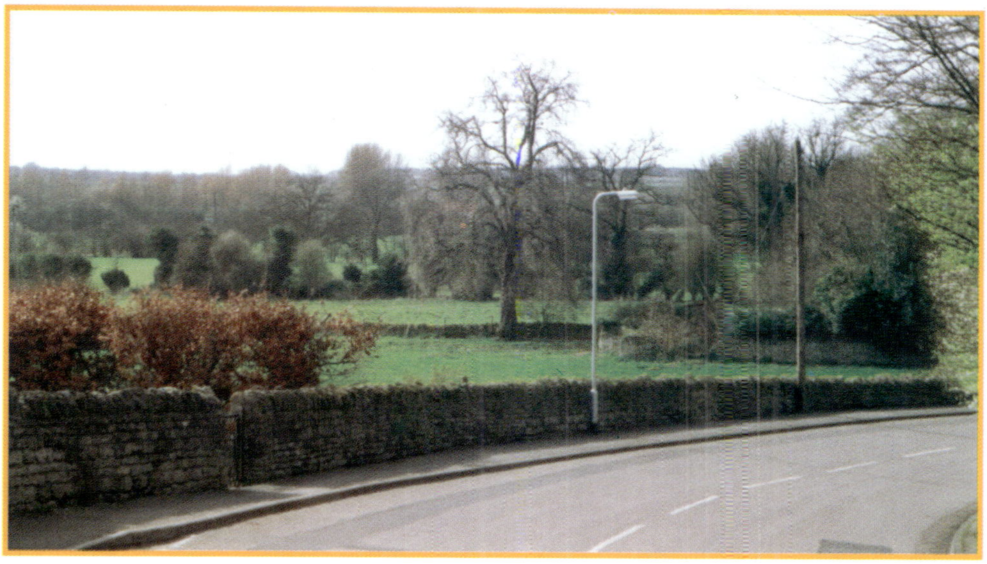

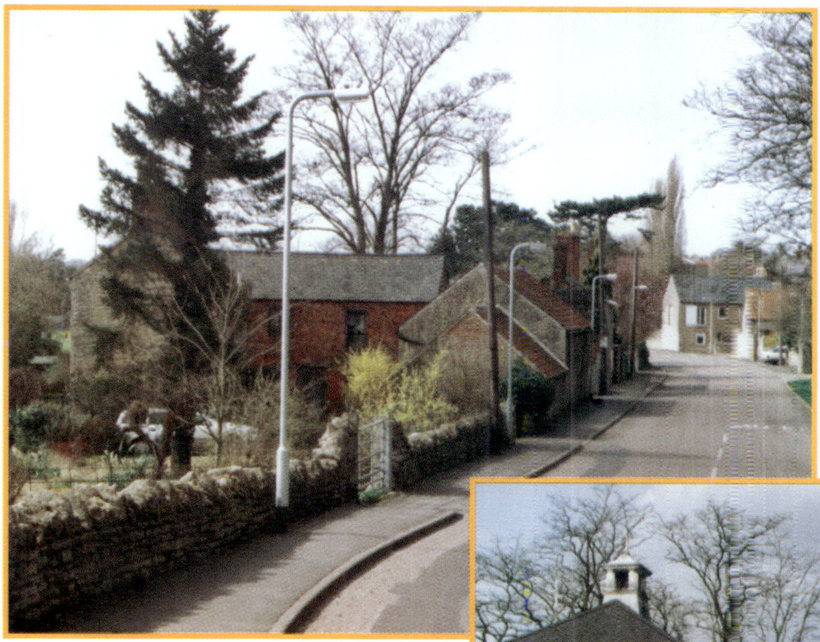

Views from the South Road. Above, looking towards the playing fields and the Nene Valley flood plain.

Left, the cottages along the road, many of these were built during the Victorian era.

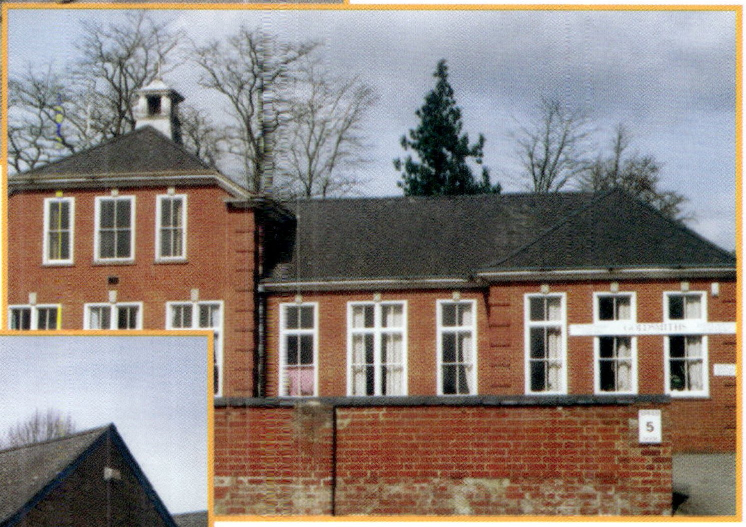

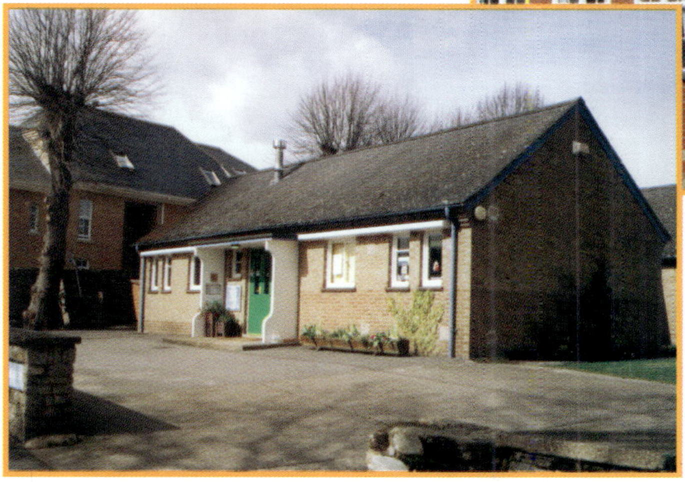

Left, an important part of Oundle's infrastructure - the Oundle Veterinary Surgery and above, the Auction Rooms, a former school at the rear of the vets.

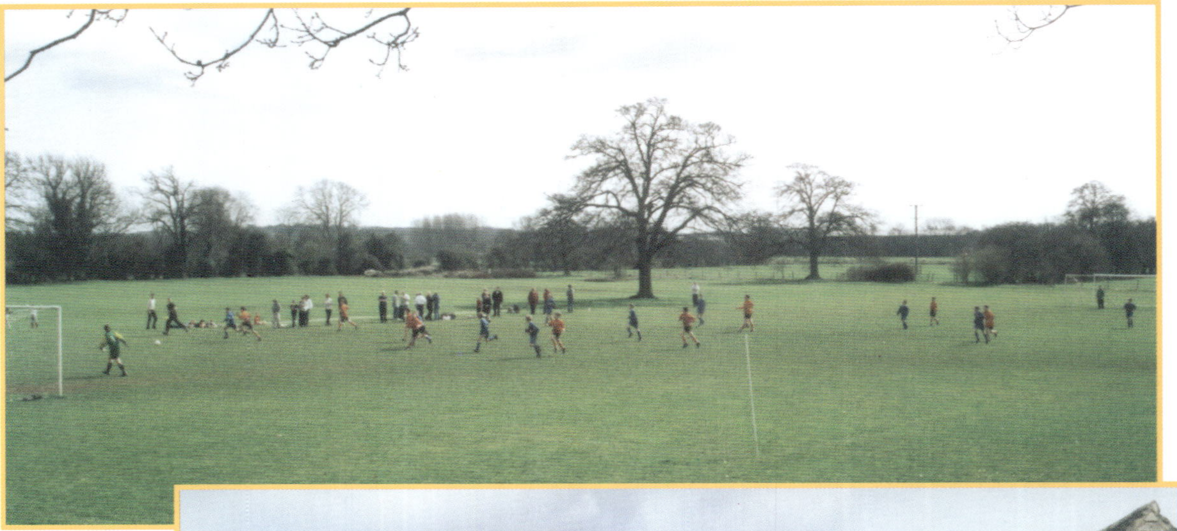

Above, South Road playing fields and right the rear of the Ship Inn, the main entrance being in West Street

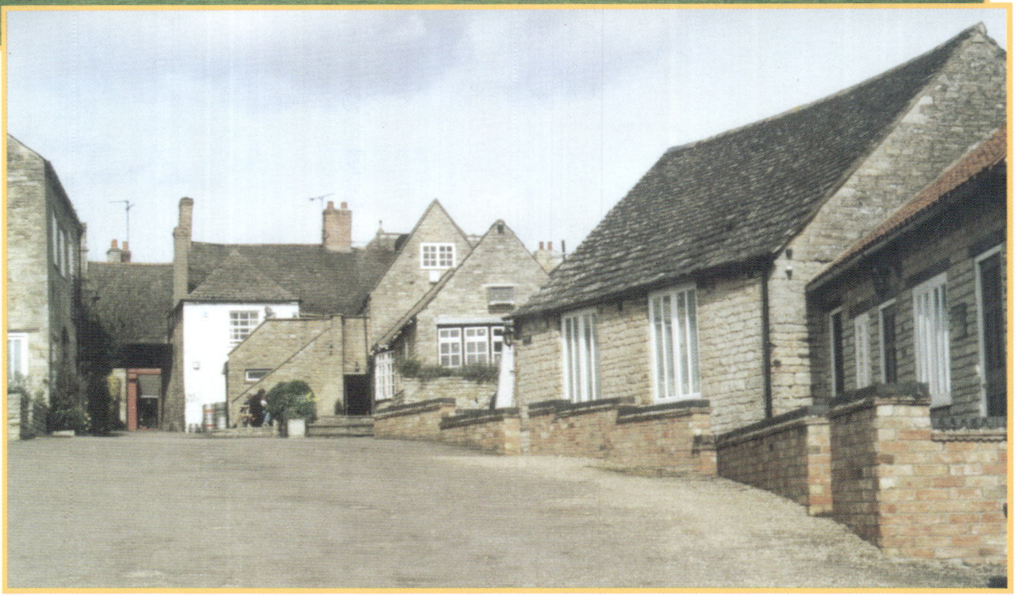

Below, the aerial view of South Bridge looking east.

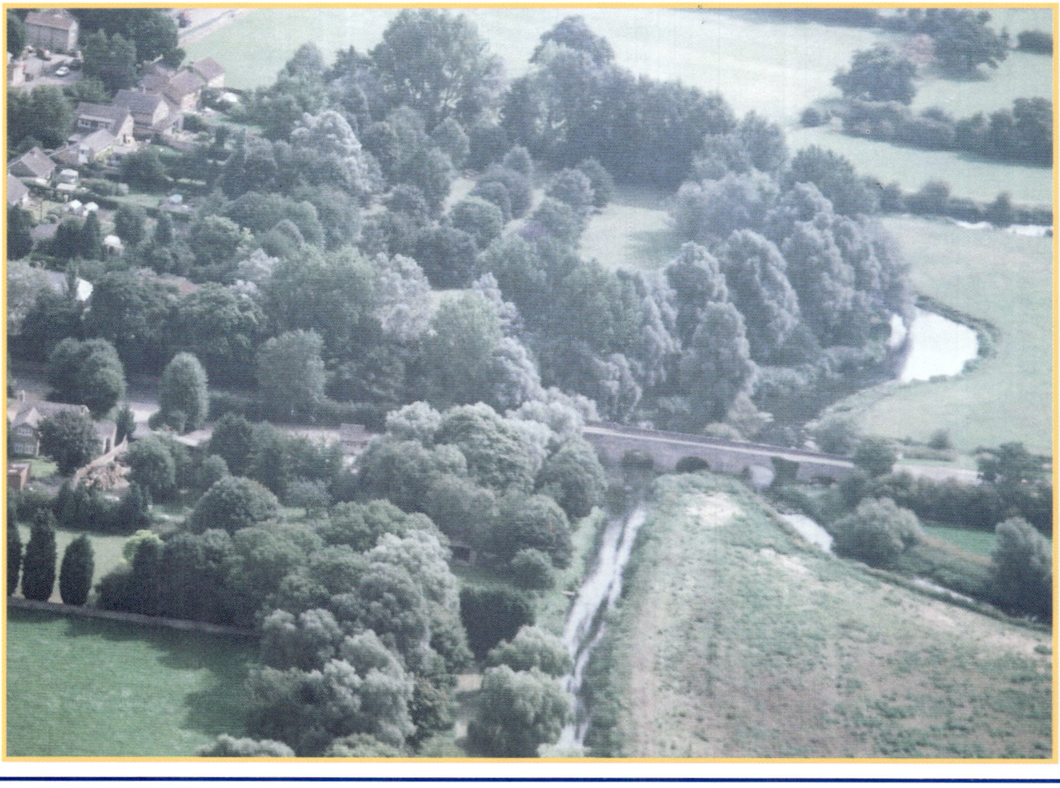

Below and left, the old Anchor Brewery at the corner of South Road and Barnwell Road was founded in 1854. Production ended fifty years later, but still visible are the Brewery House and Office.

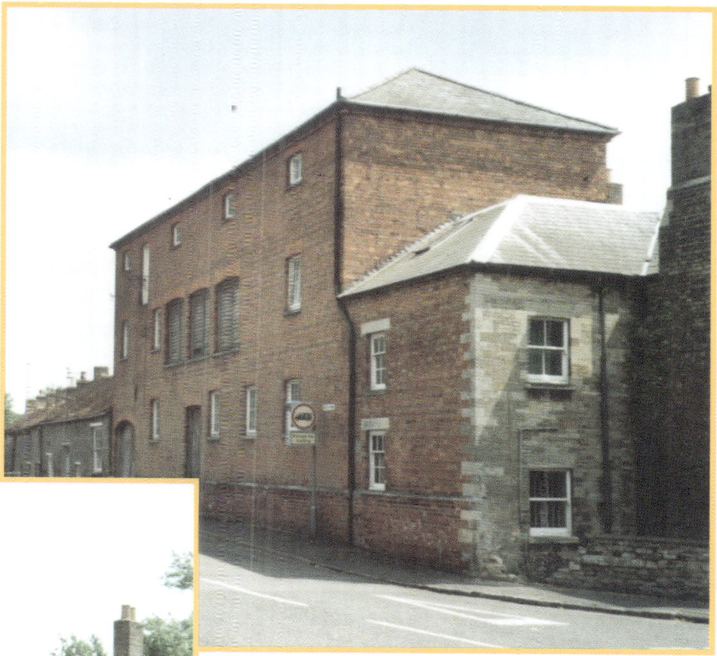

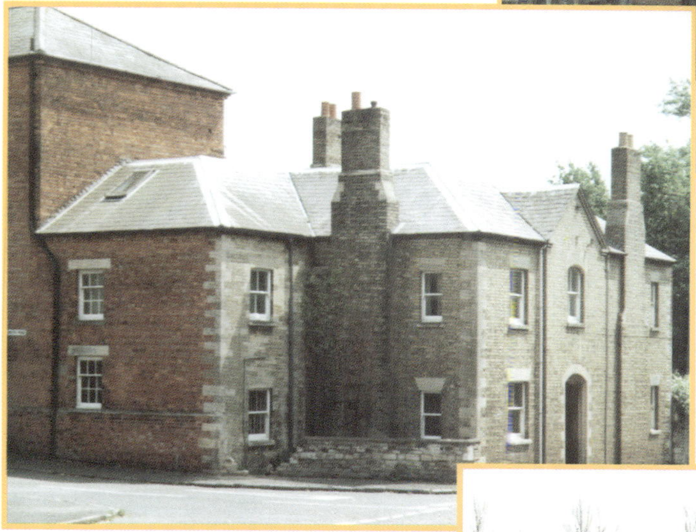

Right, the River Nene at South Bridge and below, an aerial view of South Bridge looking north.

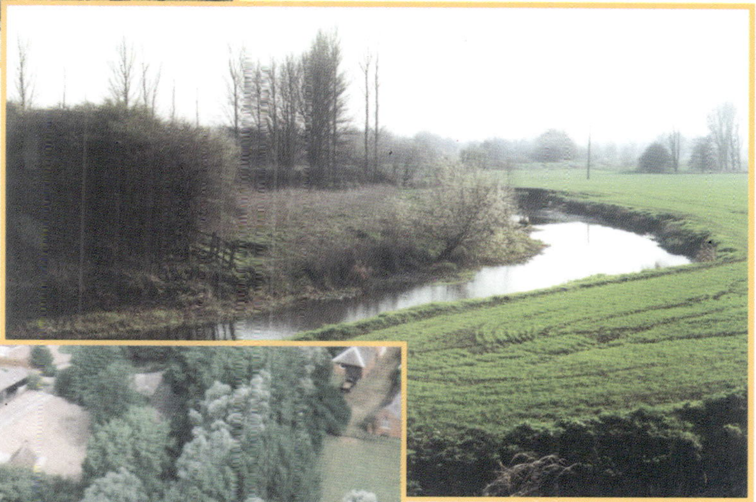

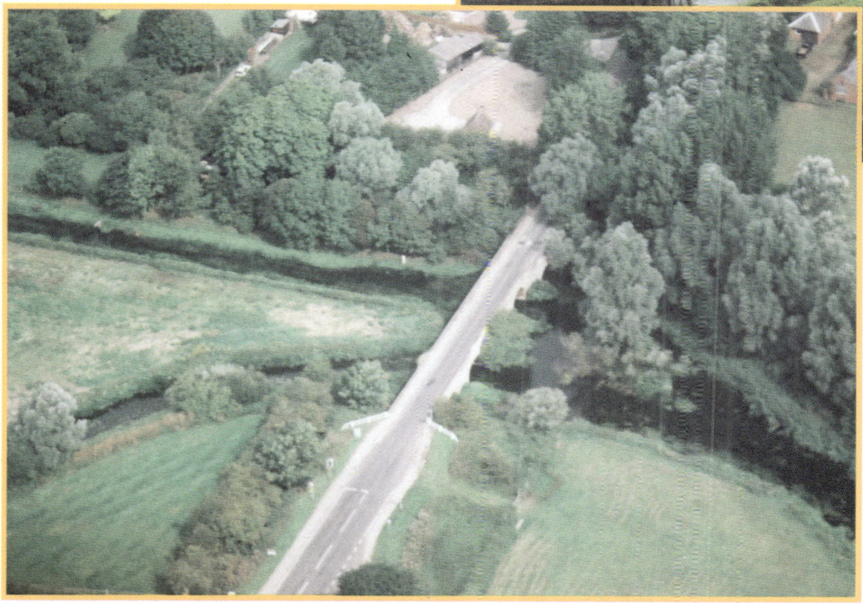

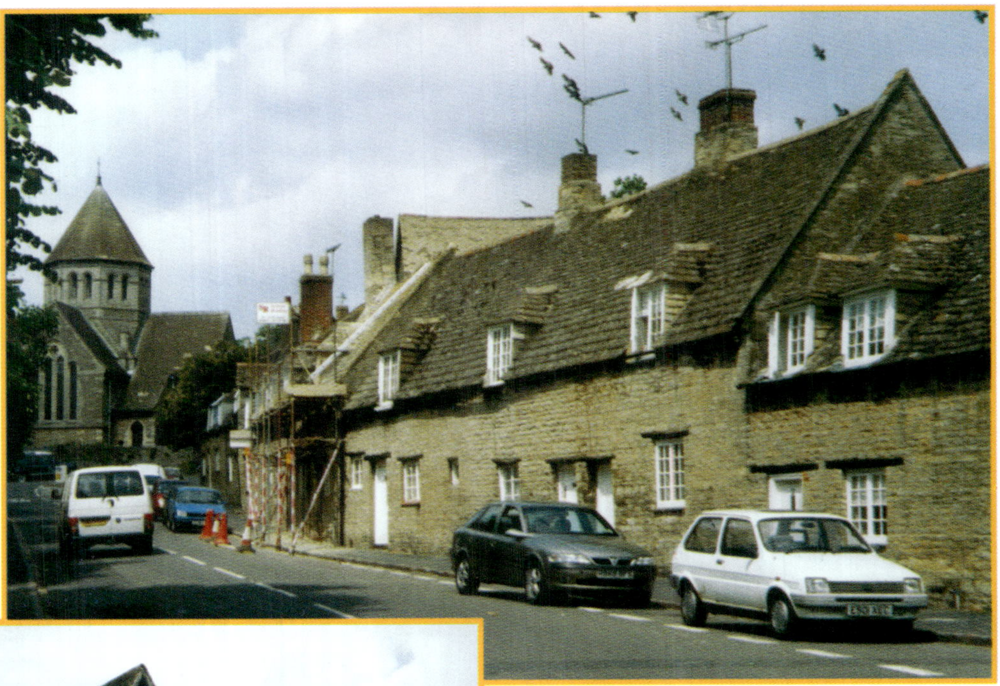

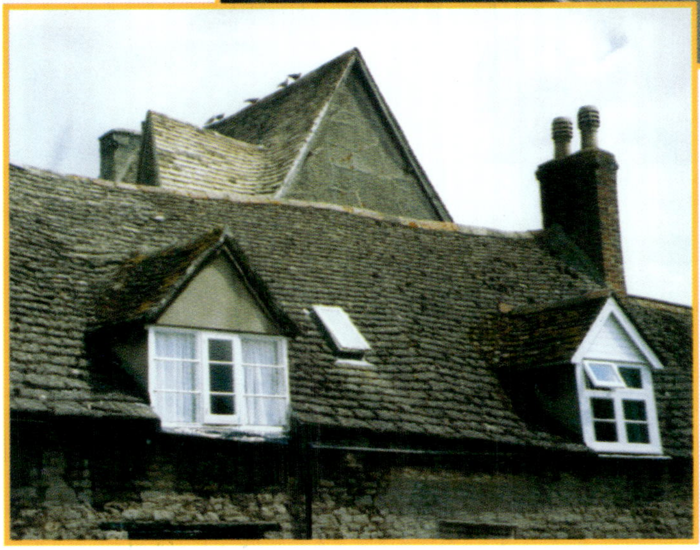

Above, Mill Road looking north towards the Roman Catholic Church. In the centre is the roof of the old 'Priest's House' visible above the roof line of the Mill Cottages. Left and to be seen clearly is the old 'Priest's House'. This is the remnant of a manor house dating from at least the sixteenth century. A mill once stood close to South Bridge.

Below, the old pumping station alongside the River Nene at the start of Barnwell Road.

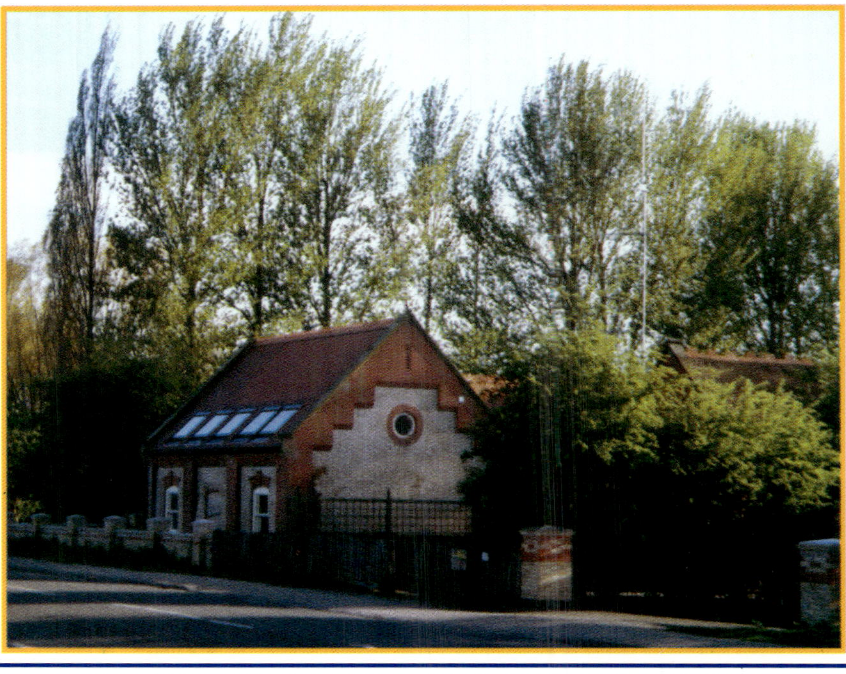

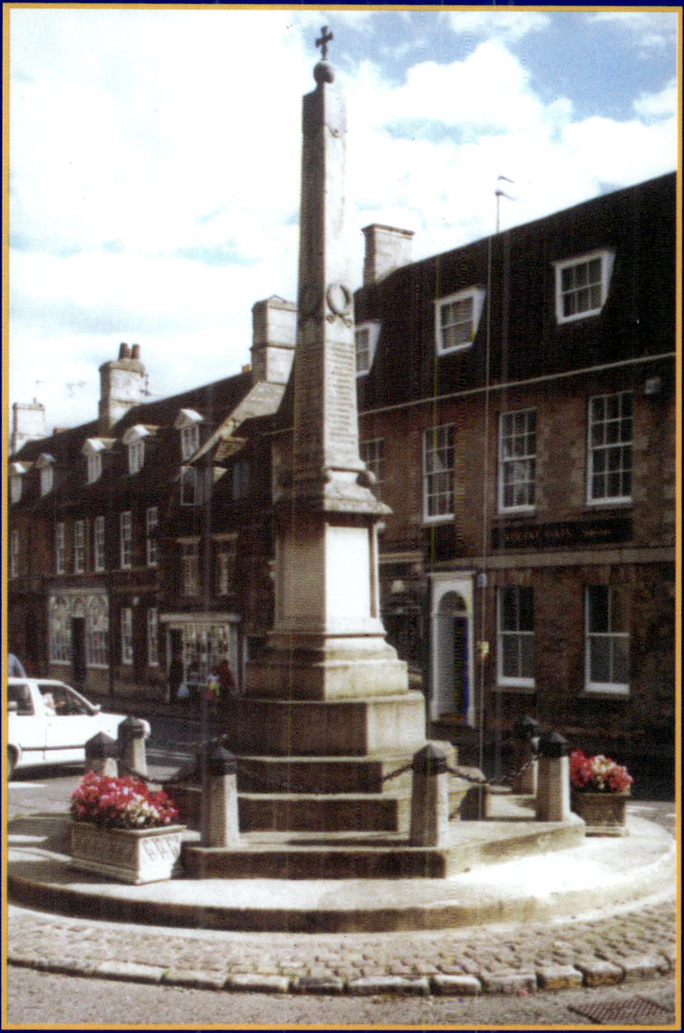

Returning to the Centre of Oundle

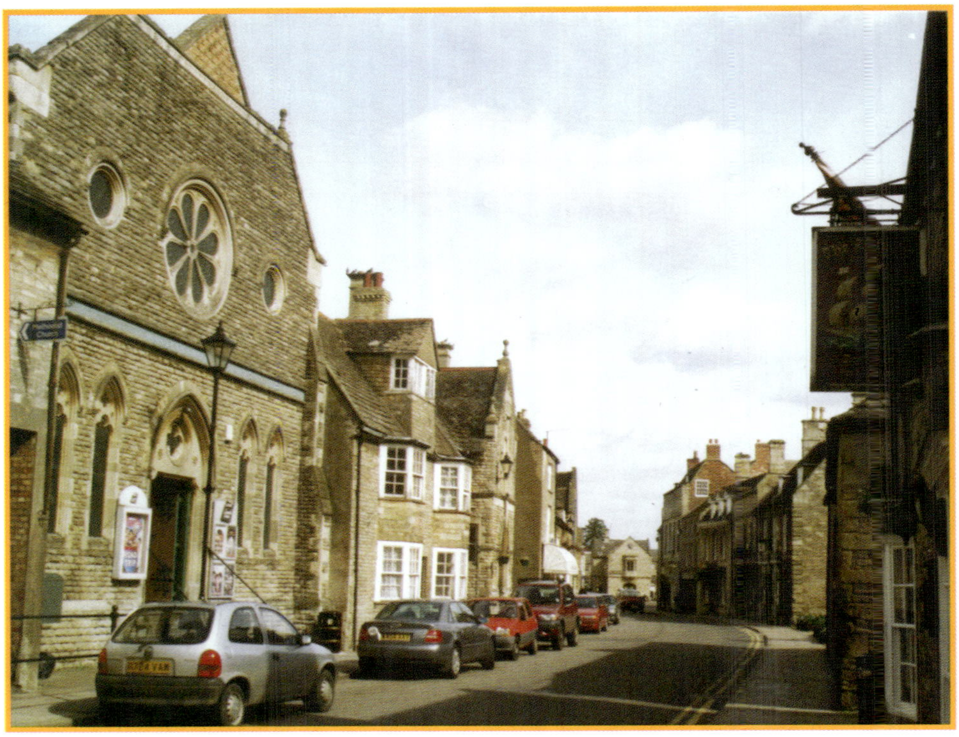

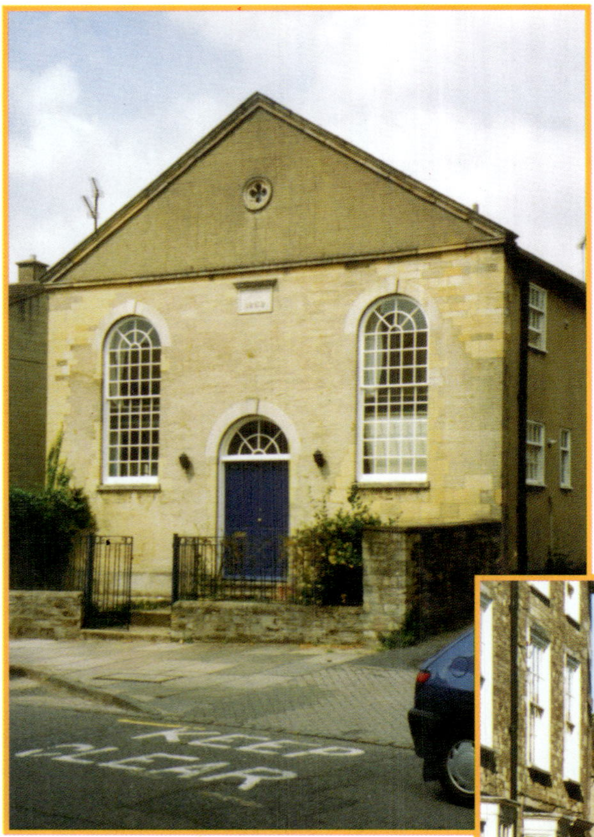

Above the old Weslyan Church now a shop unit and The Ship Inn just visible on the right, this has a large yard where there used to be a saw pit, wheelwrights, blacksmiths and plumbers shop.
Left, the old Baptist Chapel in West Street which was founded in 1852.
Below, the junction of West Street and Benefield Road - the building with the white windows facing on the left was formerly the old work house.

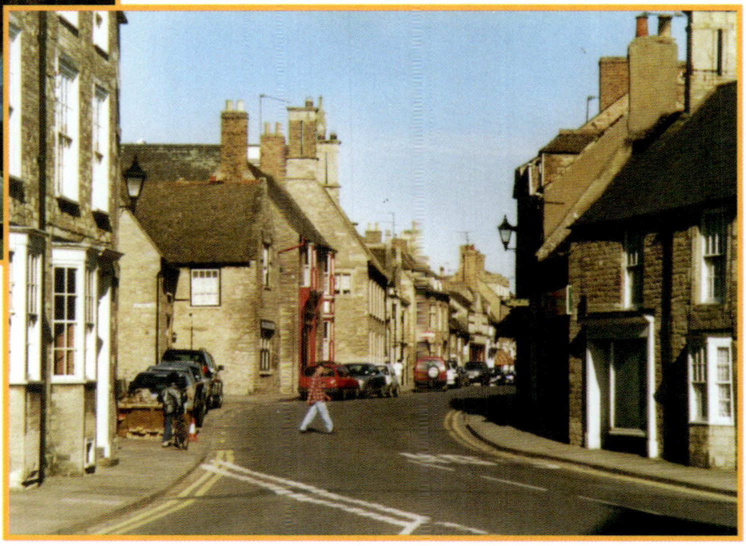

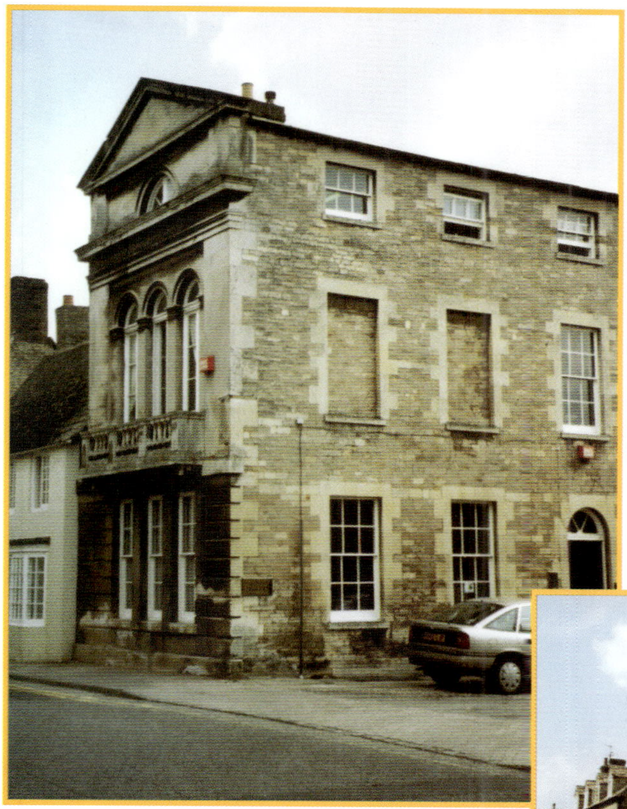

Left, the unusual Townley House, now home to Oundle's dental surgery. This was formerly the brewery house of the Oundle Union Brewery which was started in 1836 by local farmers and business men. It was sold in 1853 to Smith's Brewery.

Below, houses and shops along West Street.

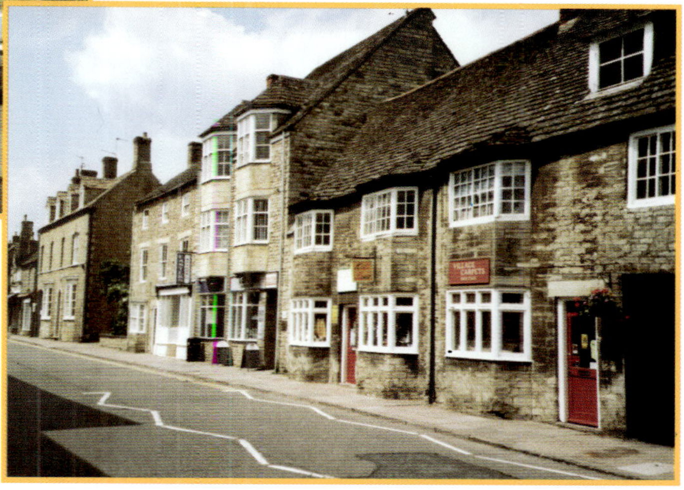

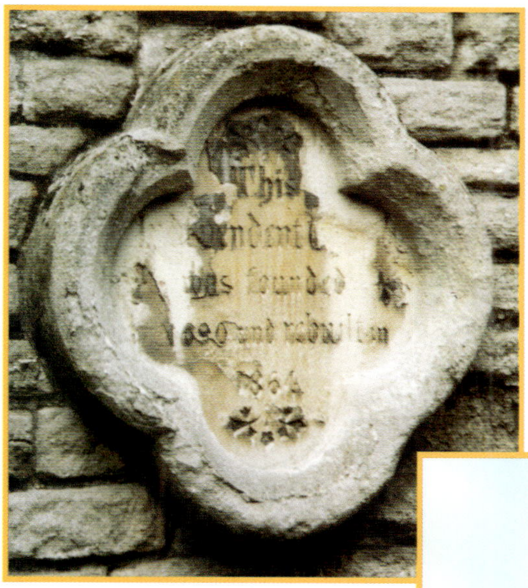

Above, the foundation stone on the Rodolphe Stahl Theatre.

Below, a unique photograph showing Paine's Cottages with their ornate entrance, the old Congregational Manse and the Chapel (1834) which was converted in 1979 to the Rodolphe Stahl Theatre by a bequest from an American who had attended Oundle Public School.

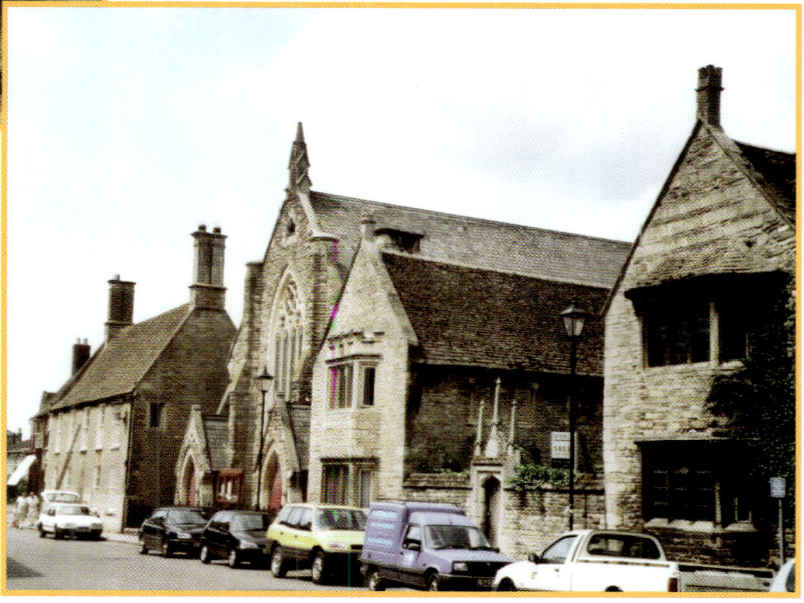

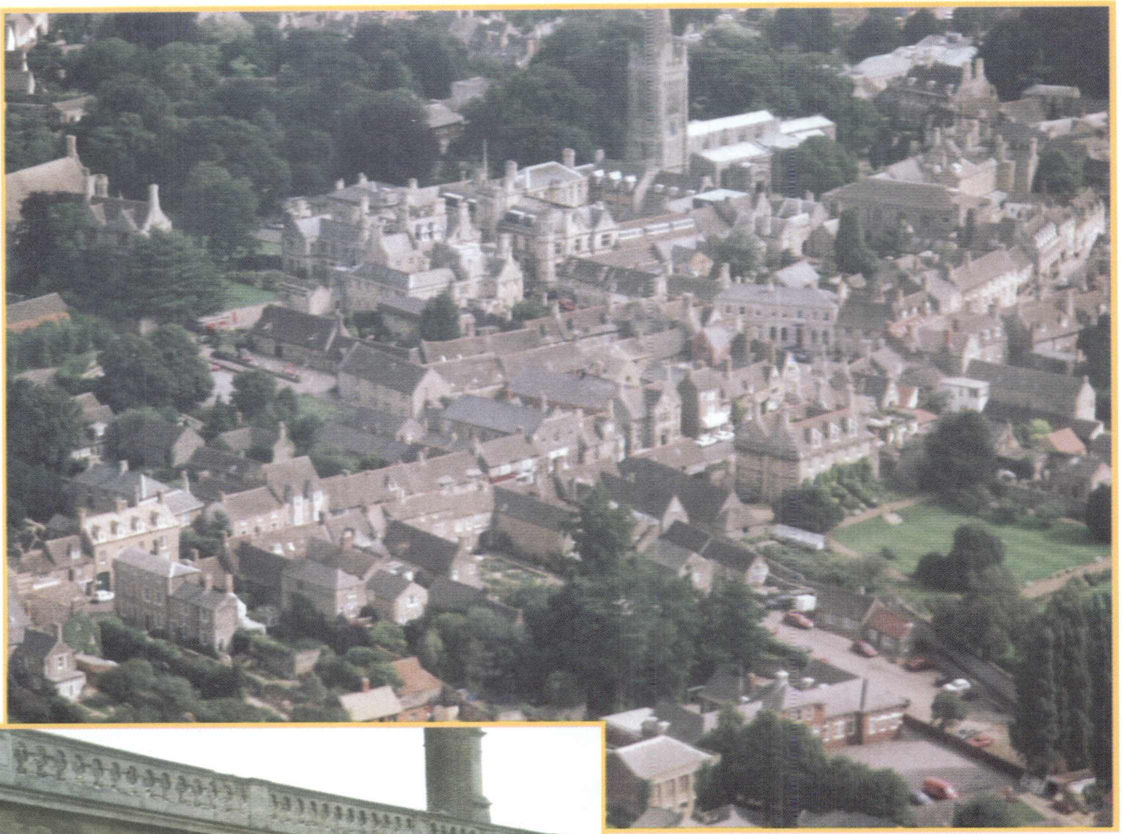

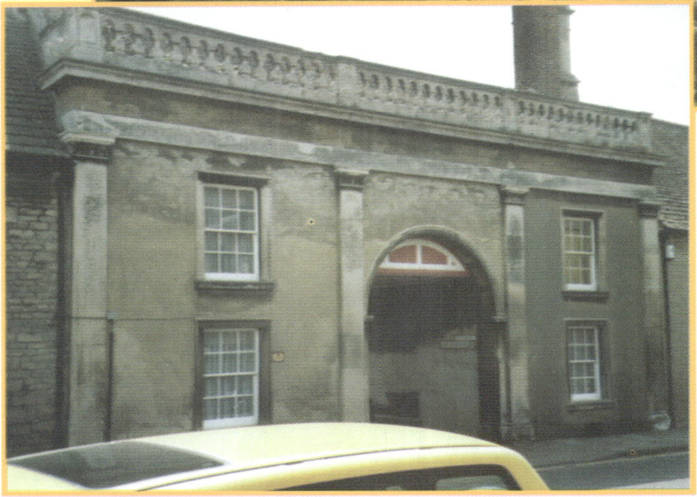

Above, an aerial photograph showing West Street looking north towards Oundle School Cloisters and St Peter's Church.

Left, Danfords. The extraordinary facade was built in the 1830's but this pretentious facade with the central arch and balustrade only leads to a yard with cottages and Danford's Close below.

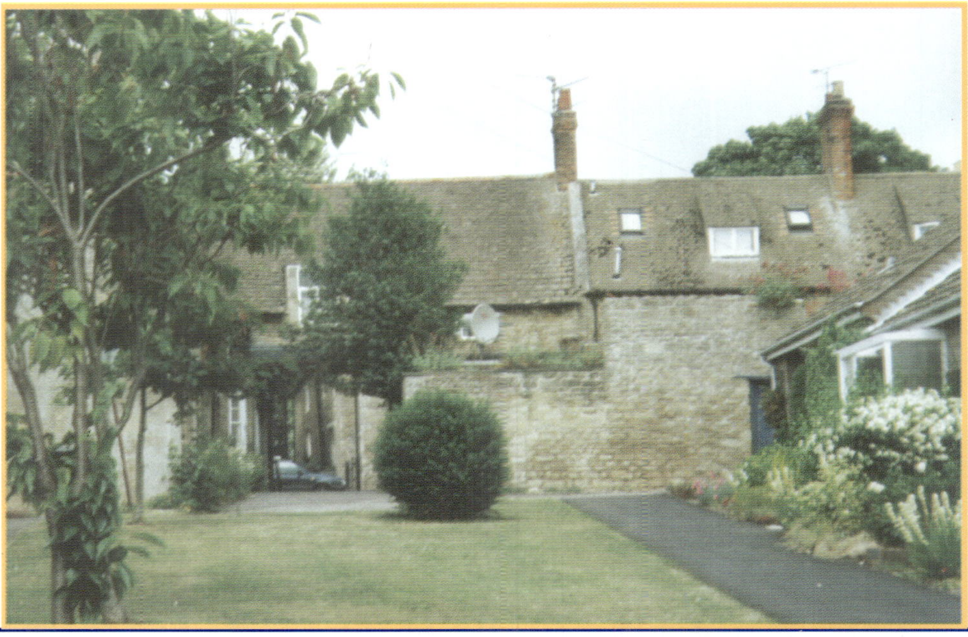

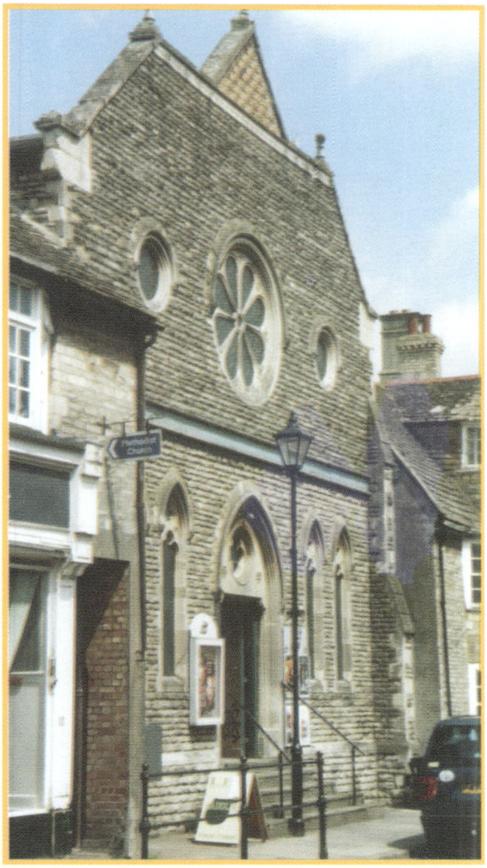

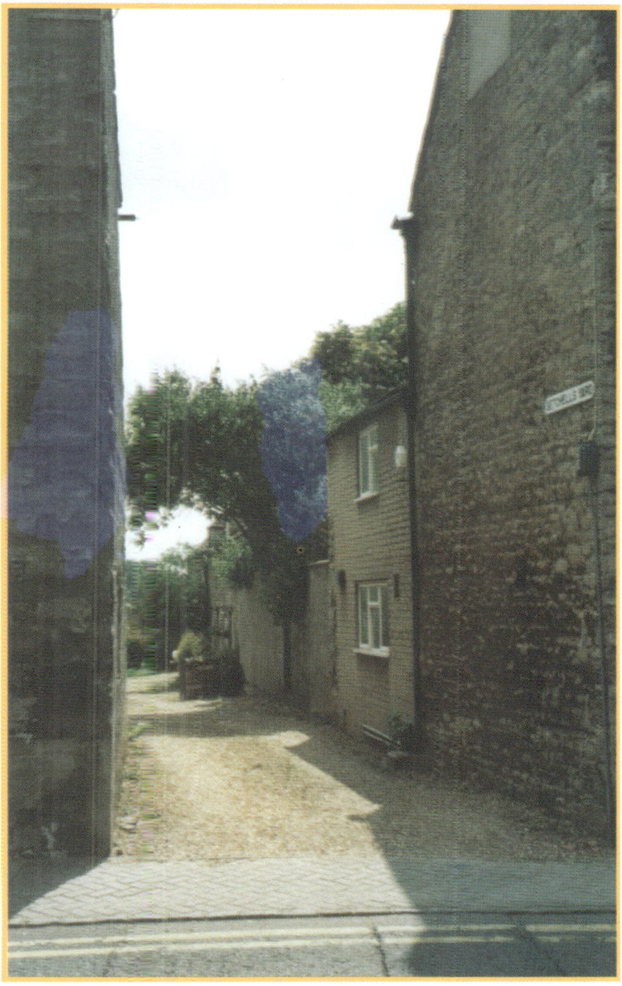

Above, the Weslyan Church clearly marked across the blue band and now a shop unit.

Right, Setchells Yard

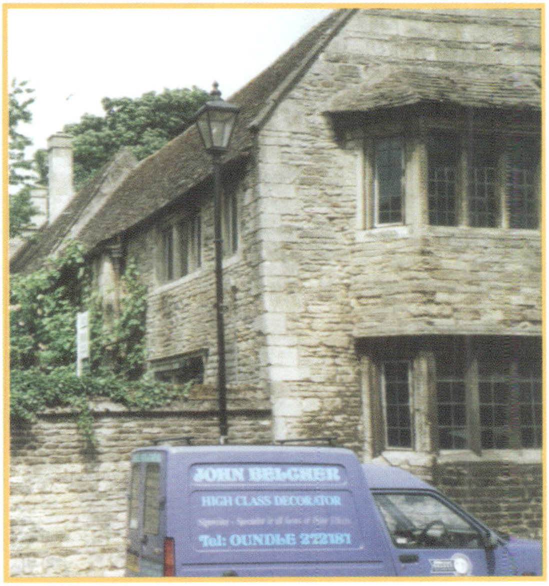

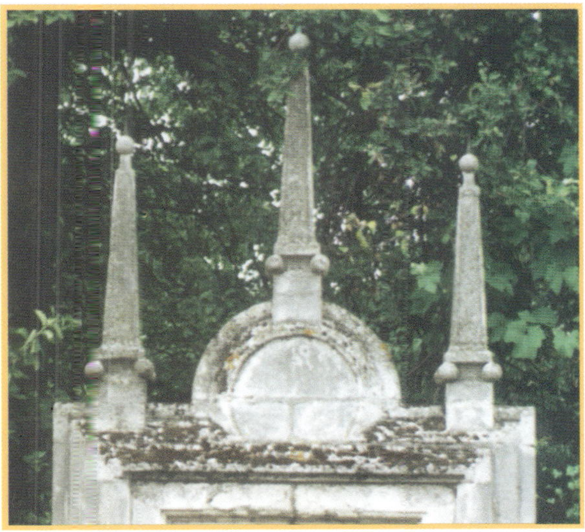

Above, Paine's Cottage with the distinctive Elizabethan doorway (right) with the crown decorations on the gable points. The cottage is at least fifteenth century as the fireplace is also of this year. It also has a seventeenth century bay and several other distinctive characteristics - hearths, cornice and beams and a window with wooden mullions.

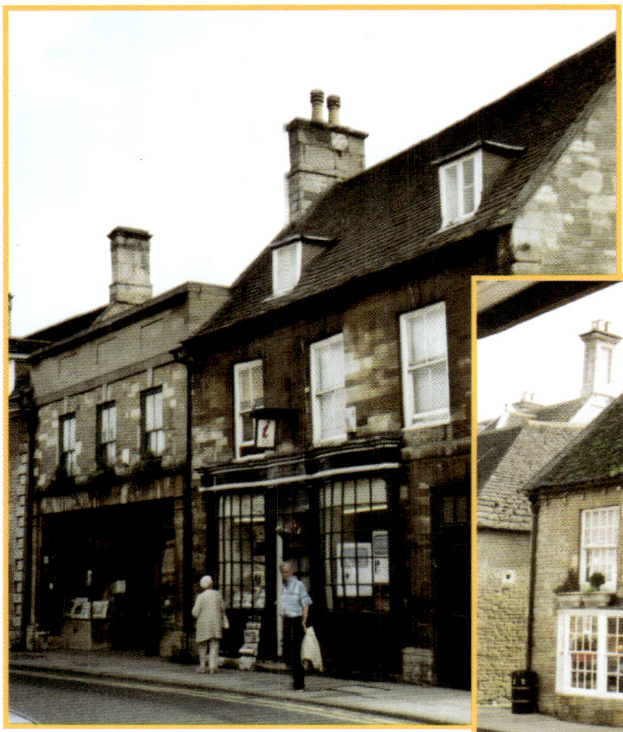

Left, the attractive building occupied by the Tourist Information Centre in West Street and below, The Ship Inn - a seventeenth century inn with an entrance large enough to admit wagons and coaches.

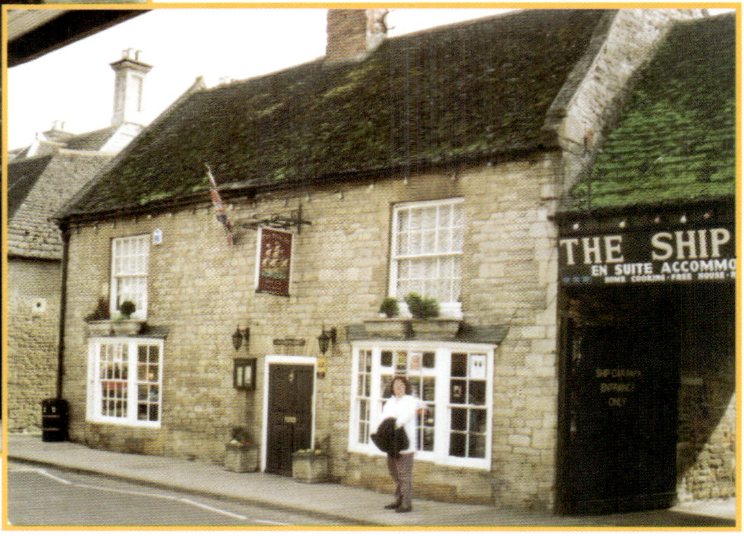

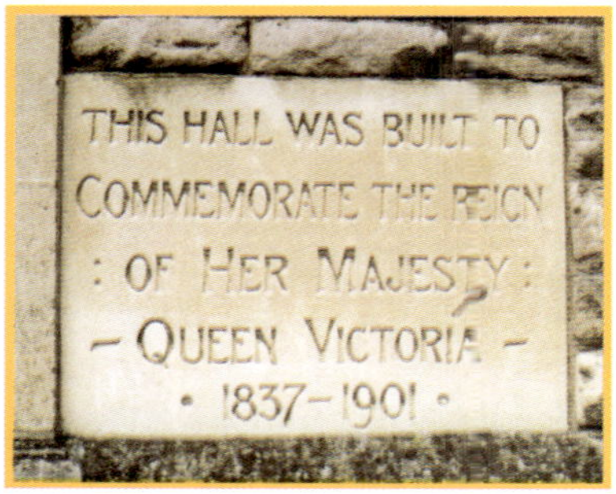

The Queen Victoria Hall below, built in 1902, commemorates the reign of the monarch and now houses the council offices as well as a hall for a variety of functions. The two stones set either side of the doorway commemorate the monarch's reign (1837 -1901) and the laying of the foundation stone on Coronation Day in August 1902.

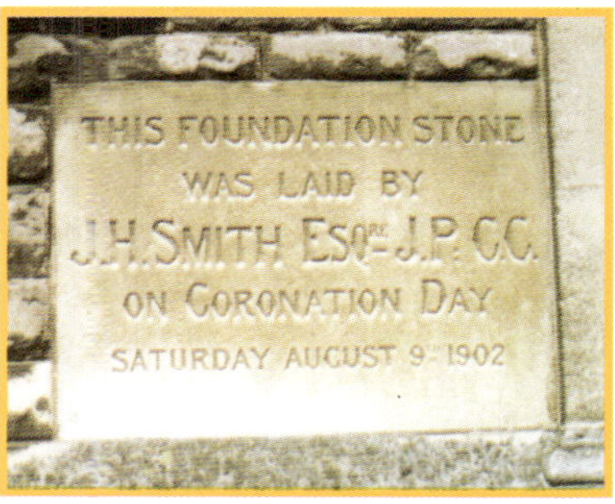

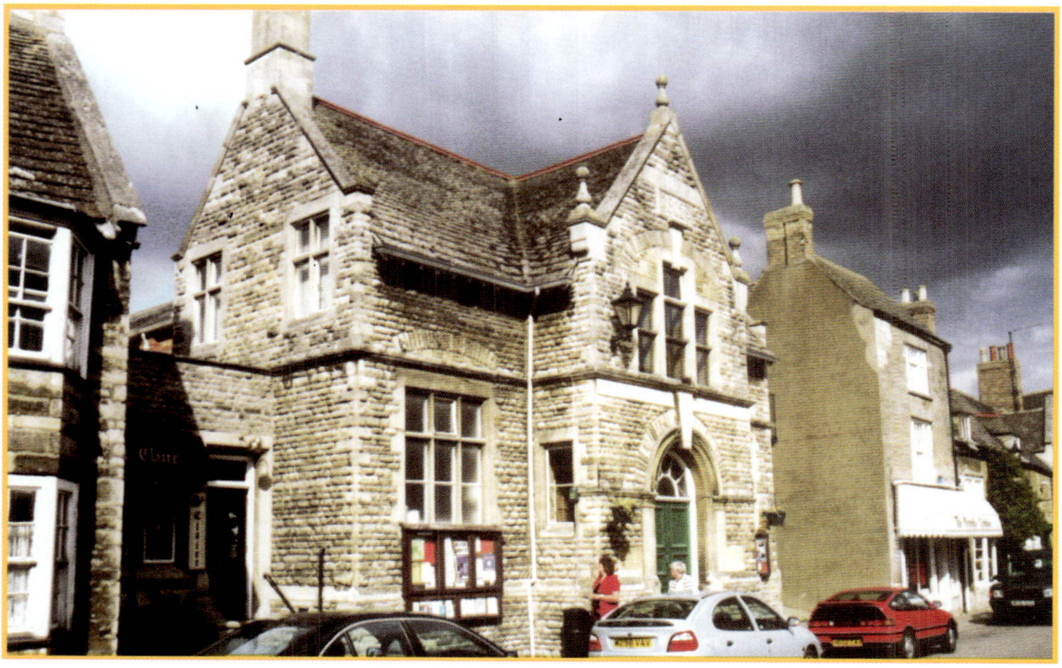

The War Memorial (right), standing at the junction of West Street, New Street and the Market Place was erected after the First World War and prior to this the site was occupied by a water pump.

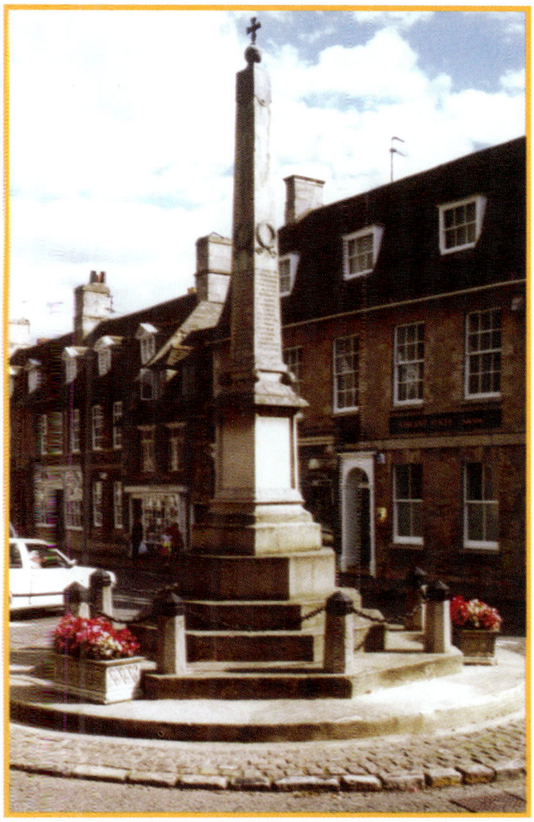

Below, Cobthorne standing close to the War Memorial in West Street is an elegant seventeenth century town house built by Major General William Butler who was a close aide to Oliver Cromwell. The house was later owned by John Creed, a friend of Samuel Pepys and related to the poet John Dryden of Aldwincle village. In 1827 the building passed into the hands of John Smith, Brewers who started in Oundle. Cobthorne is now the residence of the headmaster of Oundle Public School.

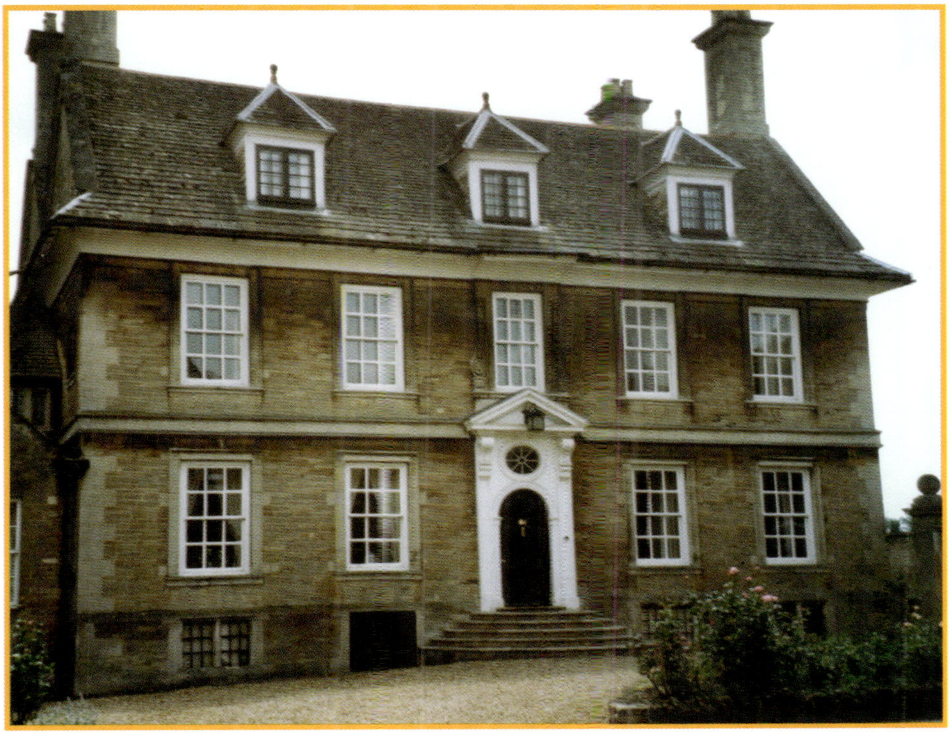

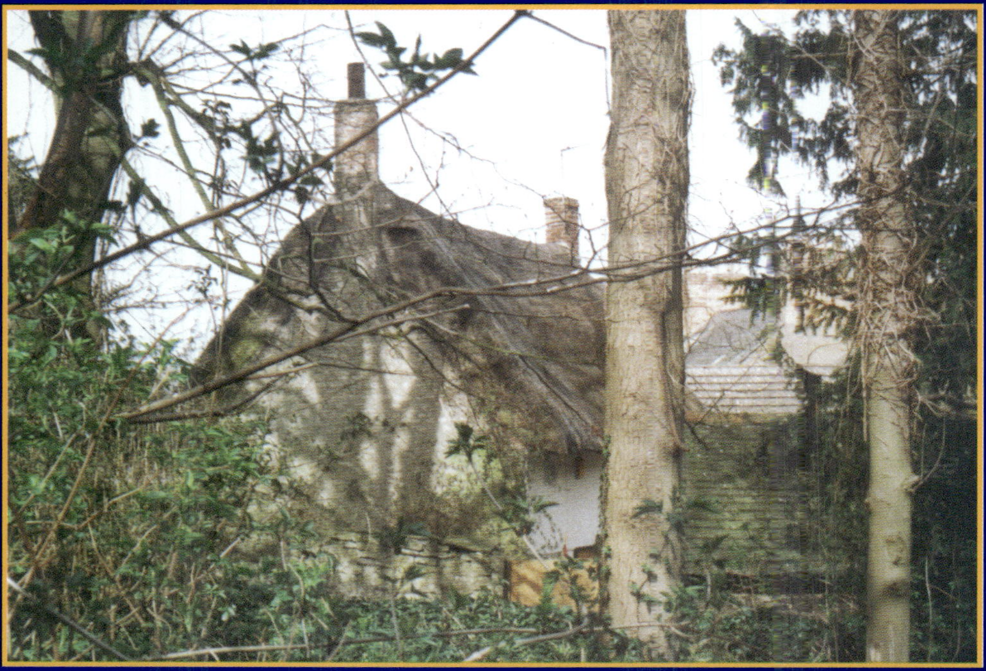

North Street Area

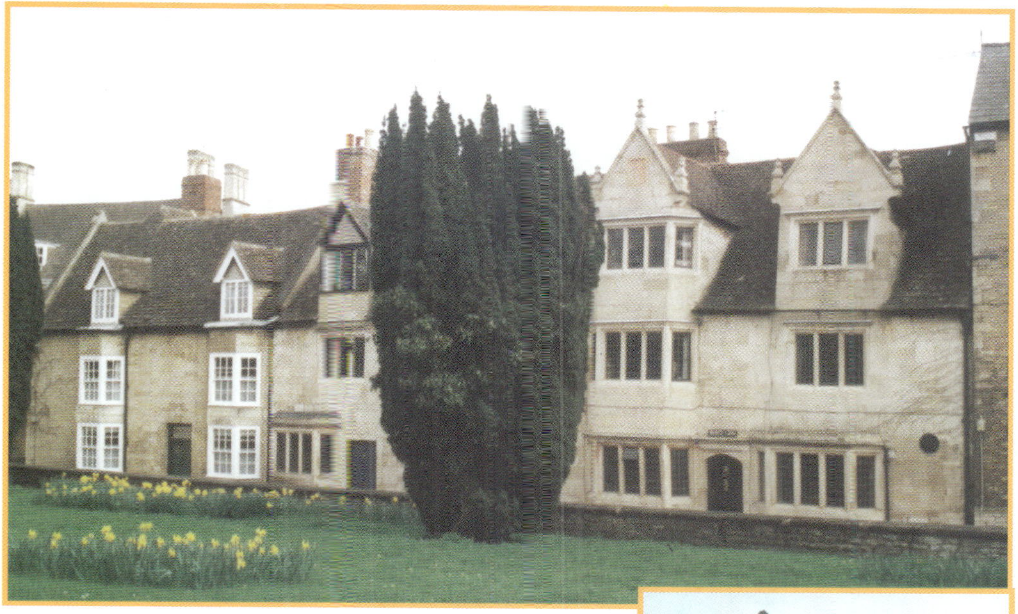

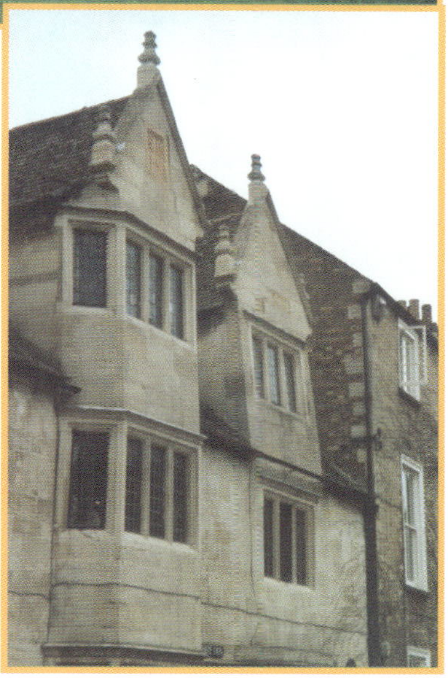

Three photographs of the 'Old White Lion'

At one time Oundle had over forty inns and public houses but only four remain today, although many have seen a new lease of life as private houses. The White Lion in North Street was partly rebuilt in 1641. Look at the western most gable (right) to see the pronounced lean from the vertical. At one time the building was Laxton School's Headmaster's House.

Below is a view of the adjacent buildings. The large building in the distance with blue doors is the soon-to-be-replaced Laxton Junior School and was once the Dolphin Inn.

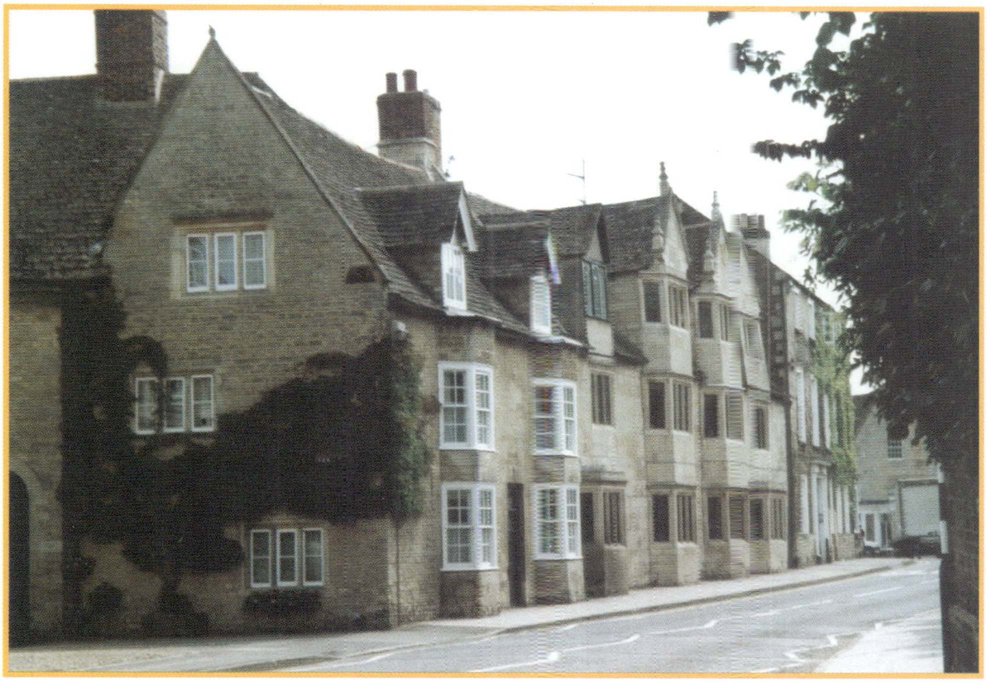

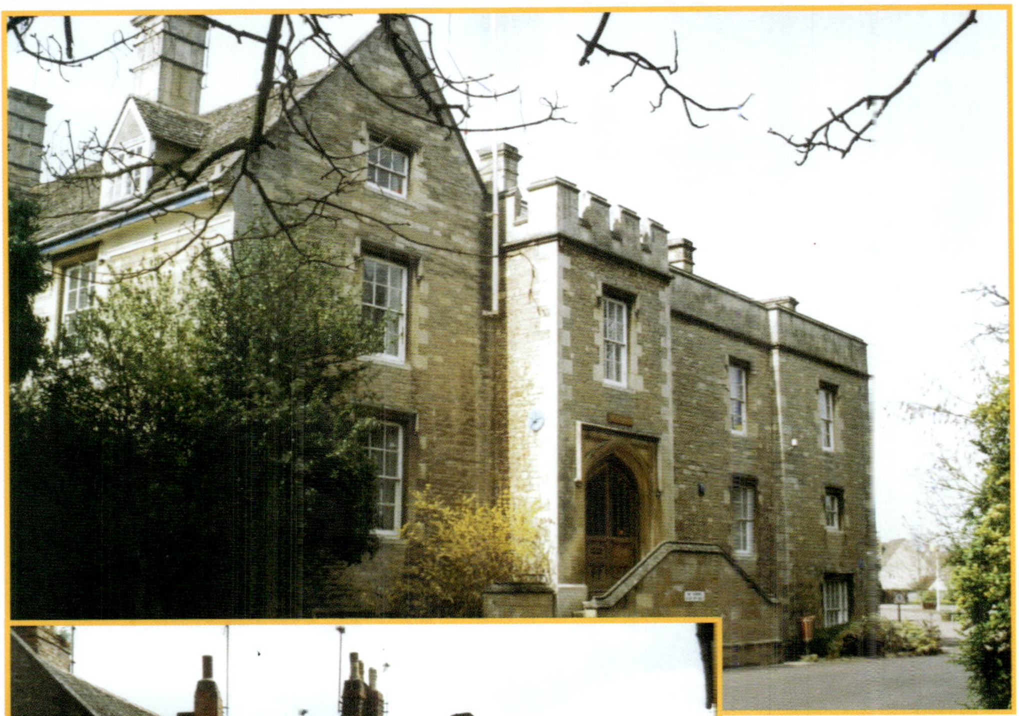

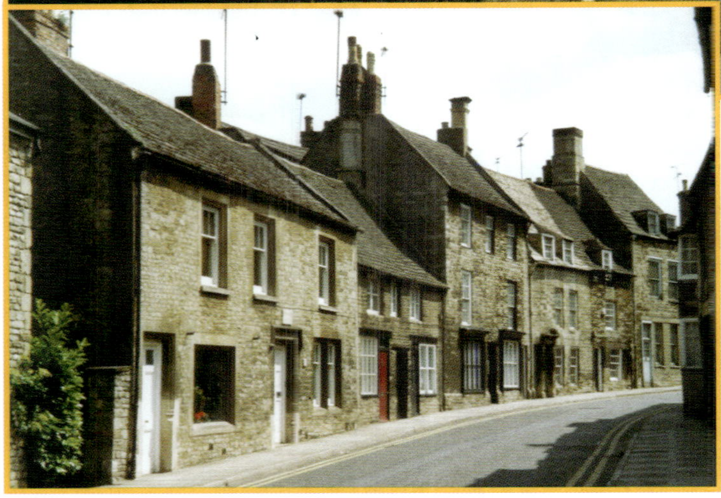

Known once as 'The Old Rectory' Oundle School's Gascoigne building (above) is used as the main music department. During the Second World War the building was used as a billet for the troops.

Left are the medieval buildings along North Street. Behind these on the opposite side is a thatched property - a rare sight in Oundle where there is a dearth of thatched properties.

Below and looking along North Street is Laxton School on the left with Laxton Junior School on the right.

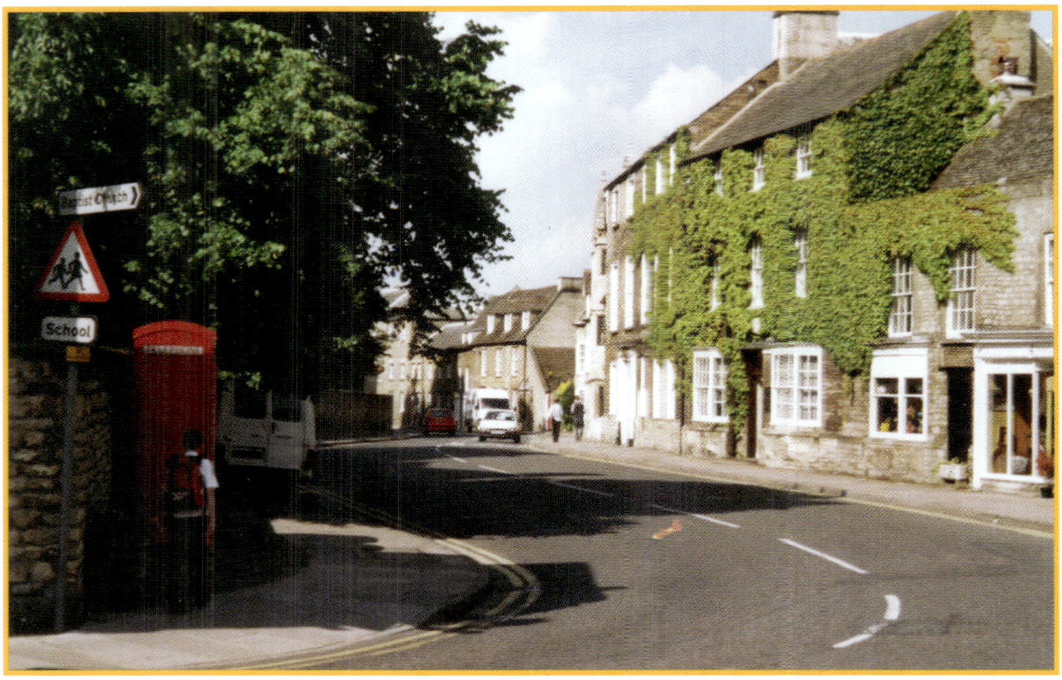

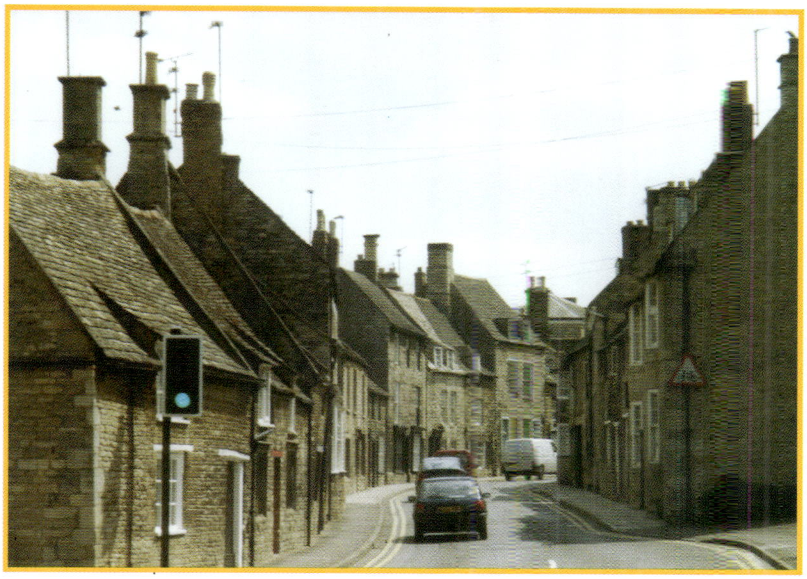

Further views of North Street, the old main street in Oundle. Hidden behind number 7 is one of only two thatched cottages left in Oundle. In common with many of Oundle's buildings most roofs are of Collyweston Slate - thin limestone slates each held by a single peg to wooden laths.

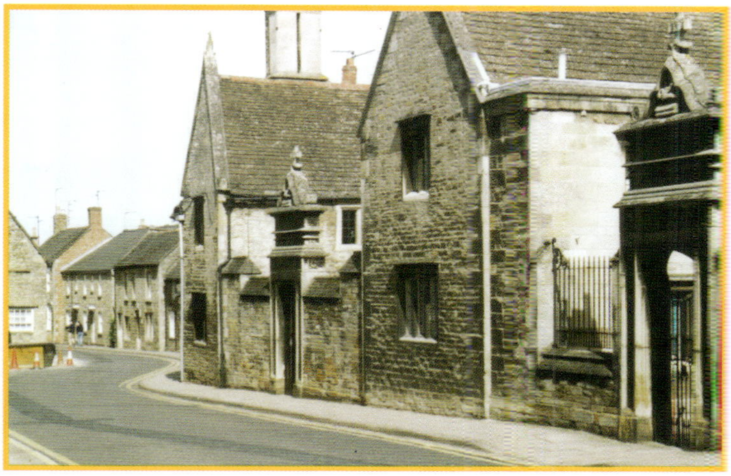

Latham's Hospital (left) is an early seventeenth century building much of which has been added to as the years have progressed. The two courtyards are entered by stone gates decorated above by the symbol of Christ, a cross and a pelican on her nest. The north courtyard still has the original high wall and was once a Blue Coat School and an almshouse - today it is still an old people's home. Laxton's was originally a hospital and school. Below Laundimer House, one of fourteen boarding houses belonging to Oundle Public School.

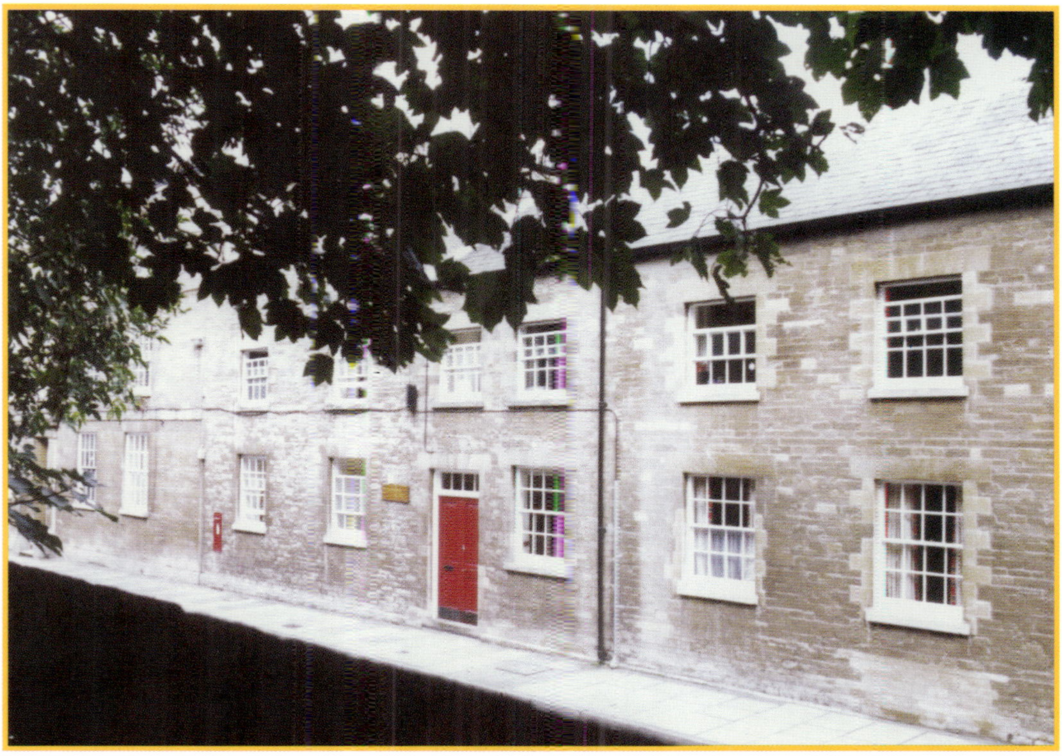

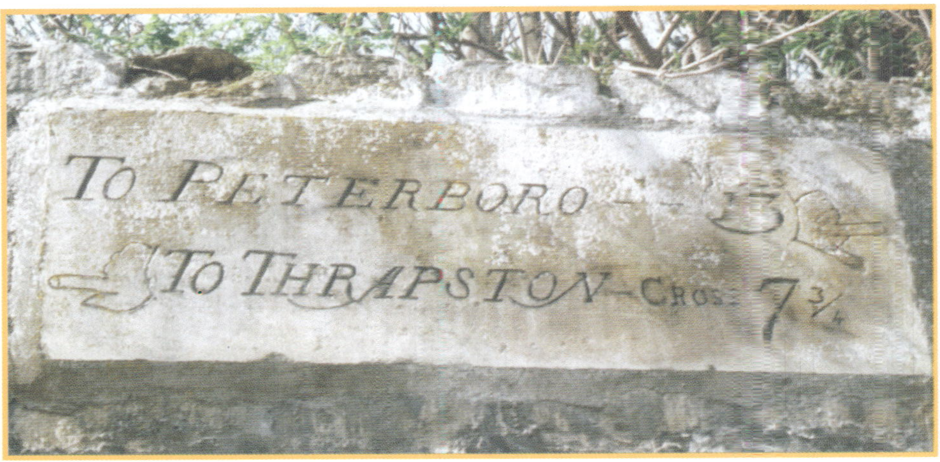

Left, a mileage indicator carved into the wall of the old rectory and opposite the Berrystead.

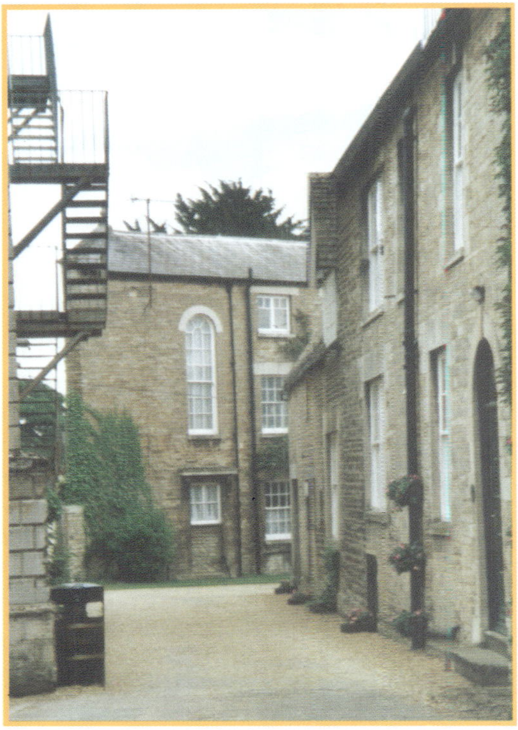

Two views of Duck Lane. Left, the Berrystead in the background, with the immediate building having an unusual counterbalanced fire escape, which stopped at the first floor level. Only with the weight of the escapees would it touch the floor! Below a further view of Duck Lane from the gates to the Gascoigne building. St Peter's churchyard is adjacent.

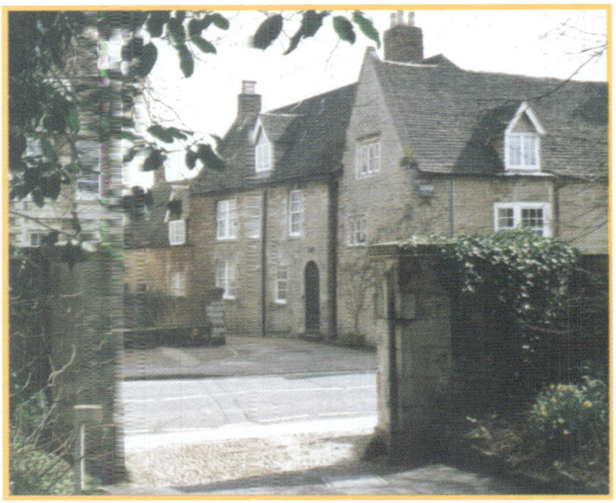

Below, Laxton with the replica long room (furthest away). The building beyond the tree was once one of Oundle's many inns. Perhaps this photograph will be remembered for the two old telephones, the type now rarely seen.

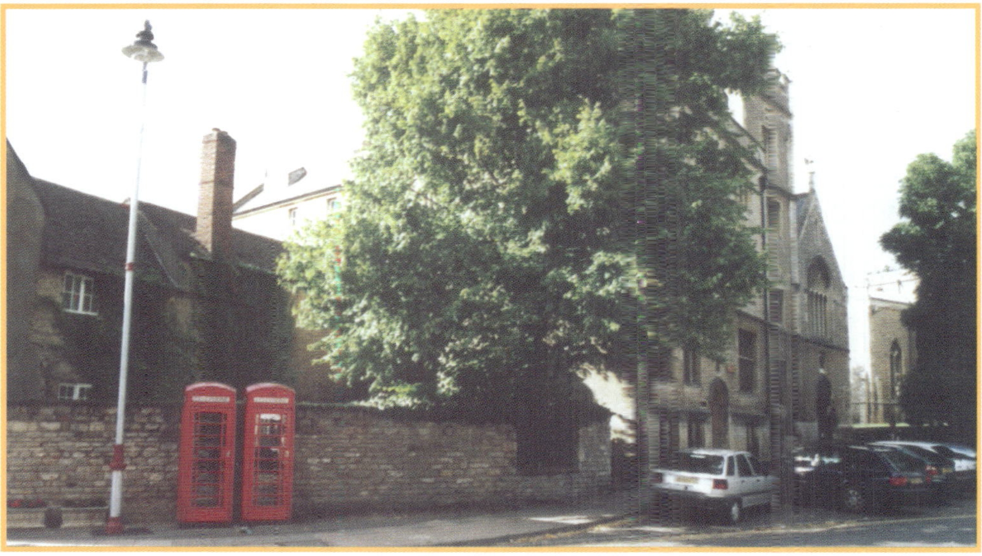

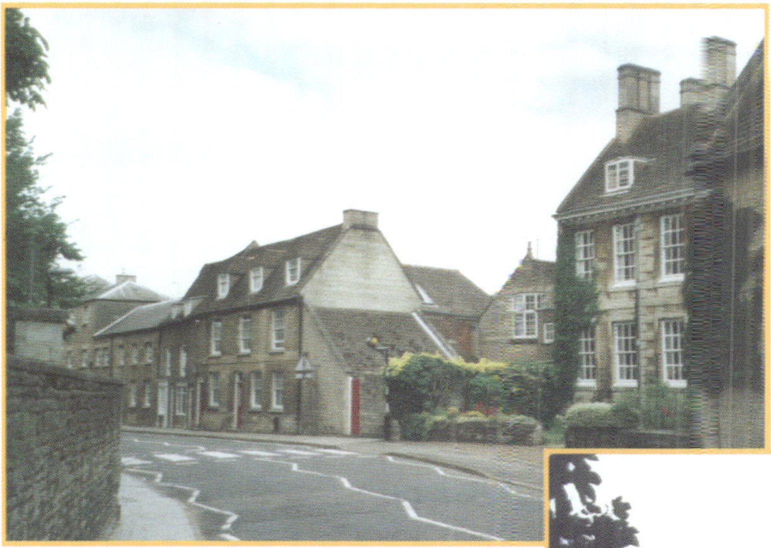

Two views, above and right, showing the unique town house the Berrystead. It was built in the late seventeenth century by the wealthy William Whitwell. The rear of the building used to be the front entrance and as such is equally imposing as the current view.
Below, the aerial view of the North Street area with the Berrystead dominating the centre and the Laxton Long Room and tower visible in the top left hand corner.

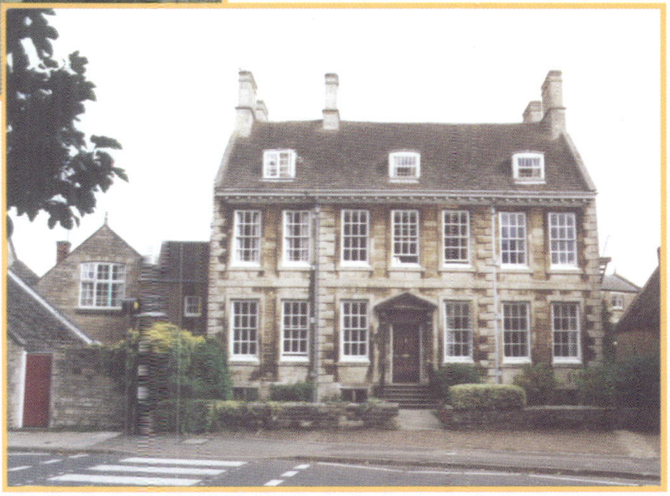

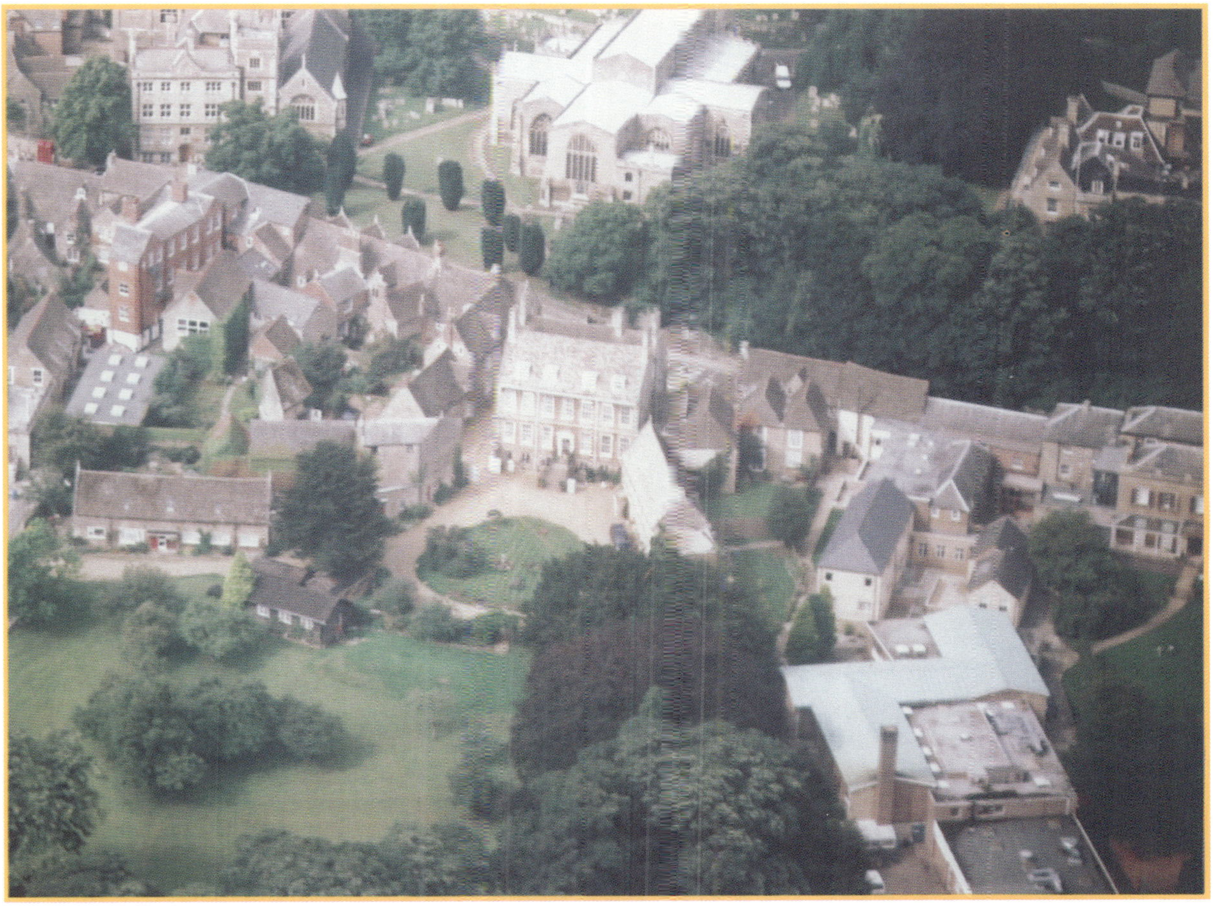

An unusual gatepost, right, at the end of the old Anglian Water property in North Street. O/R's directed, meaning "other ranks" to the Rectory, now the Gascoigne building of Oundle School. This was the wartime area base for the Royal Army Service Corps (RASC).

Below an aerial view of the town centre with Oundle Public School Cripps Library in the centre. The tower and spire of St Peter's Church can be seen because the dead walnut tree which used to obscure it has been cut down. The blue huts and cleared land near the top are the site of the new Laxton Junior School.

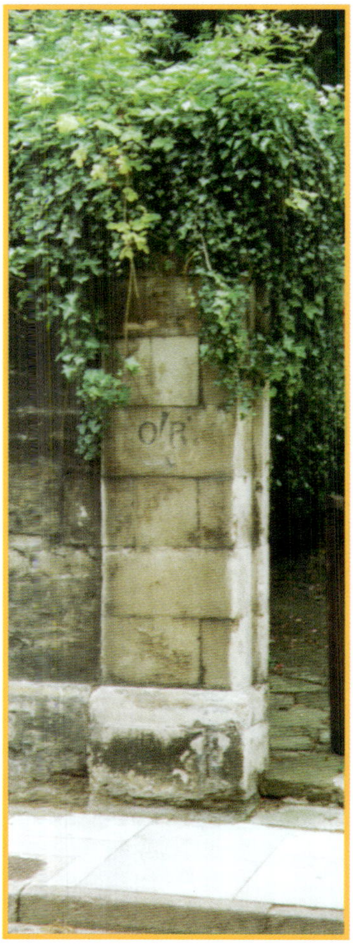

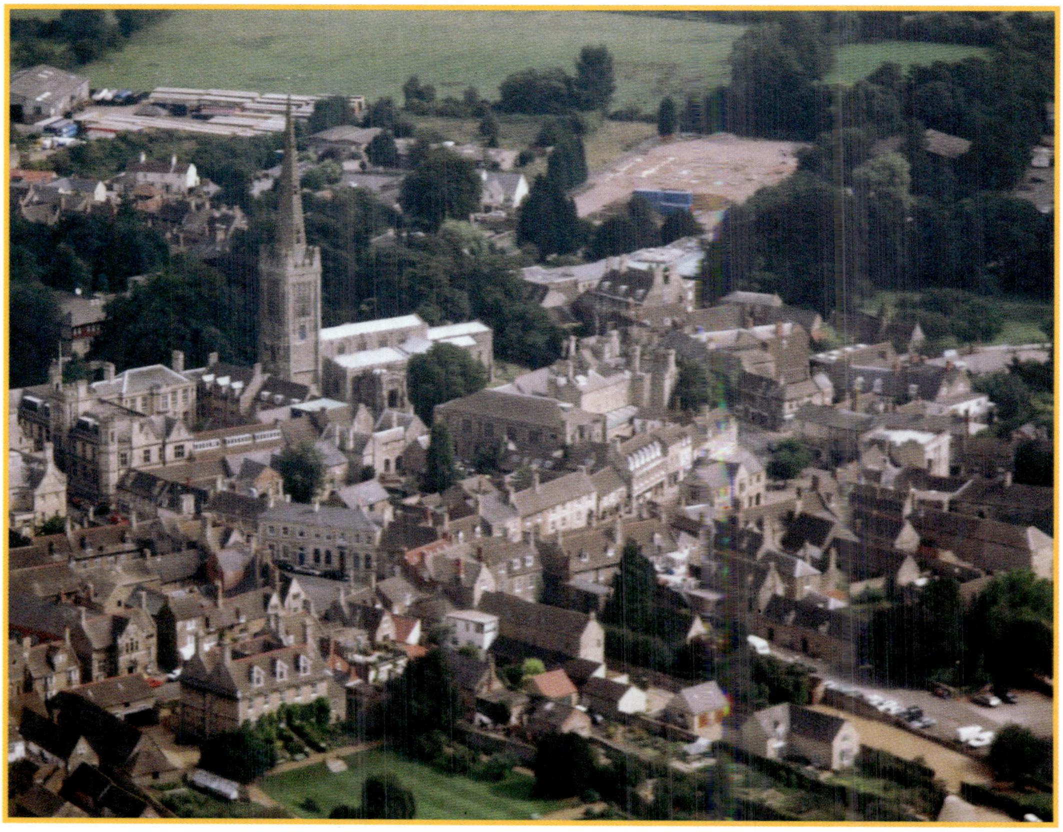

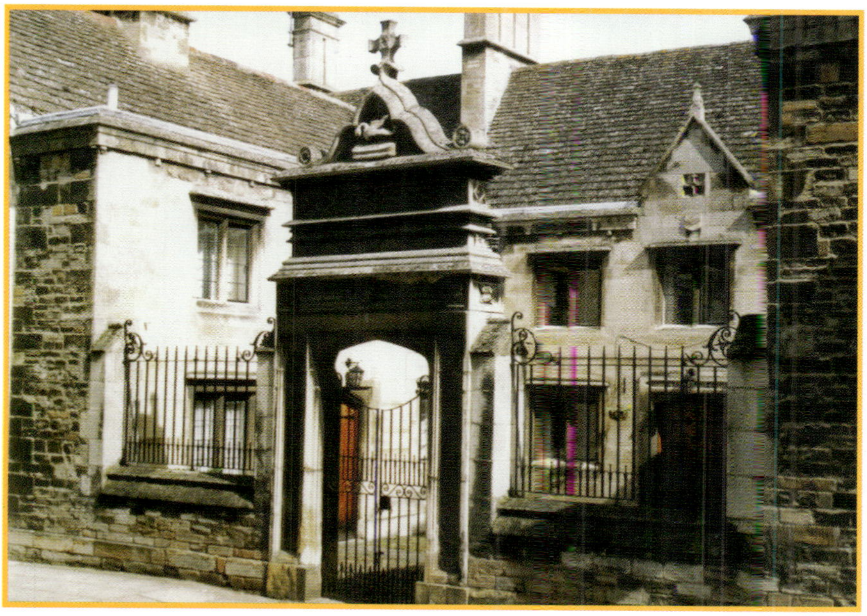

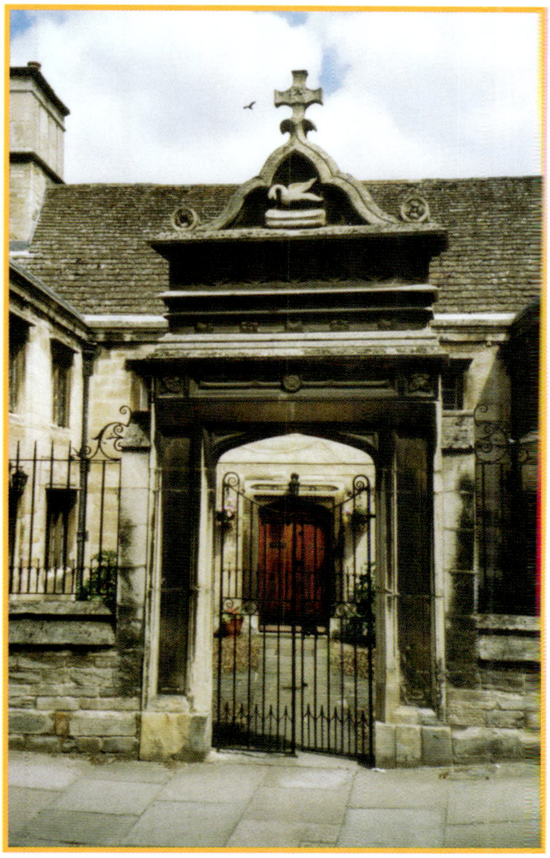

Three photographs showing Latham's Hospital. Two views of the front vividly show the cross of Jesus Christ adorning the top of the gate and the symbolic pelican on her nest which is also an old symbol of Christ.
Nicholas Latham founded an almshouse and Blue Coat School here in 1611 and the building is still used as a home for the elderly. Interestingly Latham also built further hospitals and schools close by at Barnwell (1607) and Weekly (1611). Below shows the rear of Lathams Hospital.

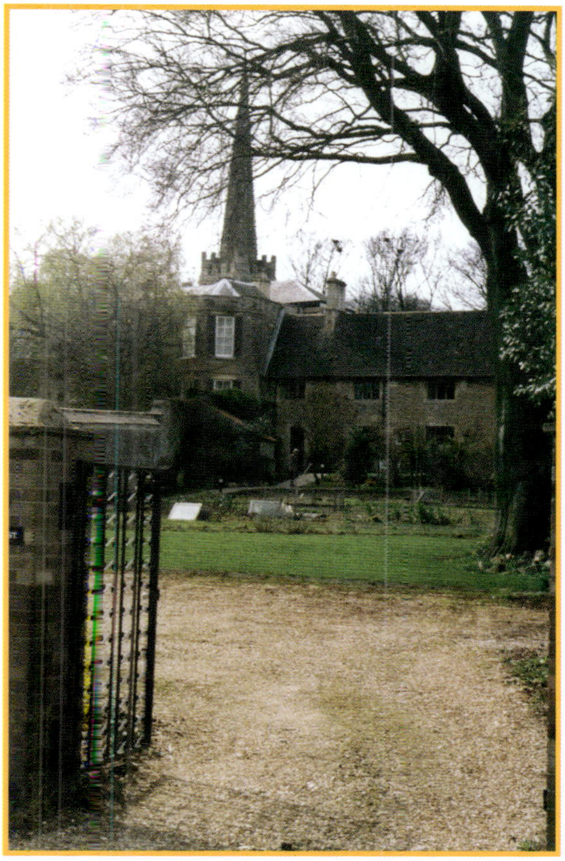

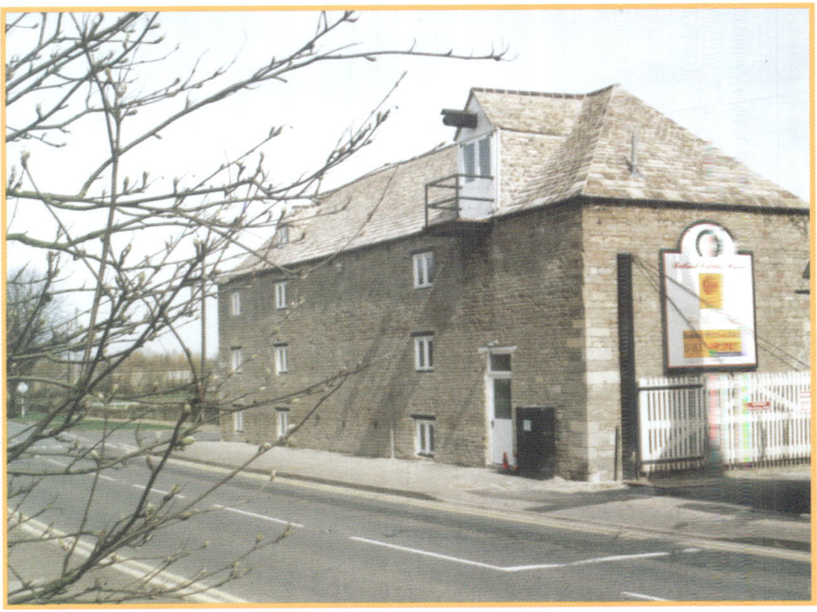

The site of John Smith's No 2 Brewery at the junction of east Road and North Street. This was formerly the base for Oundle School's Clerk of Works but has now been converted into dwellings. Smith's Brewery started in 1775 until 1955 when it was purchased by a company from Newark-on-Trent. In 1962 the new company merged with John Smith's Tadcaster Brewery Ltd, but although the name of the founder there was no family connection.

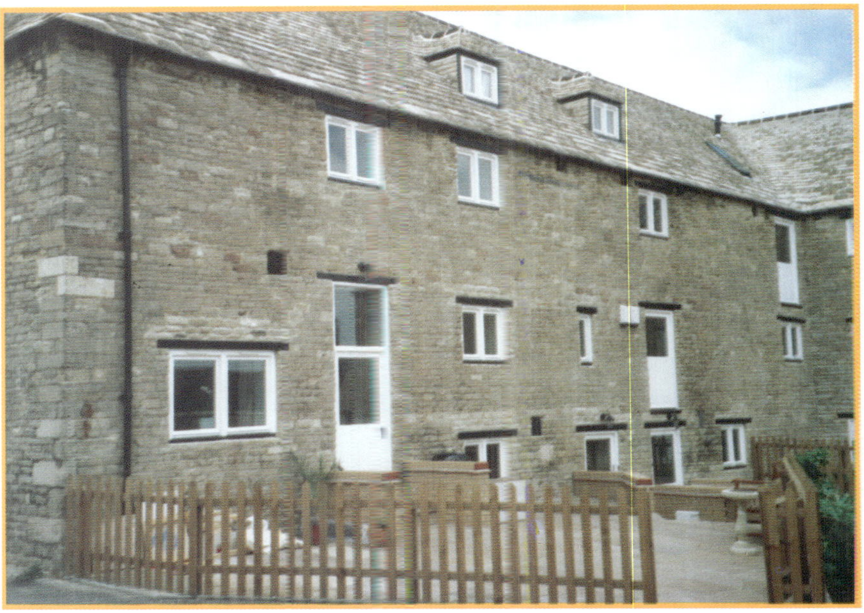

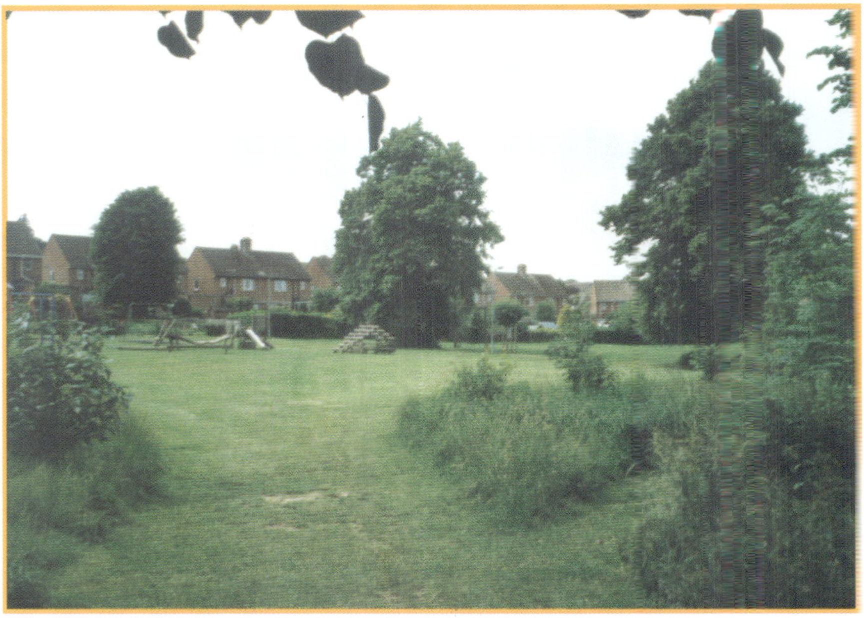

Oundle's Pocket Park off New Road and Gordon Road. Pocket Parks have been encouraged and developed throughout the county during the nineties and provide local areas for recreation and habitat for flora, fauna and wildlife.

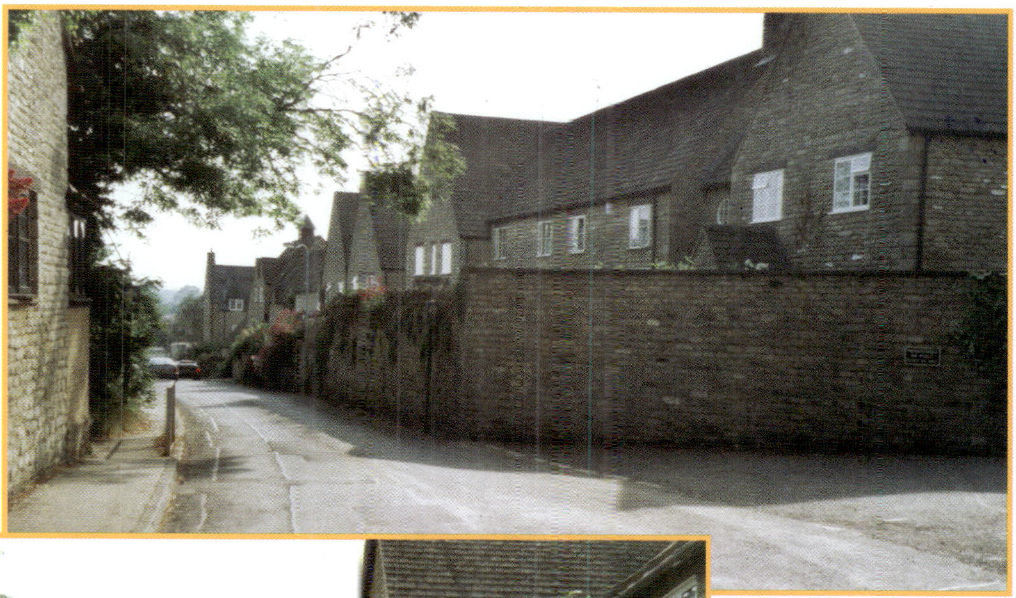

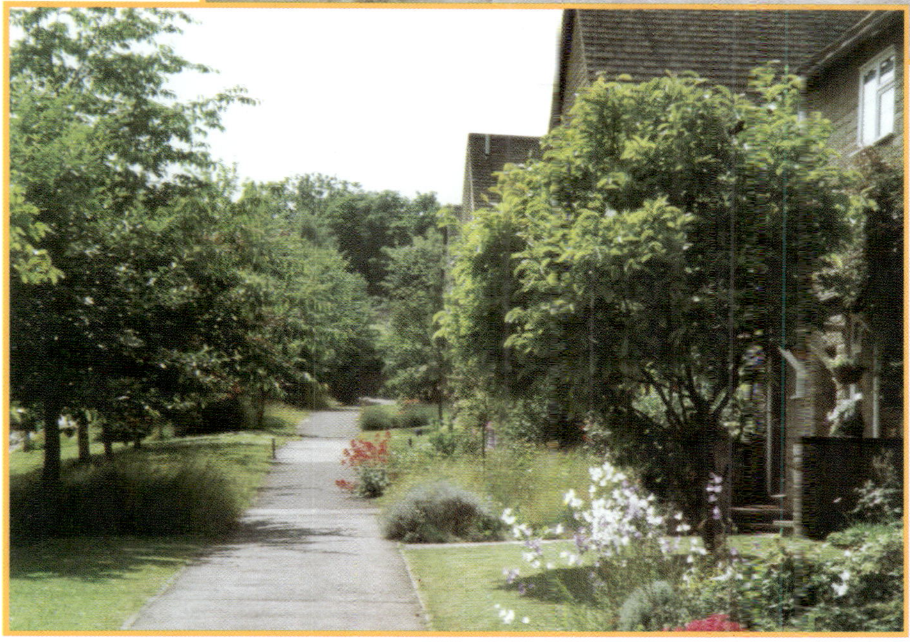

Blackpot Lane seen from outside the Oundle Public School car park. Few newcomers to the town could guess at the origin of its name, caused by the heavy industrialisation in the nineteenth century. A gas works and John Smith's main brewery were in the street of attractive housing and leafy gardens

A clock on the garage of 'Gardenways', a private house in Blackpot Lane.

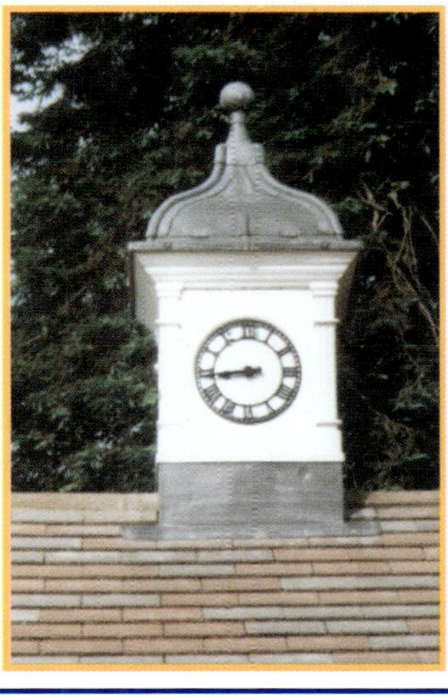

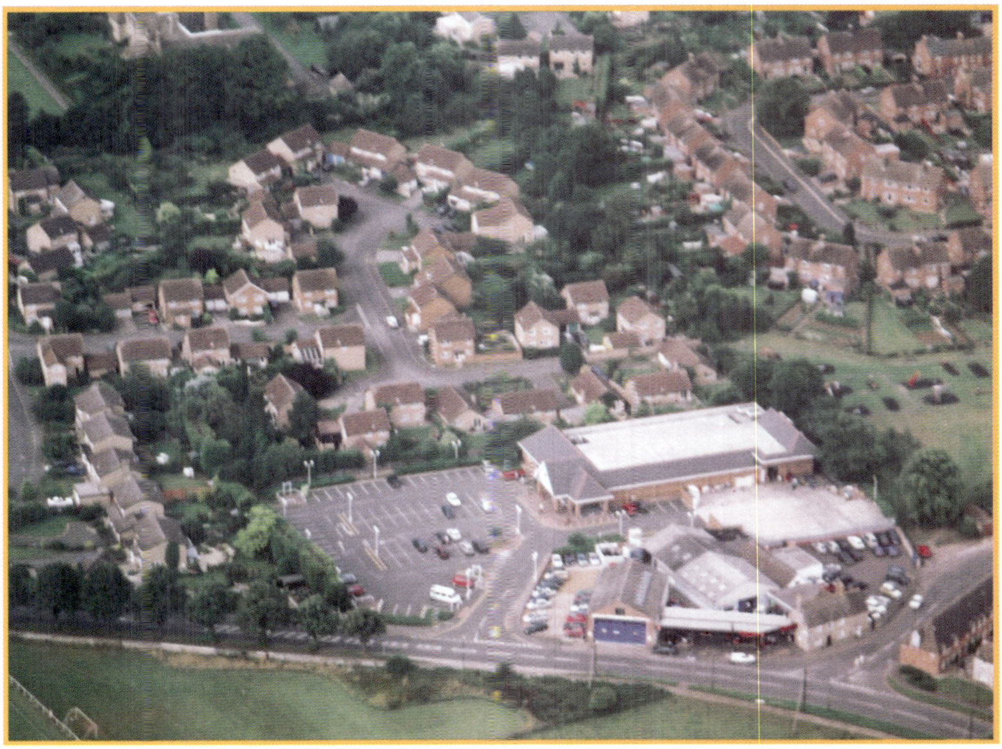

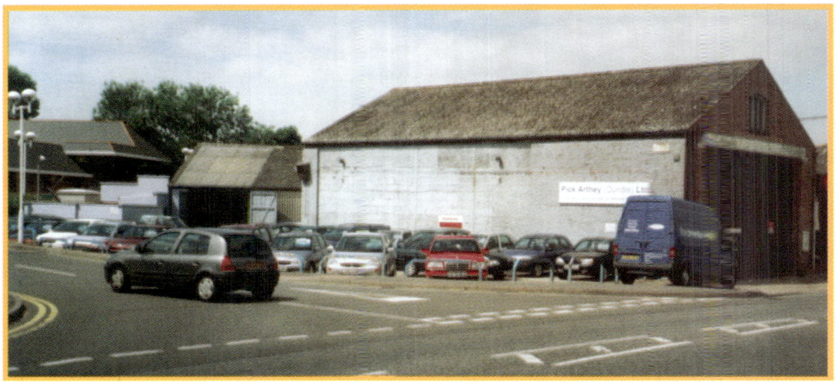

The commercial area of Oundle includes Oundle's Bus Garage (left), a supermarket now in St Osyths Lane with the Cooperative Store (below) closing mid 2001 and the filling station currently remaining!

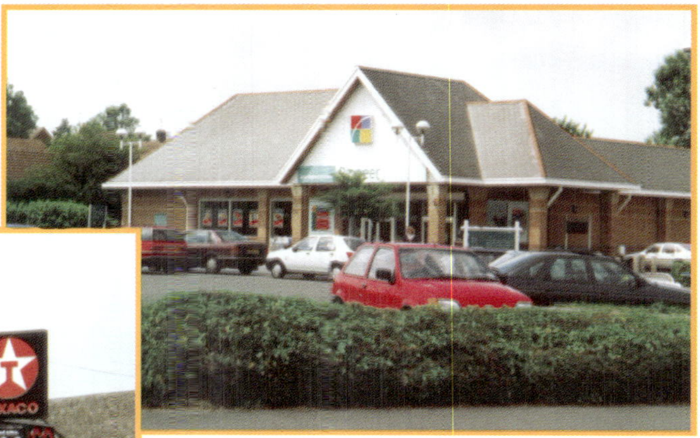

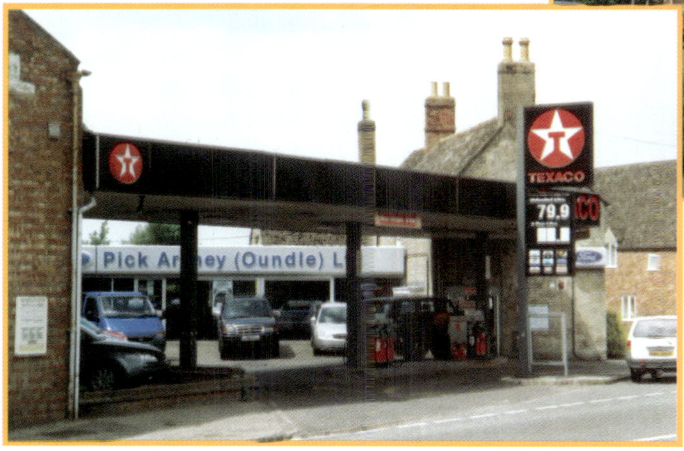

Occupation Road, right, is the home to Oundle tennis, bowling and rugby clubs.

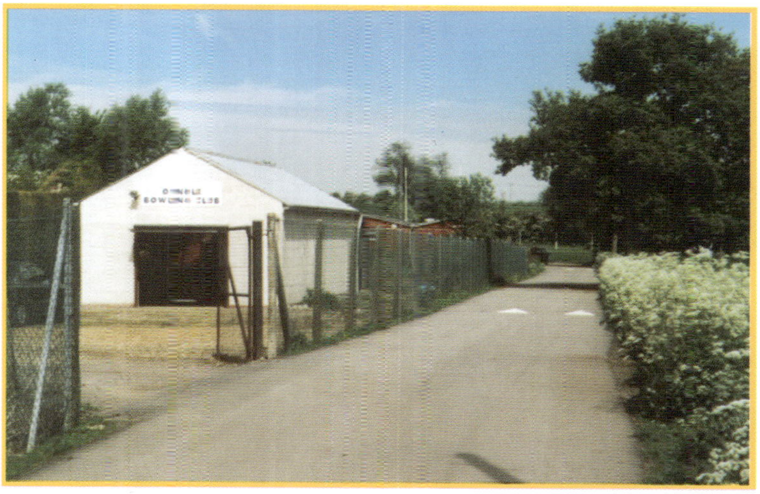

Throughout the country there has been a variety of housing development over the last decade, two photographs show sheltered housing developed at the corner of New Road and North Street.

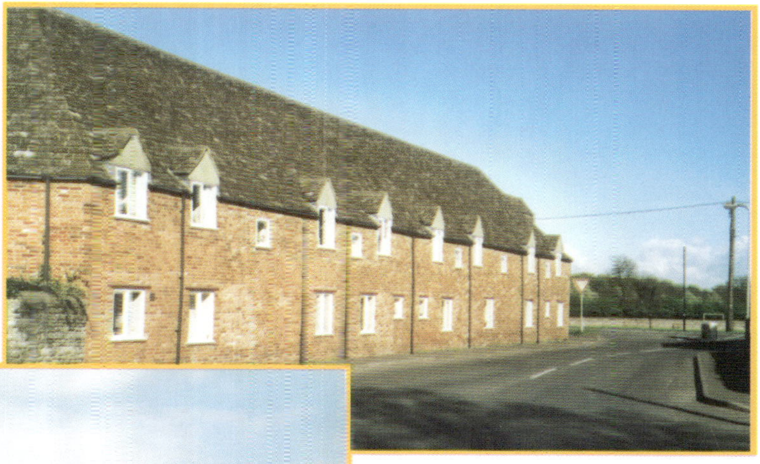

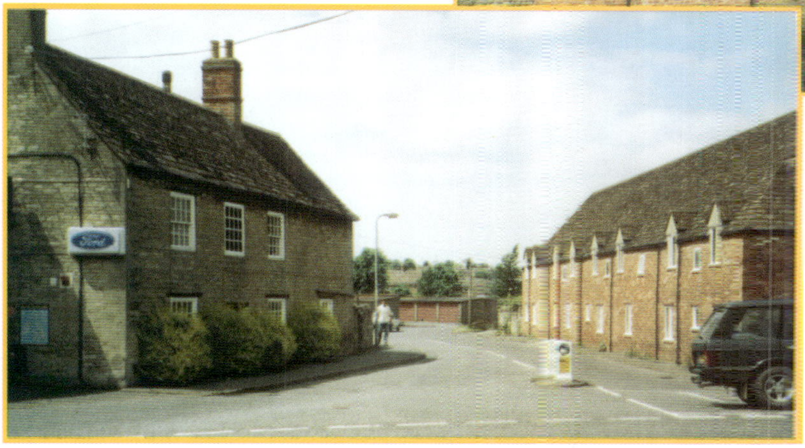

Below, Station Road from the junction with New Road.

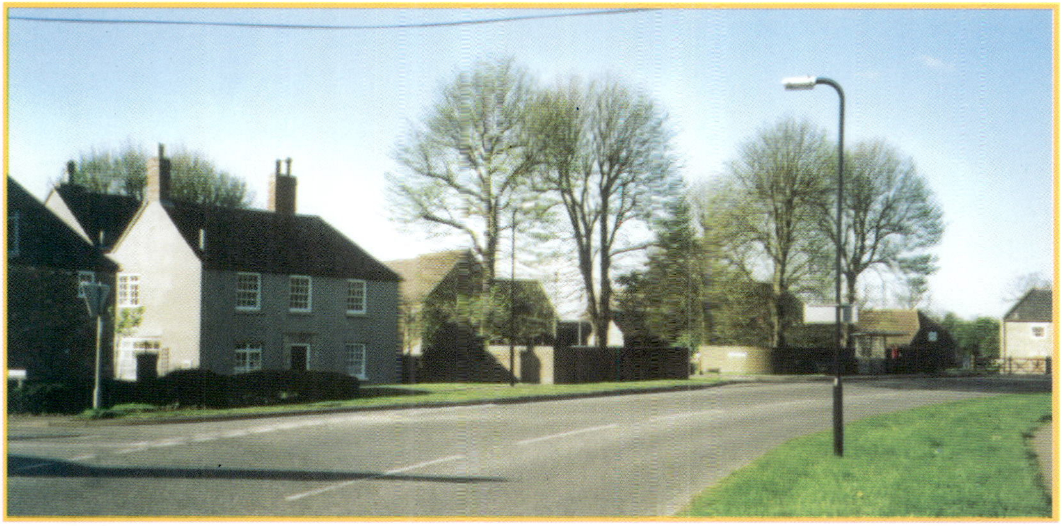

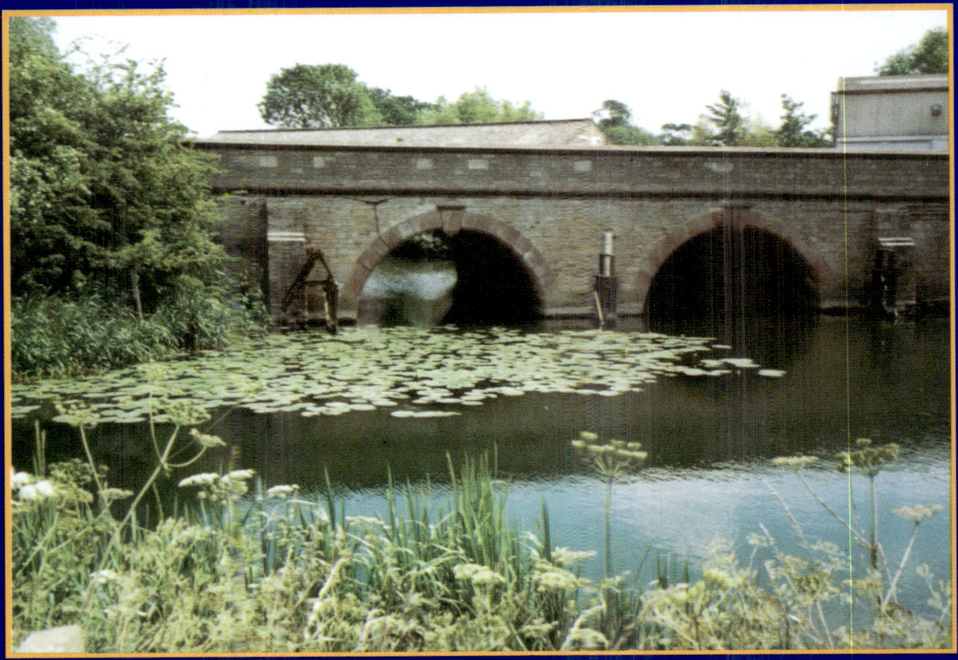

North Bridge and the River Nene

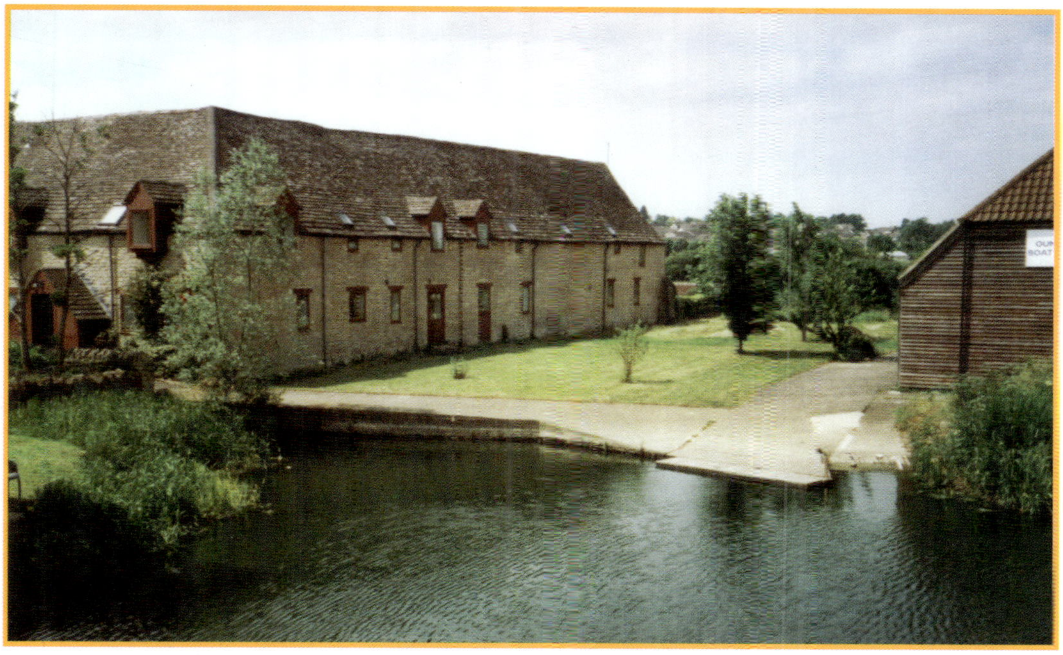

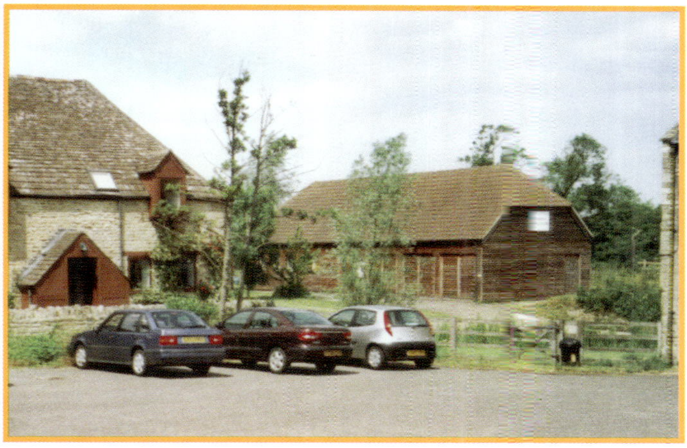

Views along Station Road and close to the North Bridge. The Old Maltings now converted to retirement homes and the slipway for the Oundle's boat club, with the boat house on the right of the photograph above. The centre picture shows a fuller view of the boat house and below farmland opposite the Old Maltings.

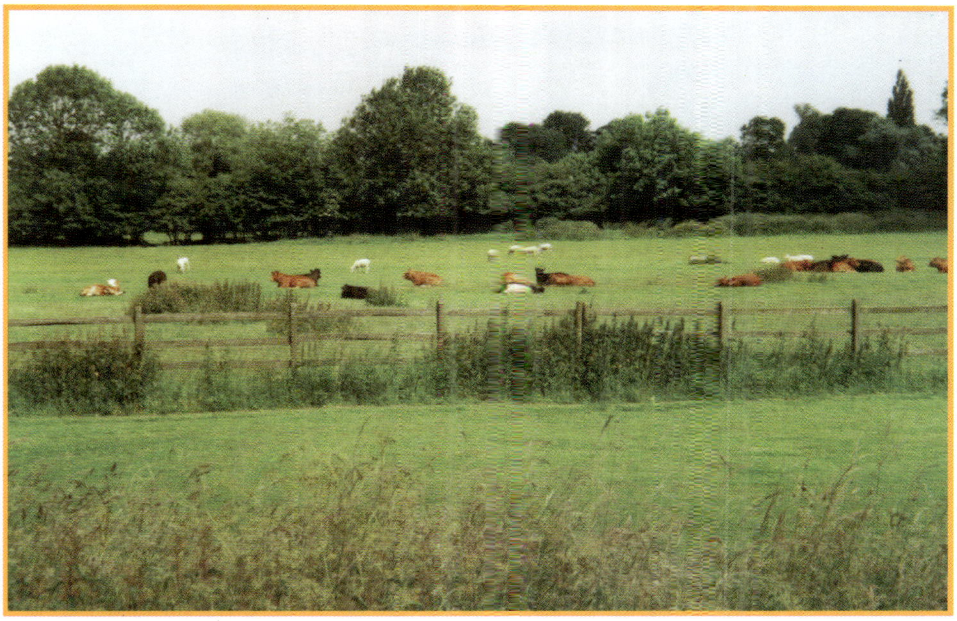

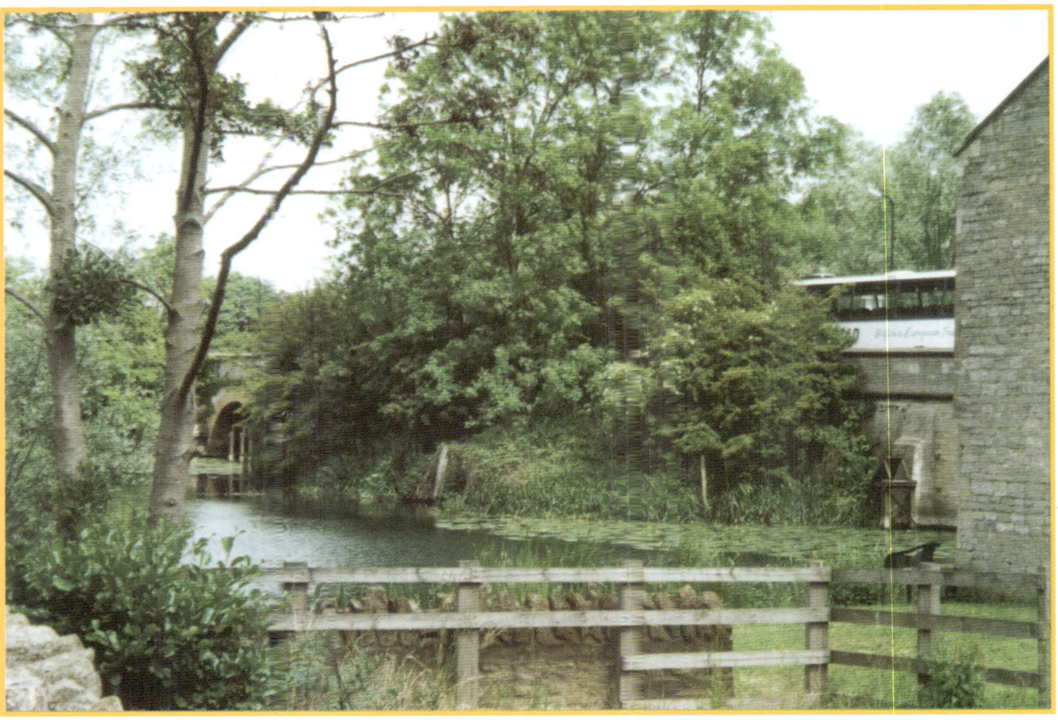

Further views of the medieval North Bridge, including the renovated foundation stone. The bridge was rebuilt after destruction by the floods of 1570. There are actually two bridges with separate inscriptions. The nearest to the town reads:

IN
THE YERE OF
OVRE LORD 1570
THES ARCHES WER
BORNE DOWNE BY THE
WATERS EXTREMYTIE
IN THE YERE OF OVRE
LORD 1571 THEY WER
BVLDED AGAYN WITH
LYME AND STONNE
THANKS BE TO GOD

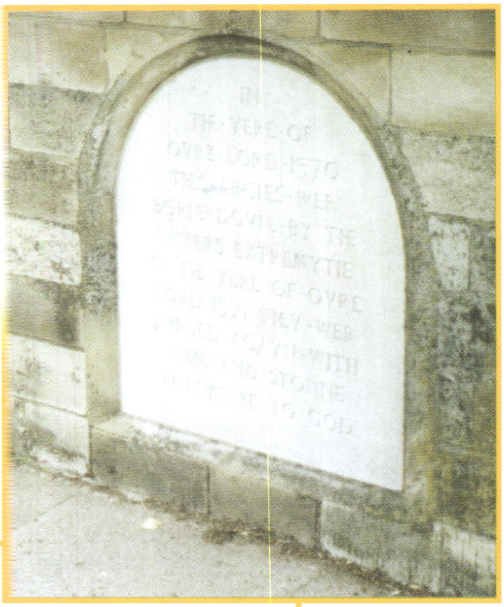

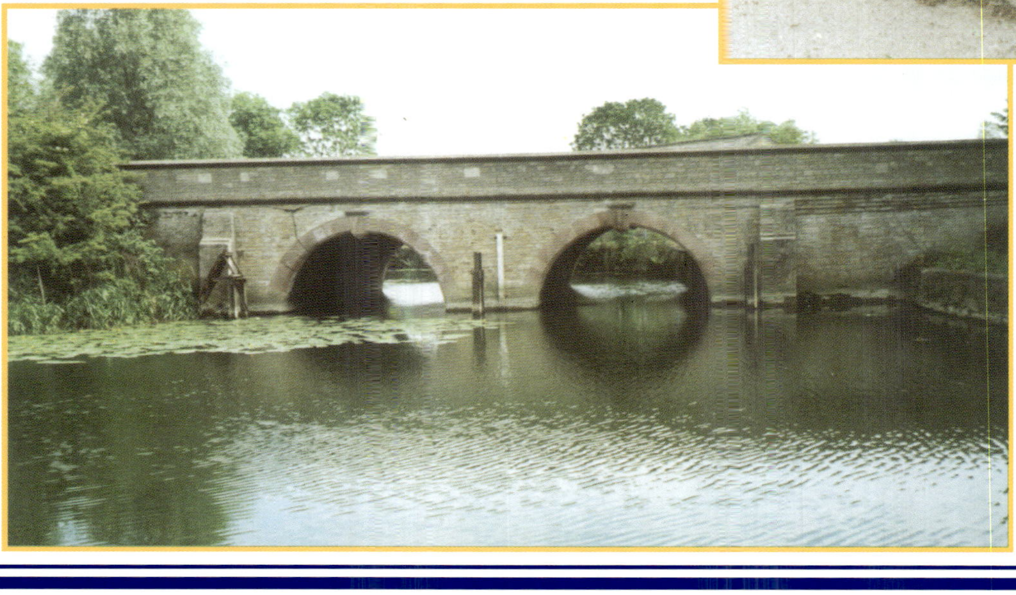

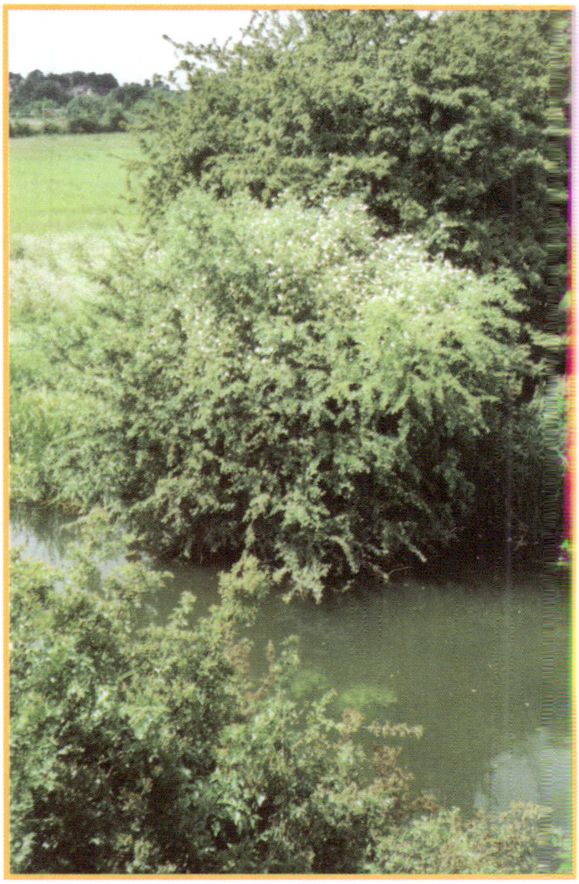

The River Nene has been the County's main waterway for centuries, although the Grand Union Canal has been an important routeway since the late eighteenth century. Approximately 10000 years ago, as the last Ice Age receded it left behind the familiar broad and fertile Nene Valley. Later, Saxon and Viking invaders navigated the river and settled nearby. By 1761 the was made navigable for commercial use, but this type of transport was never really viable for commercial use. So today we have the broad valley creating a beautiful tranquil setting where fisherman, canoeists, narrowboat owners and many others make use of its recreational facilities.

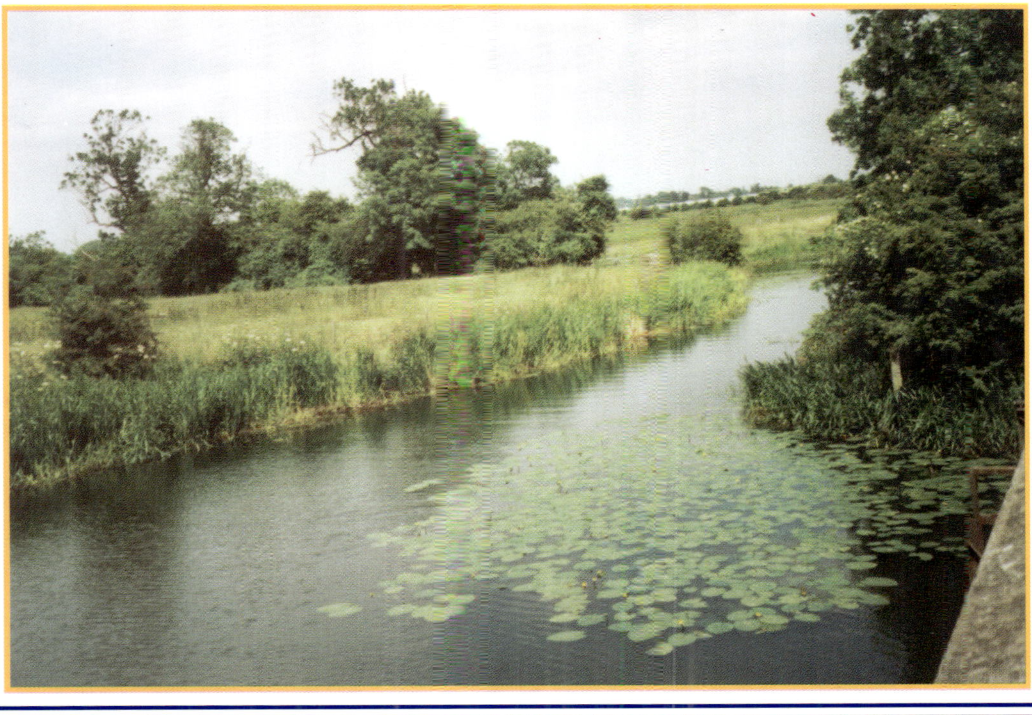

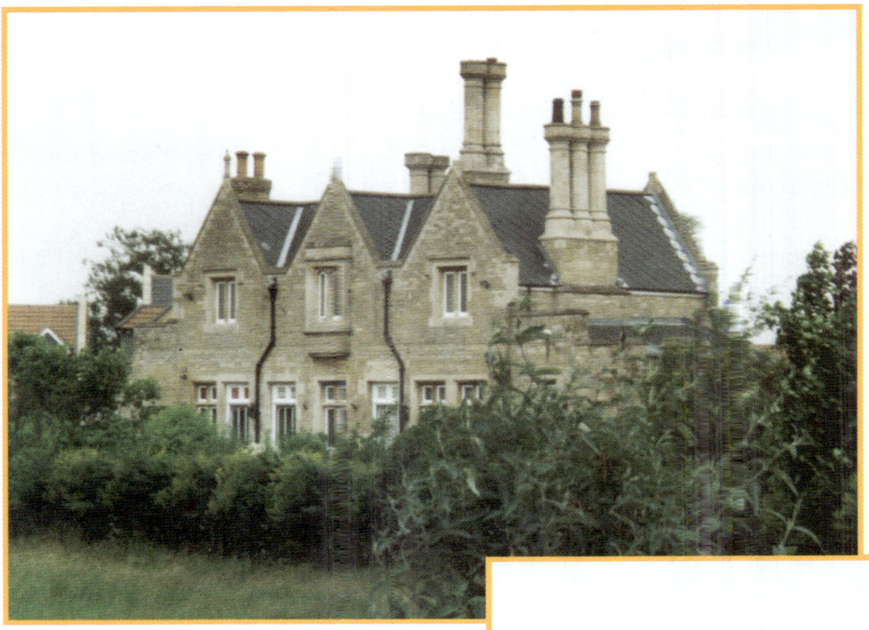

The London and North Western Railway (later the LMS) ran through the Nene Valley, roughly following the line of the A605 near Oundle. Built in local stone the old station (left) and the Riverside Hotel, below, which needs restoring are situated at the northern entrance to the town.

Though the canopy of the station has disappeared the line of it can be traced on the brickwork above. John Betjemen described it as, "one of the finest examples of domestic railway station architecture in England".
Built in 1845 the line closed in the 1960's.
Below the River Nene from the North Bridge and looking across the flood plain with the white flood level markers.

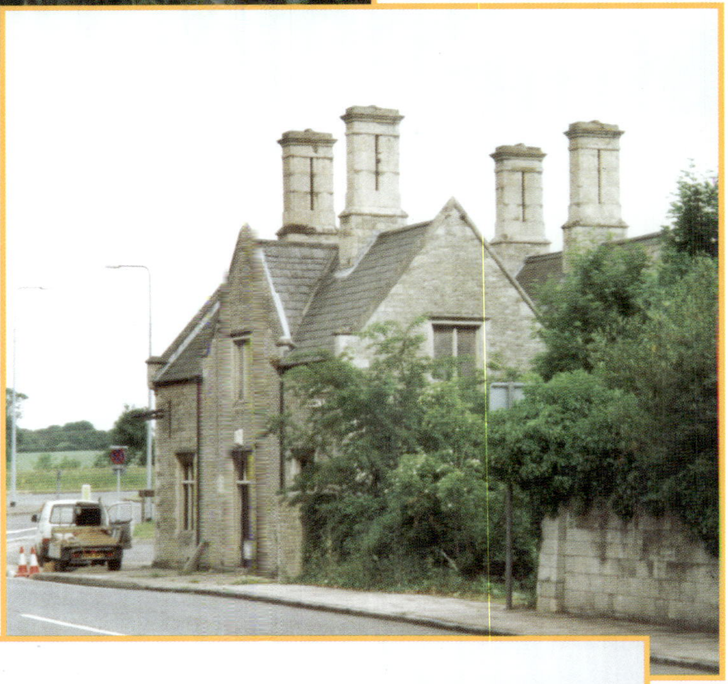

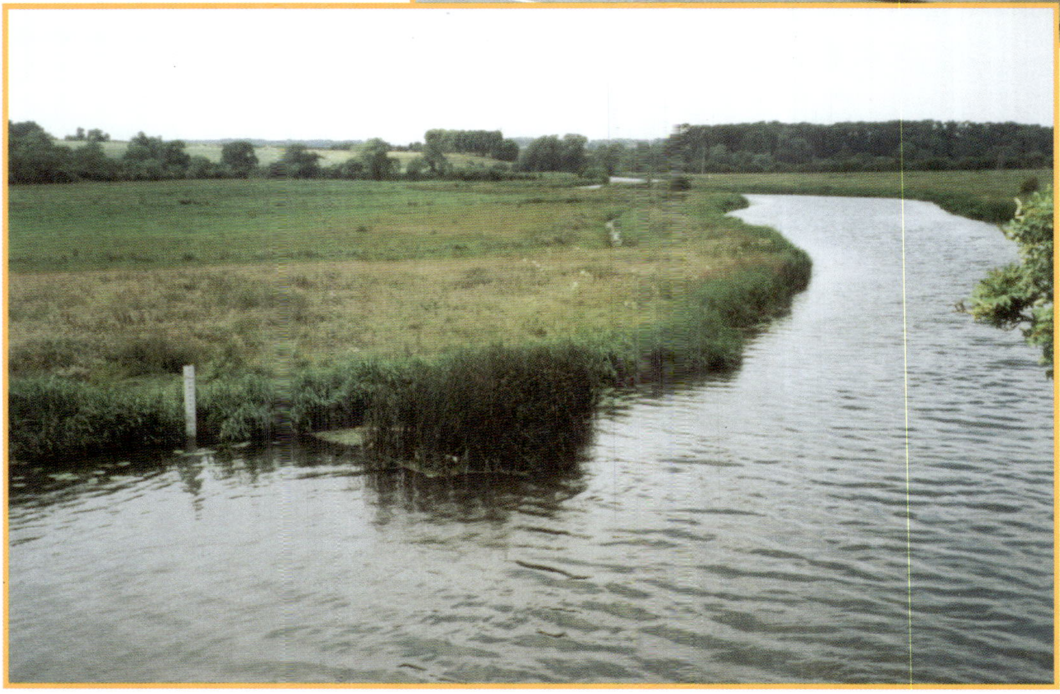

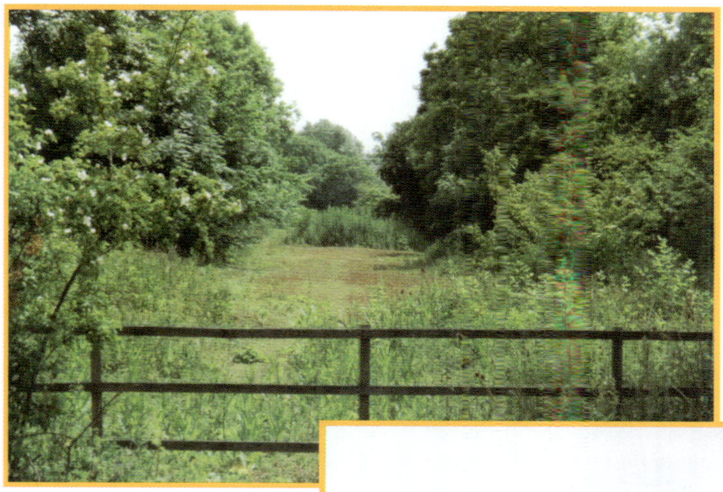

The course of the old railway, (left), runs directly behind the Riverside Inn (below).

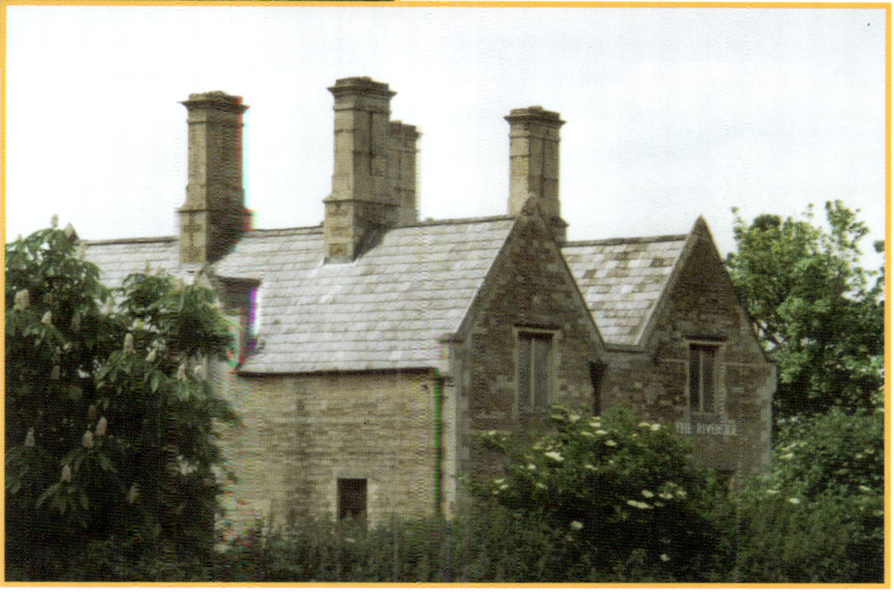

Below, a slightly hazy photograph of northern Oundle. The tennis courts and bowling green on Occupation Road are in the foreground. Glapthorn Road, is top right.

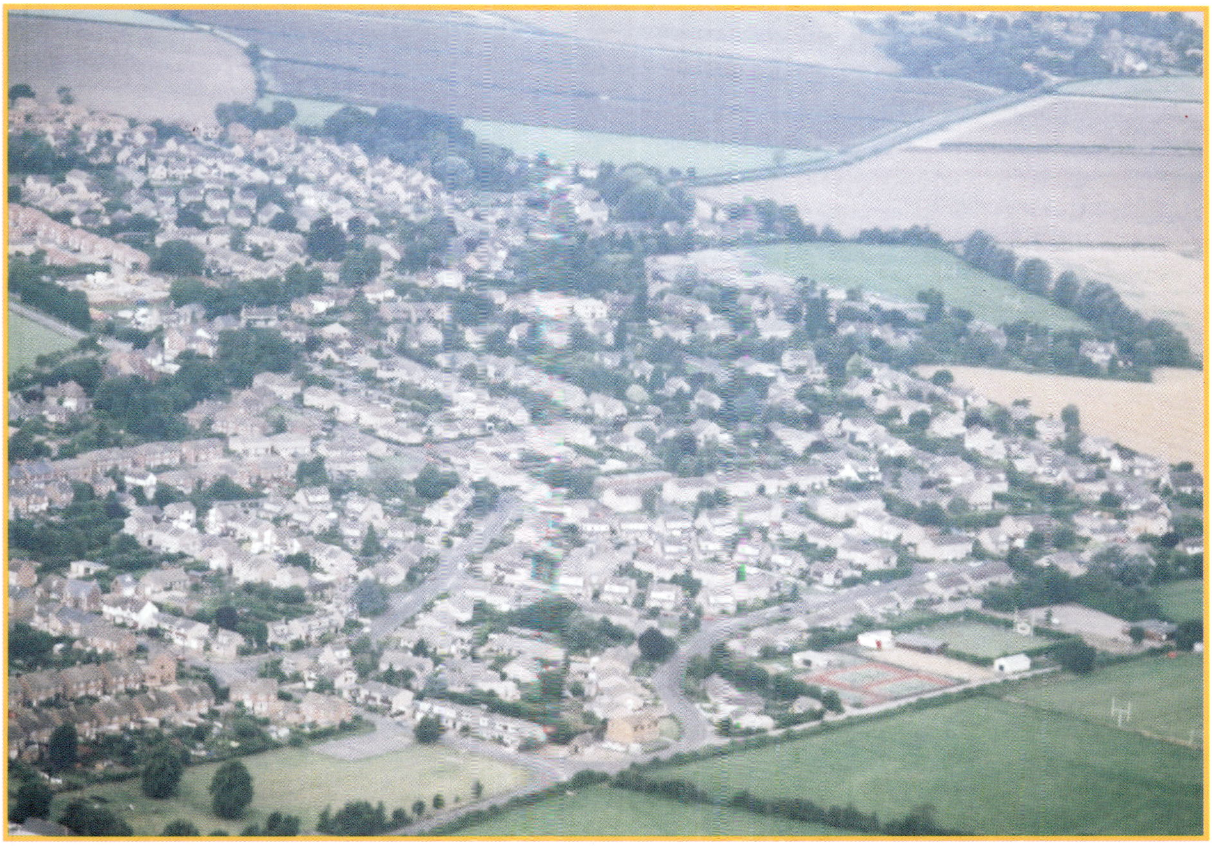

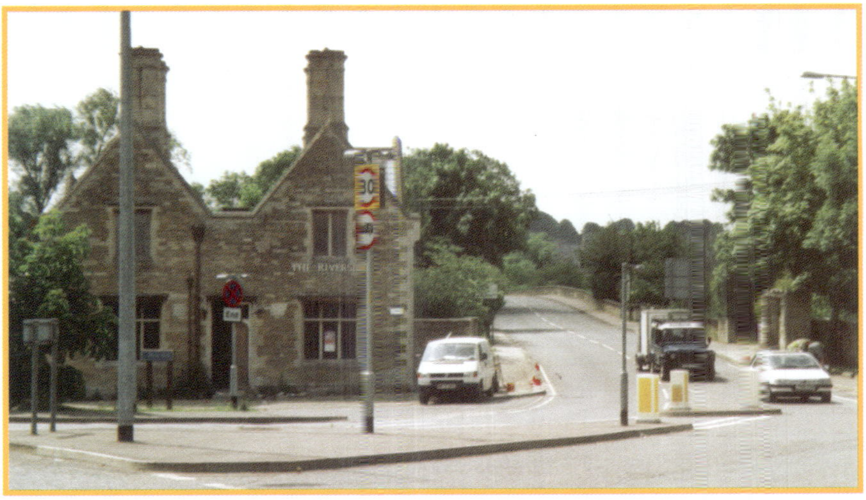

Left, the Riverside Inn and North Bridge viewed from the A605 roundabout.

Below, the Nene flood plain with the North Bridge in the background taken from the A605.

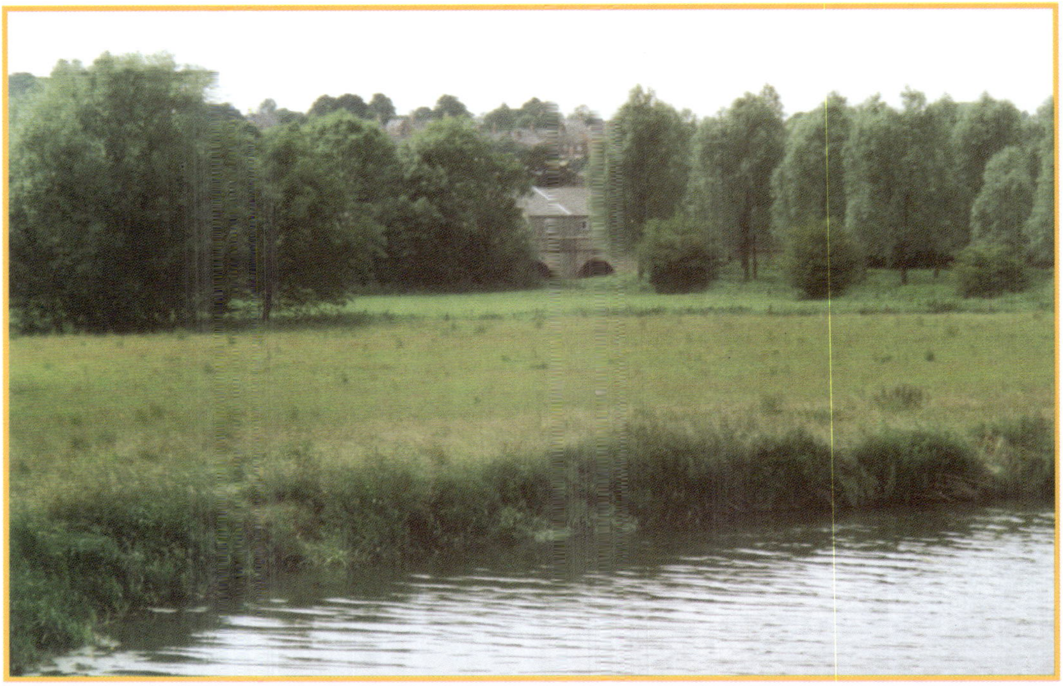

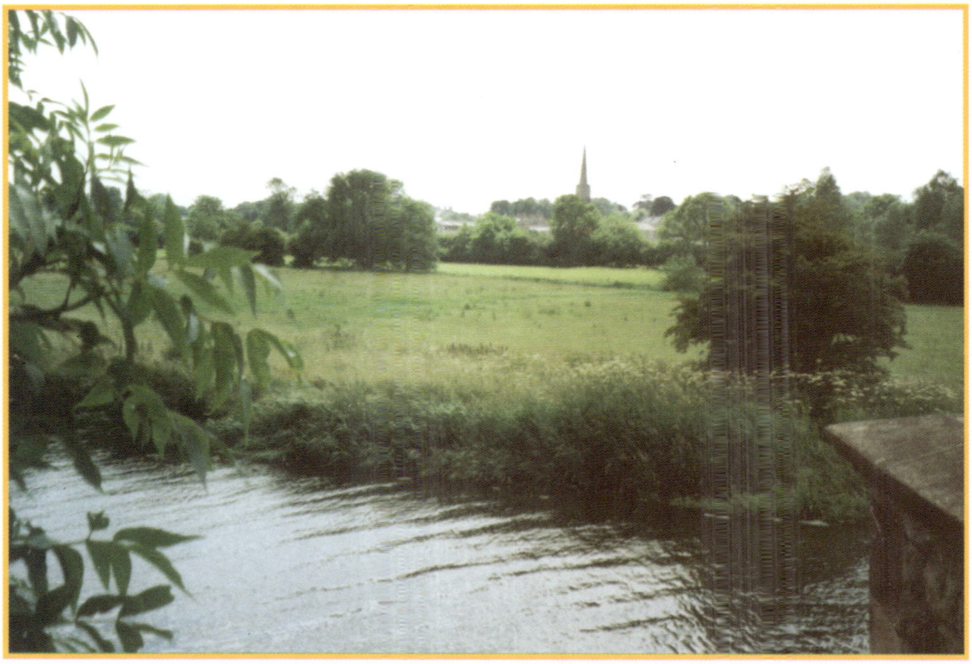

Left, a further view across the Nene flood plain and looking towards Oundle.

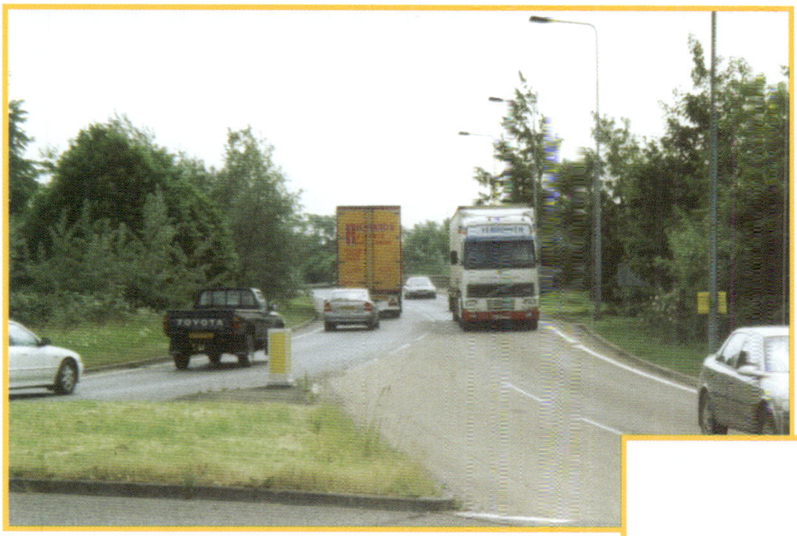

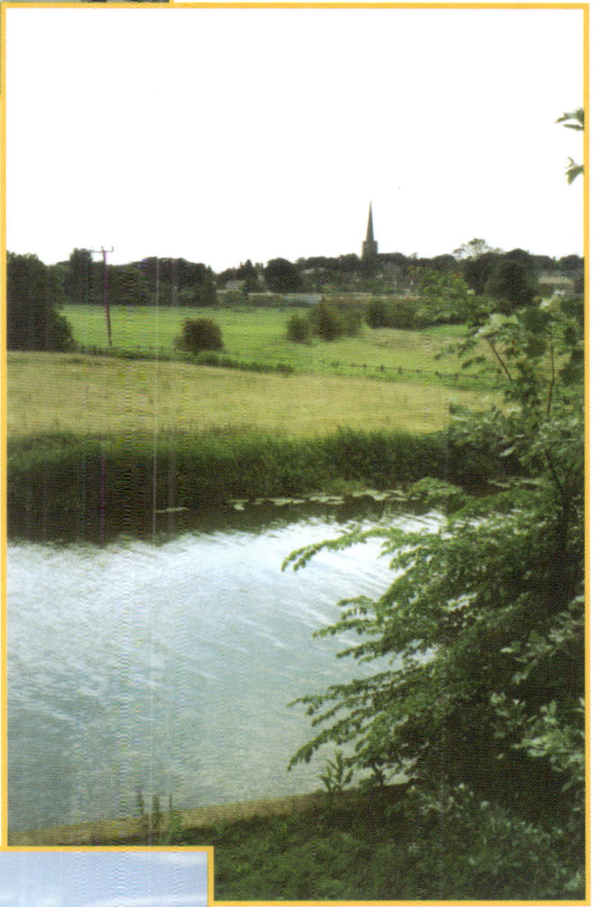

Above, looking south down the bypass from the roundabout on the A605. The road is continuously busy with a variety of traffic.

Right and below, two further views of the Nene flood plain - such a picturesque sight but can be a problem when the weather is continuously wet.

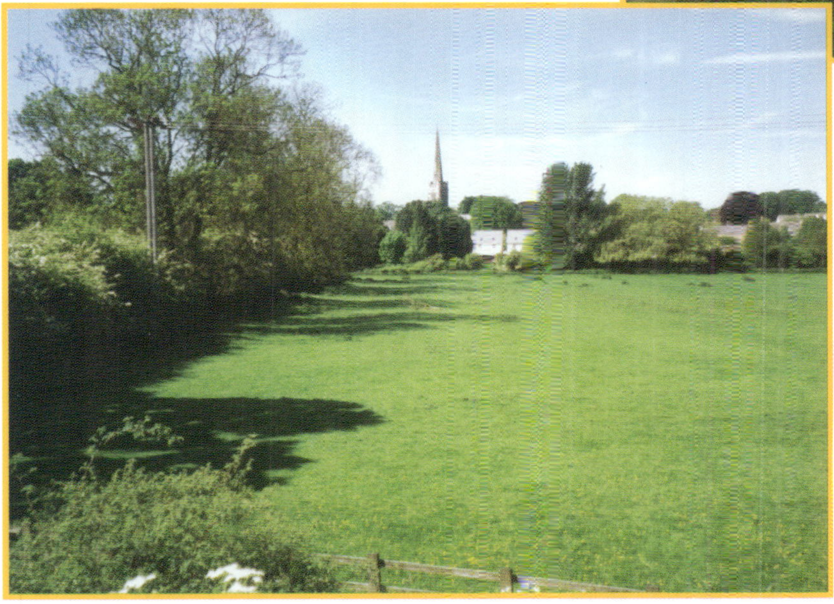

Oundle has been fortunate to have had a bypass built towards the end of the twentieth century and like many towns and villages business parks have been developed often close to such roads. Here are three photographs showing the Nene Valley Business Park. Offices include the Post Office and a yachting business, the latter no doubt complementing the marina situated close by.

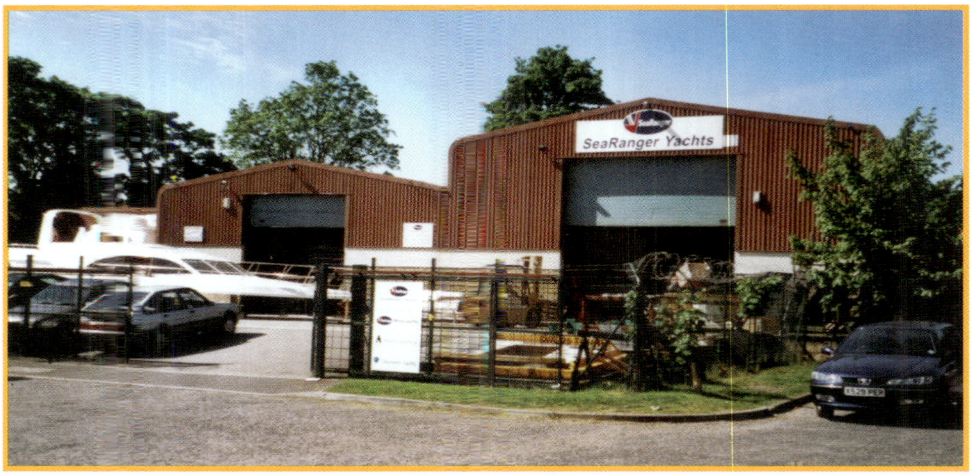

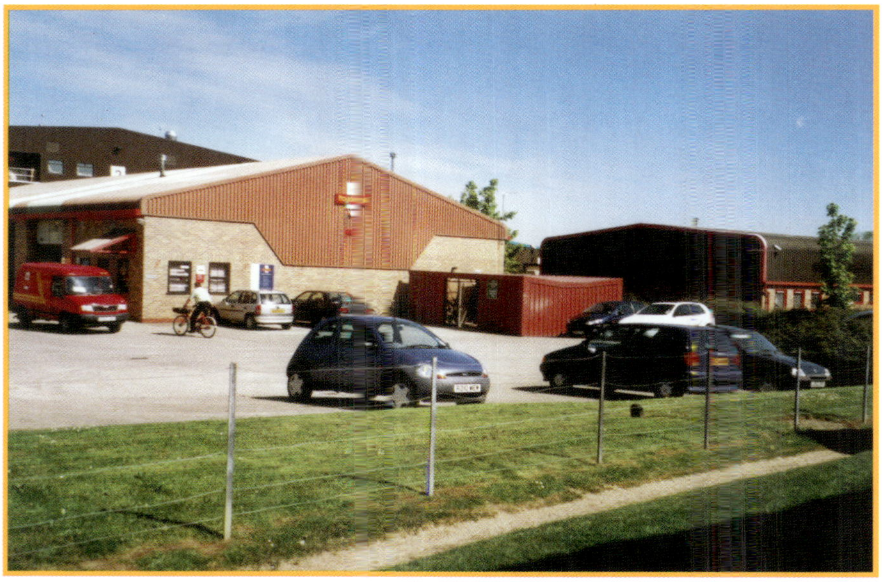

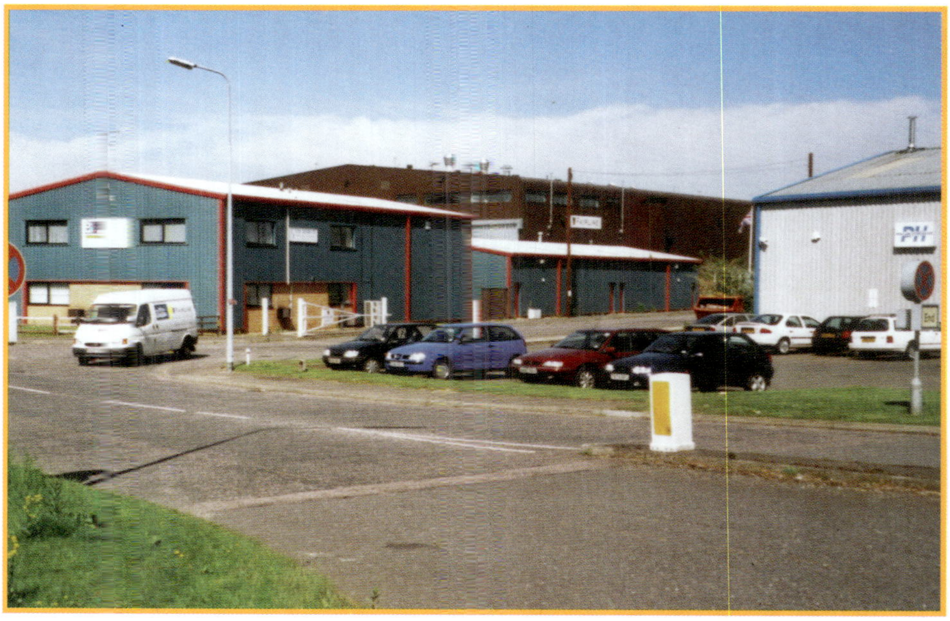

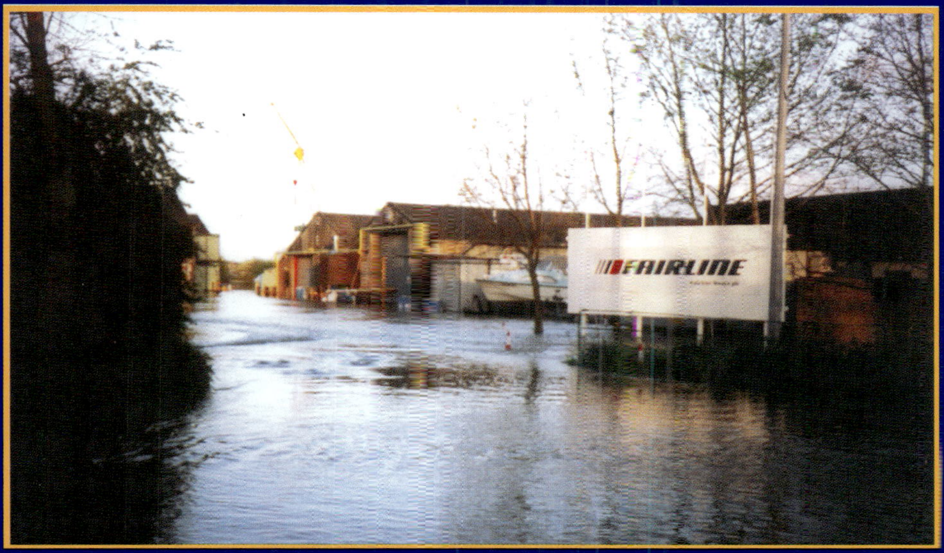

Easter Floods 1998

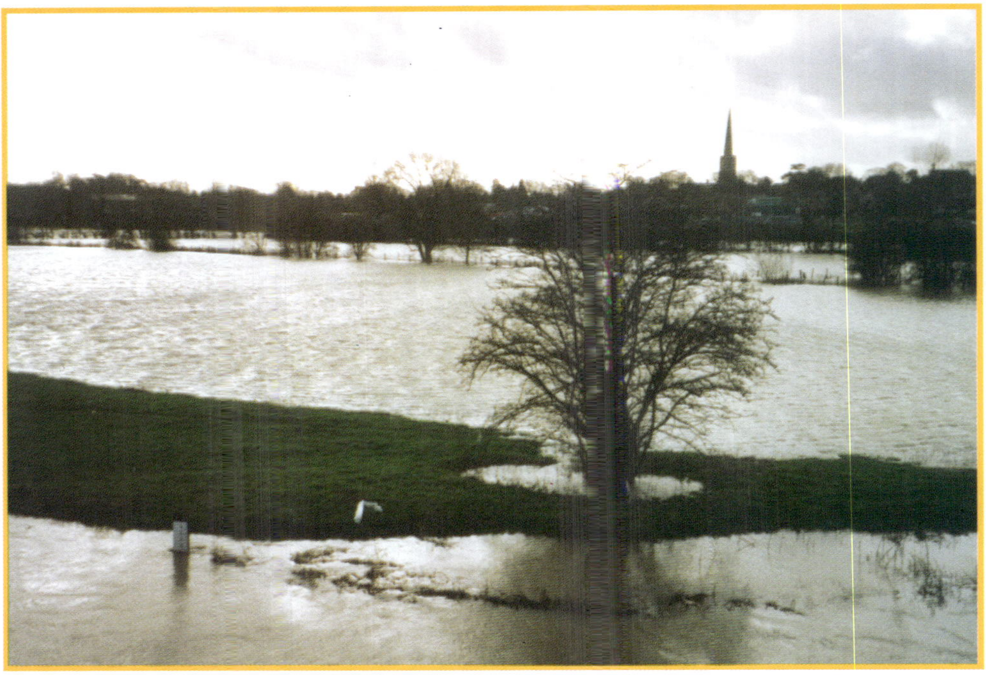

During Easter 1998 the Nene Valley suffered extensive flooding. The River Nene to the south of the town swelled to almost ten times its usual size!
Previous page. Fairline Boats situated on the Barnwell Road are one of Oundle's best known employers and sell all over the world. On this day the water came to them! The Nene was 15cm (6 inches) high as it ran through their premises.

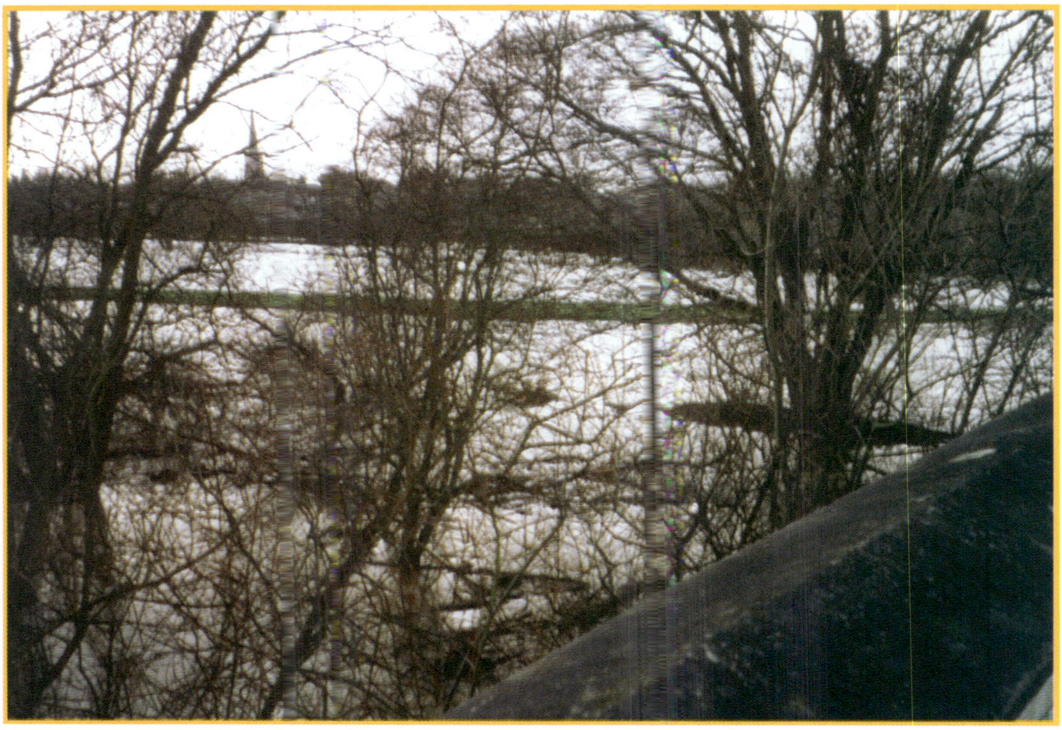

The two views show the flood plain with the town in the background. Look to see in the top photograph the white flood marker, which is considerably higher by 3-4 feet than the one shown previously in the book.

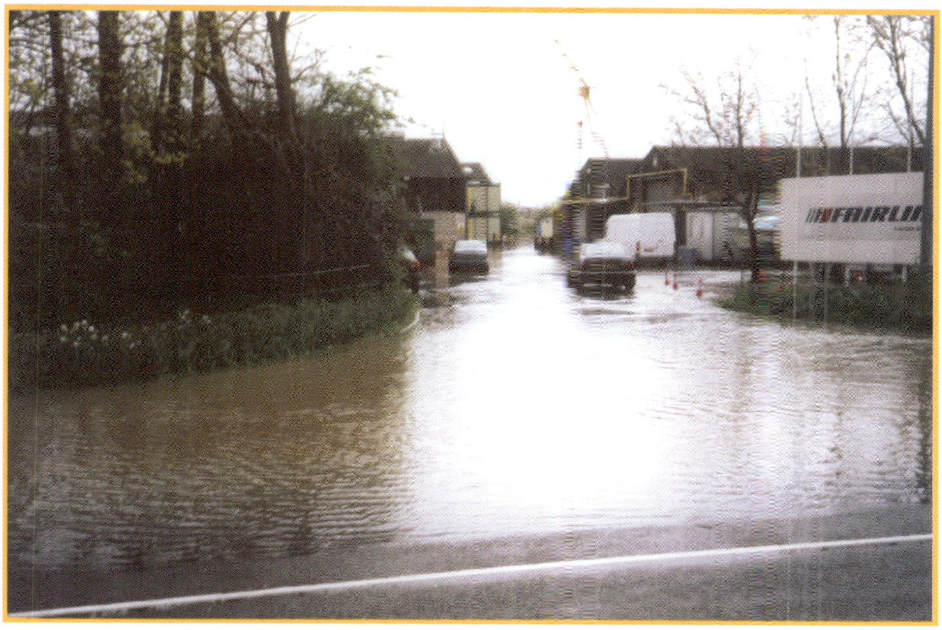

Left, the water at the entrance to Fairline Boats has subsided a little.

Below, the flood waters came to within one inch of the top step into the house at Riverside Maltings. Quite a scare for the elderly residents.

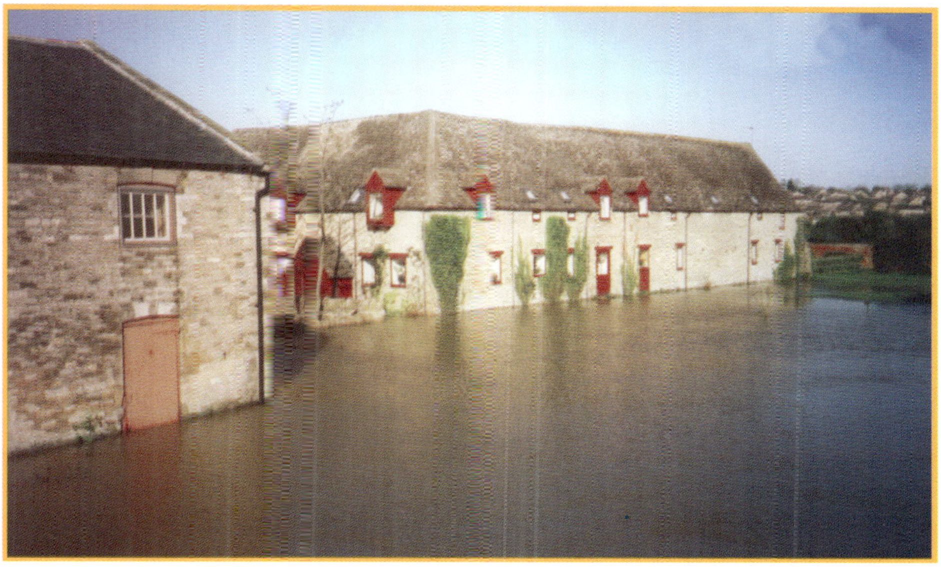

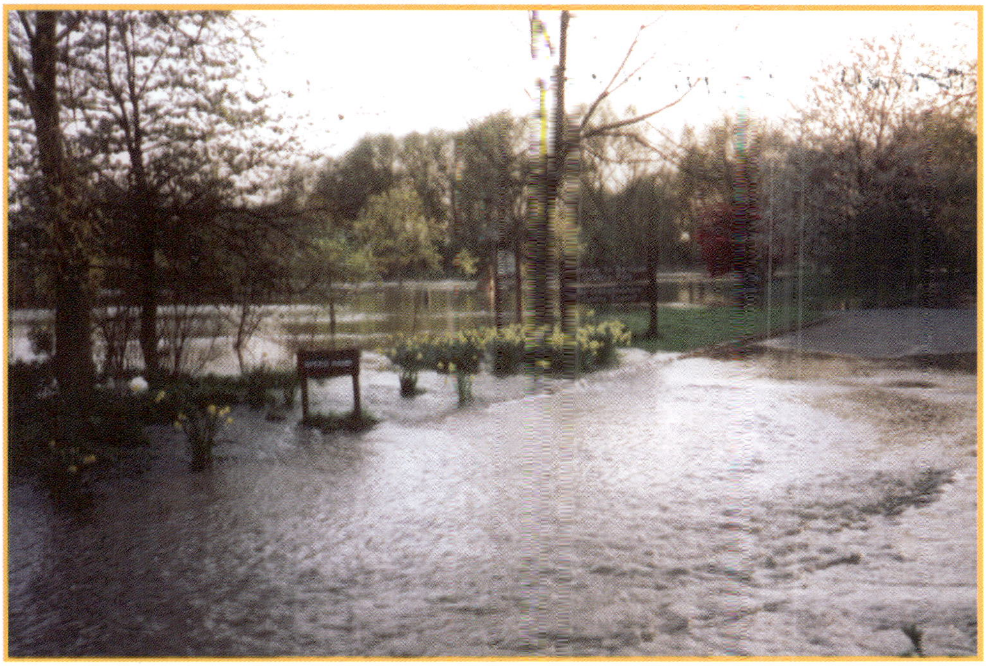

The entrance to Barnwell Country Park. This conservation area was a disaster, with nesting birds and small mammals suffering and in many cases dying.

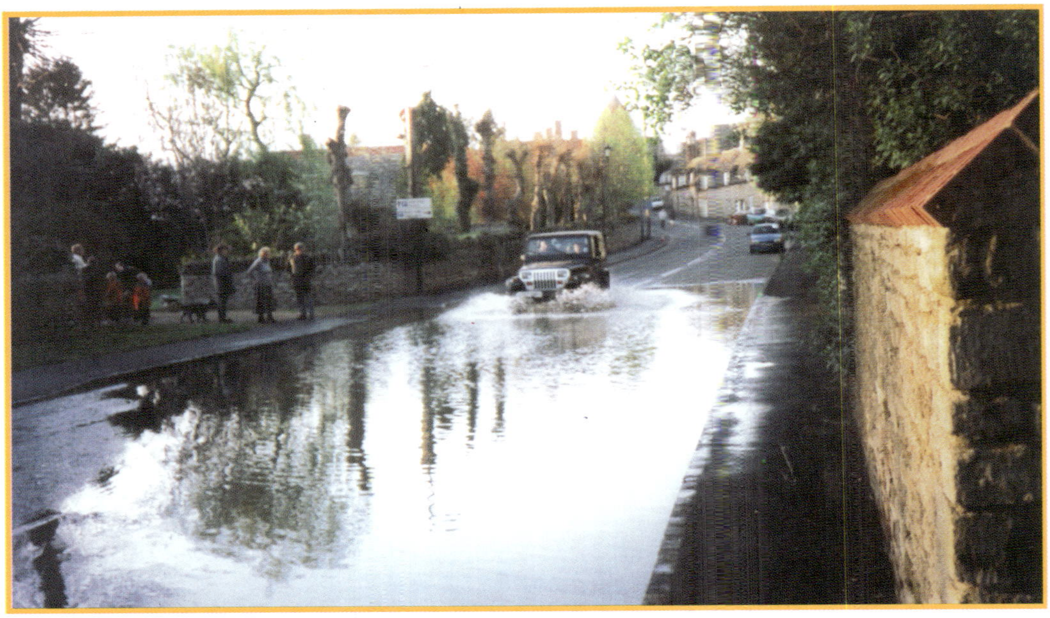

Whoosh, above, Mill Road in flood and below South Bridge before the flood covered the road. Here the water is at the top of the arches. The bottom photograph shows Lyveden Brook at Warren Bridge in full spate. Houses in the area had been flooded the night before and the weight of the water had flattened the ancient wall.

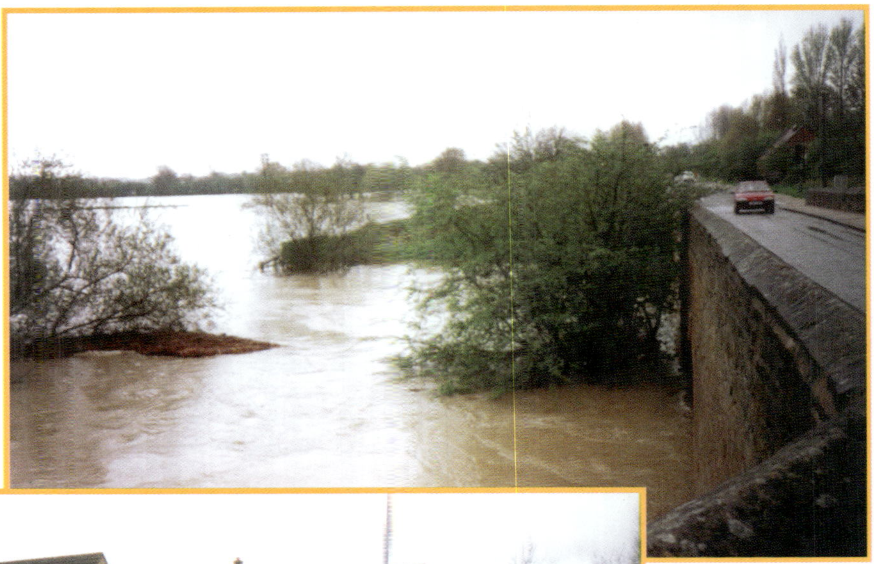

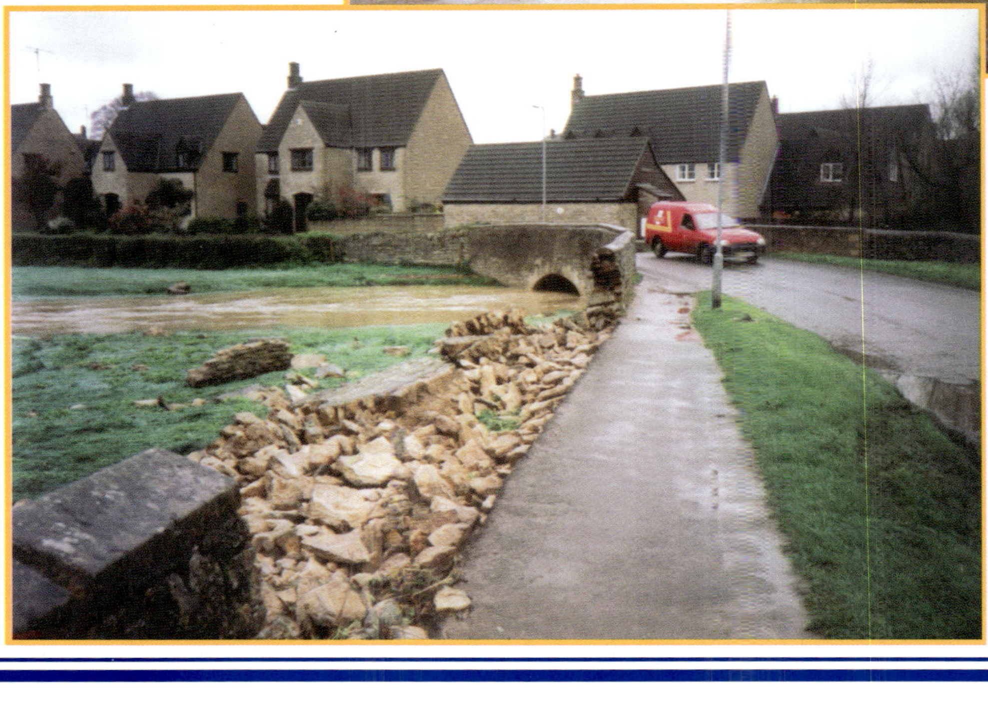